Cambridge readings in literature

George Sampson

BIBLIOLIFE

CAMBRIDGE
READINGS IN LITERATURE

EDITED BY

GEORGE SAMPSON

BOOK TWO

CAMBRIDGE

AT THE UNIVERSITY PRESS

1918

PREFACE

THESE reading books have been prepared in the first instance for use among pupils of eleven or twelve and above, and are thus suitable for the middle forms of secondary schools, the four years of central and higher grade schools, the upper standards of elementary schools and the literature courses of continuation schools. Admirable use is now made of what are called *Continuous Readers*; but these should not wholly supplant a miscellany, a collection of extracts good in themselves and representative of great or interesting writers.

Reading in schools may take three forms—audible reading by individual pupils, silent reading by all members of a class and reading by the teacher to the class. These forms represent three grades of difficulty in matter. Pupils can appreciate poetry and prose well read to them which they could not themselves read aloud with intelligence. Some parts, therefore, of the available material should reach the third grade of difficulty. It must certainly not all be kept down to the level of a stumbler's precarious fluency. Literature should be measured out to readers by their capacity to receive rather than by their ability to deliver.

Young people do not fully understand much of their reading; but they can be deeply impressed even where they do not comprehend; and their selective instincts (very different in different cases) should at least have a chance of working upon noble matter. We must take the mean, not the meanest, capacity for our standard. Difficulty is not an affair of words. Pupils of fifteen can get more from Wordsworth's *Immortality* ode than from such apparently simple poems as *The Fountain* and *The Two April Mornings*—more, even, from the great narrative passages of *Paradise Lost*, than from the exquisite traceries of *Lycidas*. They can understand, in a sense, a scene from *Prometheus*, but they will hardly understand in any sense a *Conversation* of Landor. The nearer prose or verse lies to the elemental, the nearer it lies to the young reader's understanding.

The present collection is purely a miscellany. Some hints of a purpose in the choice and arrangement of passages will be discerned, but this is not emphasised, and, generally, the collection may be said to exist for its parts rather than for any fanciful wholeness. It does not in the least pretend to be representative of any special age or country, or to exhibit the main types of literature, or to have one inflexible standard of inclusion. It is certainly not a selection from the "hundred best books." The editor's aim has been to give young readers the pleasure that is also a profit— to afford them the varied excitements (and incitements) of miscellaneous reading, to introduce to their notice certain poems, passages, books and writers great, or famous, or merely entertaining, and to associate with these a few pictures, drawings and engravings of widely differing schools and periods. Perhaps it may be added that special care has been given to the text.

The general tendency of school reading nowadays is towards a more ordered and therefore more restricted range of English literature, and away from the mis-

cellaneous knowledge that amused the youth of older
people. Much has been gained by the change; but
something, too, has been lost. It is better, certainly,
to know some poems in particular than to know something about poetry in general. The pupil of to-day
gets a first-hand acquaintance with some selected
examples of English literature, but he misses that
general knowledge of books, which, though it may
amount to very little in present profit, is a great
investment towards future reading. The indiscrimi-
nate young reader of old at least got to know some
of the landmarks in general literature. To-day, the
student of twenty, who can read (say) Francis Thomp-
son with appreciation, has been known to refer, in the
more expansive moments of his essays, to the epic
poems of Plato and the tragic dramas of Dante. The
present volumes, as a middle course between too vague
general knowledge and too restricted selection, will
supplement, without disturbing, any chosen or pre-
scribed scheme of study.

They may even find another use; for books have
destinies of their own. The savage satire for men
becomes (after due purgation) a playbook for children;
and the children's fairy tale, with its delicate irony,
becomes the delight of the elders. Perhaps the present
volumes may achieve this extended application, and
amuse the grown-up and the growing-up as well as
instruct the children. The puzzling question, "What
ought I to read," often asked by young people with
a developing sense of responsibility, can be answered,
at least in part, by these volumes. To such inquirers
it may be said, "Here you will find many clues to
the paradise of literature: follow that which leads you
through the most attractive way." Had the collection

been designed in the first place for older readers, some passages now included might have been replaced by others less familiar. Still, the familiar has its claim, and, " in vacant or in pensive mood," even a special charm for experienced readers. The day-book of the boy may be welcome as a bedside book for the man.

The variety of the entertainment is part of the plan. Neither man nor boy can live by the sublime alone, and so the range of the selection has been made very wide. Modern and even contemporary work has been drawn upon, though one's liberty of choice is here very restricted. Whether we are teachers or learners, we must not be fearful of the new. For us there should be no "battle of the antient and modern books," but one great stream of literature with all its lesser waters, as full and noble now as ever.

GEORGE SAMPSON

August 1918.

CONTENTS

CONTENTS

LIST OF PICTURES

LIST OF PICTURES

The design on the cover is taken from the *Luttrell
Psalter*, a Latin *Psalter* of the fourteenth century.

WILLIAM BLAKE

WILLIAM BLAKE (1757–1827), painter, engraver and poet, was born in London. His volumes *Poetical Sketches*, *Songs of Innocence* and *Songs of Experience* contain some beautiful poems. He wrote a series of long works—"prophetic books" in Biblical style—from one of which, *Jerusalem*, the first of the following extracts is taken. The second occurs in *Milton*, another long poem. Many of Blake's volumes were elaborately illustrated by his own hand, and he drew some remarkable illustrations for other books He had a strong and simple imagination; and, in the sincerity of his faith, believed that he saw visions of angels and other spiritual beings.

I

ENGLAND AWAKE!

(From *Jerusalem*)

England! awake! awake! awake!
    Jerusalem thy Sister calls!
Why wilt thou sleep the sleep of death,
    And close her from thy ancient walls?

Thy hills and valleys felt her feet
    Gently upon their bosoms move:
Thy gates beheld sweet Zion's ways;
    Then was a time of joy and love.

And now the time returns again:
    Our souls exult: and London's towers
Receive the Lamb of God to dwell
    In England's green and pleasant bowers.

II

(From *Milton*)

And did those feet in ancient time
    Walk upon England's mountains green?
And was the holy Lamb of God
    On England's pleasant pastures seen?

And did the Countenance Divine
   Shine forth upon our clouded hills?
And was Jerusalem builded here
   Among these dark Satanic Mills?

Bring me my bow of burning gold!
   Bring me my arrows of desire!
Bring me my spear: O clouds, unfold!
   Bring me my chariot of fire!

I will not cease from mental fight,
   Nor shall my sword sleep in my hand,
Till we have built Jerusalem
   In England's green and pleasant land.

ADDISON

JOSEPH ADDISON (1672-1719), the son of a Wiltshire clergyman, was educated at Charterhouse and Oxford. He wrote many poems, including *The Campaign*, which celebrates the victory at Blenheim. He is specially admired for the pleasant, good-humoured and charming essays written—some of them in association with Richard Steele—for two famous periodicals, *The Tatler* and *The Spectator*. Of these essays those which deal with the life of an imaginary country gentleman Sir Roger de Coverley are perhaps the most popular. Addison was active in political life and held several important offices. Thackeray's novel *Esmond* includes Addison and Steele among its characters. The essay which follows is No. 159 of *The Spectator* (1 Sept. 1711).

THE VISION OF MIRZAH

Omnem, quæ nunc obducta tuenti
Mortales hebetat visus tibi, et humida circum
Caligat, nubem eripiam.   VIRG *Æn* ii. 604.

The cloud, which, intercepting the clear light,
Hangs o'er thy eyes, and blunts thy mortal sight,
I will remove.

   When I was at Grand Cairo, I picked up several oriental manuscripts, which I have still by me. Among others I met with one entitled, The Visions of Mirzah, which I have read over with great pleasure. I intend to give it to the public when I have no other entertainment for them; and shall begin with the first vision, which I have translated word for word as follows:

"On the fifth day of the moon, which according to the custom of my forefathers I always keep holy, after having washed myself, and offered up my morning devotions, I ascended the high hills of Bagdad, in order to pass the rest of the day in meditation and prayer. As I was here airing myself on the tops of the mountains, I fell into a profound contemplation on the vanity of human life; and passing from one thought to another, 'Surely,' said I, 'man is but a shadow, and life a dream.' Whilst I was thus musing, I cast my eyes towards the summit of a rock that was not far from me, where I discovered one in the habit of a shepherd, with a little musical instrument in his hand. As I looked upon him he applied it to his lips, and began to play upon it. The sound of it was exceeding sweet, and wrought into a variety of tunes that were inexpressibly melodious, and altogether different from any thing I had ever heard. They put me in mind of those heavenly airs that are played to the departed souls of good men upon their first arrival in Paradise, to wear out the impressions of their last agonies, and qualify them for the pleasures of that happy place. My heart melted away in secret raptures.

"I had been often told that the rock before me was the haunt of a genius; and that several had been entertained with music who had passed by it, but never heard that the musician had before made himself visible. When he had raised my thoughts by those transporting airs which he played, to taste the pleasures of his conversation, as I looked upon him like one astonished, he beckoned to me, and by the waving of his hand directed me to approach the place where he sat. I drew near with that reverence which is due to a superior nature; and as my heart was entirely subdued by the captivating strains I had heard, I fell down at his feet and wept. The genius smiled upon me with a look of compassion and affability that familiarised him to my imagination, and at once dispelled all the fears and apprehensions with which I approached him. He lifted me from the ground, and taking me by the hand, 'Mirzah,' said he, 'I have heard thee in thy soliloquies; follow me.'

"He then led me to the highest pinnacle of the rock, and placing me on the top of it—'Cast thy eyes eastward,' said he, 'and tell me what thou seest.'—'I see,' said I, 'a huge valley, and a prodigious tide of water rolling through it.'—'The valley that thou seest,' said he, 'is the Vale of Misery, and the tide of water that thou seest is part of the great tide of eternity.'—'What is the reason,' said I, 'that the tide I see rises out of a thick mist at one end, and again loses itself in a thick mist at the other?'—'What thou seest,' said he, 'is that portion of eternity which is called time, measured out by the sun, and reaching from the beginning of the world to its consummation.'—'Examine now,' said he, 'this sea that is bounded with darkness at both ends, and tell me what thou discoverest in it.'—'I see a bridge,' said I, 'standing in the midst of the tide.'—'The bridge thou seest,' said he, 'is human life; consider it attentively.' Upon a more leisurely survey of it, I found that it consisted of threescore and ten entire arches, with several broken arches, which, added to those that were entire, made up the number about a hundred. As I was counting the arches, the genius told me that this bridge consisted at first of a thousand arches: but that a great flood swept away the rest, and left the bridge in the ruinous condition I now beheld it. 'But tell me further,' said he, 'what thou discoverest on it.'—'I see multitudes of people passing over it,' said I, 'and a black cloud hanging on each end of it.' As I looked more attentively, I saw several of the passengers dropping through the bridge into the great tide that flowed underneath it: and, upon farther examination, perceived there were innumerable trap-doors that lay concealed in the bridge, which the passengers no sooner trod upon, but they fell through them into the tide, and immediately disappeared. These hidden pit-falls were set very thick at the entrance of the bridge, so that throngs of people no sooner broke through the cloud, but many of them fell into them. They grew thinner towards the middle, but multiplied and lay closer together towards the end of the arches that were entire.

"There were indeed some persons, but their number was very small, that continued a kind of hobbling march on the broken arches, but fell through one after another, being quite tired and spent with so long a walk.

"I passed some time in the contemplation of this wonderful structure, and the great variety of objects which it presented. My heart was filled with a deep melancholy to see several dropping unexpectedly in the midst of mirth and jollity, and catching at every thing that stood by them to save themselves. Some were looking up towards the heavens in a thoughtful posture, and in the midst of a speculation stumbled and fell out of sight. Multitudes were very busy in the pursuit of bubbles that glittered in their eyes and danced before them; but often when they thought themselves within the reach of them, their footing failed, and down they sank. In this confusion of objects, I observed some with scimitars in their hands, and others with vessels, who ran to and fro upon the bridge, thrusting several persons on trap-doors which did not seem to lie in their way, and which they might have escaped had they not been thus forced upon them.

"The genius seeing me indulge myself in this melancholy prospect, told me I had dwelt long enough upon it. 'Take thine eyes off the bridge,' said he, 'and tell me if thou yet seest any thing thou dost not comprehend.' Upon looking up, 'What mean,' said I, 'those great flights of birds that are perpetually hovering about the bridge, and settling upon it from time to time? I see vultures, harpies, ravens, cormorants, and among many other feathered creatures several little winged boys, that perch in great numbers upon the middle arches.'—'These,' said the genius, 'are Envy, Avarice, Superstition, Despair, Love, with the like cares and passions that infest human life.'

"I here fetched a deep sigh. 'Alas,' said I, 'man was made in vain! how is he given away to misery and mortality! tortured in life, and swallowed up in death!' The genius, being moved with compassion towards me, bid me quit so uncomfortable a prospect. 'Look no more,' said he, 'on man in the first stage of his existence, in his setting out for eternity; but cast thine eye on that thick mist into which the tide bears the several generations of mortals that fall into it.' I directed my sight as I was ordered, and (whether or no the good genius strengthened it with any supernatural force, or dissipated part of the mist that was before too thick for the eye to penetrate) I saw the valley opening at the further end, and spreading forth into an immense ocean, that had a huge rock of adamant running through the midst of it, and dividing it into two equal parts. The clouds still rested on one half of it, insomuch that I could discover nothing in it: but the other appeared to me a vast ocean planted with innumerable islands, that were covered with fruits and flowers, and interwoven with a thousand little shining seas that ran among them. I could see persons dressed in glorious habits, with garlands upon their heads, passing among the trees, lying down by the sides of fountains, or resting on beds of flowers, and could hear a confused harmony of singing-birds, falling water, human voices, and musical instruments. Gladness grew in me upon the discovery of so delightful a scene. I wished for the wings of an eagle, that I might fly away to those happy seats· but the genius told me there was no passage to them, except through the gates of death that I saw opening every moment upon the bridge. 'The islands,' said he, 'that lie so fresh and green before thee, and with which the whole face of the ocean appears spotted as far as thou canst see, are more in number than the sands on the sea-shore; there are myriads of islands behind those which thou here discoverest, reaching further than thine eye, or even thine imagination can extend itself. These are the mansions of good men after death, who, according to the degree and kinds of virtue in which they excelled, are distributed among these several islands; which abound with pleasures of different kinds and degrees, suitable to the relishes and perfections of those who are settled in them, every island is a paradise accommodated to its respective inhabitants. Are not these, O Mirzah, habitations worth contending for? Does life appear miserable, that gives thee opportunities of earning such a reward? Is death to be feared, that will convey thee to so happy an existence? Think not man was made in vain, who has such an eternity reserved for him.' I gazed with inexpressible pleasure on these happy islands. 'At length,' said I, 'show me now, I beseech thee, the secrets that lie hid under those dark clouds which cover the ocean on the other side of the rock of adamant.' The genius making me no answer, I turned about to address myself to him a second time, but I found that he had left me: I then turned again to the vision which I had been so long contemplating; but instead of the rolling tide, the arched bridge, and the happy islands, I saw nothing but the long hollow valley of Bagdad, with oxen, sheep, and camels, grazing upon the sides of it."

TOLSTOY

Count Leo Nikolaievitch Tolstoy (1828–1910), one of the greatest of Russian writers, was born at Yasnaya Polyana, near Tula, a large town south of Moscow. He came of a famous noble family, and, after a somewhat ill-spent youth at educational institutions in Moscow and Kazan, he entered the army and fought in the Caucasus and the Crimea. His first stories, *Childhood*, *Boyhood* and *Youth*, were written at this period, and his experiences in the war produced the splendid sketches called *Sevastopol*. He left the army and devoted himself to literature. The longest and, perhaps, the finest of his books is *War and Peace*, a magnificent story of Napoleon's invasion of Russia. Other famous novels are *Anna Karénina* and *Resurrection*. In his later years, he devoted himself to re-stating the rules of life given by Jesus in the Sermon on the Mount, and to uplifting the ignorant peasants of his country. He wrote, therefore, many little books upon religious subjects, and many beautiful short stories, simple enough to be understood by all. The story which follows is one of these tales. Tolstoy lived simply and sparely as if he were himself a poor peasant. His life was so sincere that his personal example has been as great an influence as his writings.

In connection with the following story, it should be understood that the great ambition of the Russian peasants is to make a pilgrimage to Jerusalem to visit the scenes associated with the life and death of Jesus. They save money for many years and go in hundreds on this long journey, enduring all sorts of terrible hardships and discomforts.

Translated by Madame Kosnakoff and A. C. Fifield

THE TWO PILGRIMS

The woman saith unto him, Sir, I perceive that thou art a prophet. Our fathers worshipped in this mountain, and ye say that in Jerusalem is the place where men ought to worship.

Jesus saith unto her, Woman, believe me, the hour cometh, when ye shall neither in this mountain, nor yet at Jerusalem, worship the Father. Ye worship ye know not what: we know what we worship: for salvation is of the Jews. But the hour cometh, and now is, when the true worshippers shall worship the Father in spirit and in truth: for the Father seeketh such to worship him.—John iv. 19–23.

I

Two old men once agreed to go on a pilgrimage together to worship God in Jerusalem. One was a rich peasant called Yefim Shevelev, the other was not wealthy and was called Elisha Bodrov.

Yefim was a staid, respectable man, upright and severe. He neither drank brandy nor smoked tobacco, nor took snuff, and he had never in his life used bad language. Twice he had been

chosen starosta (president of the village commune), and in neither
term had he made any debts. He had a large family: two sons
and a married grandson,—and all lived together. He himself was
a hale, strong, long-bearded man, and although he was seventy
years old his figure was still erect and his beard was only just
beginning to show a few gray hairs.

Elisha was also an old man, and was neither rich nor poor;
formerly he had worked as a carpenter, but now he was old he
stayed at home and kept bees. One of his sons worked away from
home, the other lived with his father. Elisha was a kind-hearted
and jovial little old man who liked his brandy and his snuff, and
was fond of singing, but he was very peaceable and inoffensive
and lived on good terms with his family and neighbours. He was
a short and dark-haired little man, with a little curly beard and
a head as bald as that of his patron saint, Elisha the prophet.

The old men had made their vow and had agreed to go to
Jerusalem together long ago, but Yefim's time was always taken
up. There was always some business on hand. As soon as one
thing was finished, he took up another. First his grandson was to
be married; then his son was coming home from the army; and
now he had begun to build a new hut.

One festival day the old men met, and sat down on some timber
to chat.

"Well, gossip," said Elisha, "when shall we set out to fulfil
our vow?"

Yefim frowned: "I must wait," he said; "this is a hard year
for me. When I began to build this hut I thought it would cost
me about a hundred roubles (£10) and I have already spent near
three hundred, and it isn't finished yet. We must wait till next
summer. Then, God willing, we will certainly go."

"As I look at it," said Elisha, "we shouldn't put it off. We
ought to start now. Spring is the best time."

"Time! yes, that's the best time, but now that I've begun the
hut, how can I leave it?"

"Haven't you any one at home? Let your son see to it."

"Yes, I know how he would see to it. He is not to be depended
on. He sometimes takes too much to drink."

"Well, neighbour, when we die, you know, they will have to
get on without us. Let your son begin to learn now."

"No doubt, no doubt But somehow I always want to have my eye on everything and finish it myself."

"Well, you can't finish everything, my friend The other day my women were scrubbing and cleaning everything for Easter. *This* had to be done and *that* had to be done, and there was always something more to do. So my eldest son's wife, who is a sensible woman, said: 'It's a good thing,' says she, 'that the holiday doesn't wait for us, else,' says she 'we should never be done, however much we worked.'"

Yefim became thoughtful.

"I have spent a lot of money on this hut," he said, "and I can't start on this journey with empty hands either. A hundred roubles is no small sum."

Elisha laughed.

"Don't commit a sin, neighbour," he said. "You have ten times as much as I have, and yet you talk about money! Only say when you will start, and although I haven't any money, I'll get some."

Yefim smiled.

"I didn't know you were such a rich man," he said. "How will you get the money?"

"Oh, I'll scrape some of it together somehow at home, and as for the rest, I'll let a neighbour have half a score of my bee hives. He has been wanting them a long while"

"If the swarms turn out good, you'll be sorry."

"Sorry! Not I, neighbour, I have never in my life been sorry about anything, except my sins There is nothing dearer than the soul"

"Yes, that's true, but still it's bad when things go wrong at home."

"And when things go wrong with the soul? That's much worse. We have made a vow and we must go. Come, don't put it off any longer."

II

At last Elisha persuaded his friend Yefim thought and thought about it, and the next morning he came to Elisha.

"Well, let us go," he said. "You speak the truth. God is the master of our life and death. We must start while we have life and strength."

Within a week the old men were ready.

Yefim had money in his house He took a hundred roubles and left two hundred with his old wife.

Elisha also was ready; he sold his neighbour the ten hives with all the new swarms when they came. He raised seventy roubles by this. The remaining thirty roubles he collected from his family, and fairly cleaned out everyone. His old wife gave him every rouble she had saved up for her funeral; his daughter-in-law also gave him hers.

Yefim left instructions with his son concerning all household matters. how many fields to rent for haying, what land to manure, and how to finish and roof the hut. He thought about everything, and gave orders how everything was to be done.

Elisha only told his old wife to be sure to separate the young swarms that were to be sold from his own, and to give them all honestly to the neighbour; and that was all. He did not even speak of household affairs. "You will see for yourself what there is to be done," he said. "You are masters, and you will do what you think best."

At last everything was ready. The women folk baked a lot of flat cakes, sewed some bags to put them in, gave them new boots, plaited some extra shoes of birch-bark, and cut new strips of linen for the leg-bands (used by Russian peasants instead of stockings). Then the old men set out accompanied by their families as far as the end of the village. There they bade them good-bye and went on their way alone.

Elisha started with a light heart, and forgot all his cares as soon as he had left the village behind. His only thoughts were how to please his comrade, how to avoid being harsh to anyone, and how to get to the journey's end and home again in peace and love with all men. As he walked he was all the time whispering prayers to himself or repeating what lives of the saints he could remember. When he met people on the road or stopped anywhere for the night, he was always on the watch to do a kindness to anyone, and to say a good word to all. And he went on his way rejoicing. There was only one thing he could not give up. He had meant to give up taking snuff, and had even left his snuff-box at home, but he felt very bad without it,—and then a stranger on the road gave him some. So from time to time he fell behind his companion—not to lead him into temptation—and took his pinch.

Yefim also got on well. He walked steadily, said very little, and did no wrong; but there was no content in his heart. He could not free his mind from cares about his household matters. He was always thinking of how they were getting on at home. Had he forgotten to give this or that order to his son? Would his son do what was necessary? Whenever he saw potatoes being planted or manure carted along the road he would think, "Is my son doing just as I told him?" And sometimes he felt almost ready to turn back and show his son how the things ought to be done, or even do them himself.

III

Five weeks went by. They had worn out their new shoes and had to buy others. At last they came to Little Russia. All through their journey so far they had always had to buy their food and to pay for their night's lodgings, but here in Little Russia all the people seemed eager to invite them freely. They were lodged and fed, and their bags were filled with bread or cakes for the journey, and no one would take any money in return. So they made another seven hundred versts (500 miles) which cost them nothing, crossed into another government, and came to a famine-stricken district.

The people here also let them spend the nights without payment, but they got no food In some places they could not even get any bread, and no money could buy it. Last year, the people said, the crops had failed altogether. The rich peasants had been ruined, and had sold all they had; those who had been moderately well off were now in misery, and the poor had either perished utterly or had become beggars; a few only remained at home, eating ground corn-husks and tree-bark in the winter.

One morning, after spending the night in a village, the two pilgrims bought fifteen pounds of bread and started off before sunrise, so as to travel a good bit before the heat of the day. They walked about ten versts (seven miles) and then came to a brook, where they sat down to rest, filled their cups with water, soaked their bread and ate. Then they rested awhile, and changed their leg wrappers Elisha took out his snuff box. Yefim shook his head at him

"Why don't you give up that dirty habit?" he said

Elisha waved his hand in despair "I can't help it," he said; "the sin has got the better of me"

They rose and went on. After ten more versts they came to a large village which they passed through. The sun was hot by this time and Elisha was tired and wanted to rest and have a drink. But Yefim kept on steadily He was a stronger walker than Elisha, who found it difficult to keep up with him.

"I should like a drink," said Elisha.

"Well, go and get a drink. I am not thirsty."

Elisha stopped.

"Don't wait for me," he said "I'll only go into this cottage and get some water and catch you up in a moment."

"All right," said Yefim, who continued on his way alone, while Elisha turned towards the cottage.

It was a small hut with plaster walls, painted black below and white above; but the clay was crumbling away in several places and the roof had fallen in on one side It was clear the hut had not been repaired for a long time. The entrance was through the yard, so into the yard Elisha went, and there was a gaunt beardless man lying on the ground near the bench, with his shirt tucked into his trousers after the manner of the Little Russians[1]. The man had probably lain down in the shade, but now the sun was burning full upon him, and though he was not asleep he lay there without moving. Elisha called to him and asked for water but got no answer

"He is either sick or bad-tempered," thought Elisha, and he went to the door He could hear a child crying inside. He rapped with the latch ring: "Masters!" he called. No answer. He tapped the door with his stick. "Christians!" No sound. "Servants of God!" No reply. Elisha was about to turn away when he seemed to hear some one groaning inside.

"Something's wrong," he thought "I had better see" And he approached the door again.

[1] The peasants of Great Russia wear the shirt outside the trousers, after the manner of a smock frock —*Trans.*

Elisha turned the handle—the door was unfastened. He opened it and stepped into the passage The inner door was open; on the left of the room was the stove, in the corner a stand with images, and a table; near the table a bench, and on the bench sat an old woman with nothing on but a shirt, resting her bare unkempt head on the table. By her side stood a little boy with a swollen stomach, thin, and white as wax, pulling her by the sleeve, and screaming and sobbing and asking for something to eat. Elisha entered. The stench in the room was suffocating. Behind the oven, on a shelf, lay another woman, her legs twitching convulsively and her body rolling over from side to side. She lay on her face and did not look up; her throat was rattling, and the stench rose from her shelf It was clear that she was too ill and weak to get up, and that no one had been attending to her or doing anything for her. The old woman raised her head and saw Elisha.

"What do you want?" she muttered in Little Russian. "What do you want? We've nothing for you"

Elisha understood and came near to her "I want some water, friend," he said.

"There's no one to get any. And we have none. We have nothing. Go your way."

"Is there no one to look after this woman?" said Elisha.

"No, no one. Our man is dying in the yard and we are dying here."

The boy, who had stopped crying when he saw the stranger, caught the old woman by the sleeve again as soon as she began to talk—"Bread, granny, bread," he cried, sobbing, "give me some bread."

Elisha was going to question the old woman further, when the man staggered into the hut, and tried to reach the bench by clinging to the wall; but he tottered and fell down in the corner near the door, and lay there unable to rise. Then he began to speak. He brought out one word at a time, gasping for breath between each

"We are ill..." he muttered, "and starving... Look...he is dying...of hunger!" And he pointed to the little boy and burst into tears.

Elisha slipped his arms free from the straps, slung his bag to the floor, lifted it to the bench and opened it He took out a loaf of bread and a knife, cut off a slice and offered it to the peasant. The peasant shook his head and pointed to the boy; "Give it to them." Elisha offered the bread to the boy, who stretched out his arms, seized it with both hands, and began to eat it ravenously. Then a little girl crawled out from behind the oven and stared at the bread. Elisha gave her a piece also Then he cut another slice for the old woman. She took it and tried to munch it. "Will you get some water?" she said: "their throats are parched. I tried to get some—I don't remember when,—yesterday or to-day,—but I fell down—and could not get there, and the pail must be there still, if no one has taken it."

Elisha asked where the well was and she told him. He went out, found the pail, and brought water and gave them some to drink. The children and the old woman ate some more bread with the water, but the man refused "I can't eat," he said

The other woman was still unconscious, and lay tossing from side to side on the shelf

Elisha went into the village and bought meal, salt, flour and butter Then he found a hatchet, chopped some wood and lighted the fire; the girl helped him and he made some soup and gruel and fed them all

v

The man ate, and the old woman also, and the children licked the bowl clean and then lay down to sleep in each other's arms. Then the peasant and the old woman began to tell Elisha how it had all happened.

"We were never rich," said the peasant, "and last year all the crops failed, and since autumn we have been living on what we had laid by When we had spent everything we had, we asked the good people around to help us At first they gave, but after a time they refused. Even those who would have been glad to help us had nothing themselves. And we were ashamed to go on begging—we owed everyone—money, flour and bread I tried to get work, but there was none to be had. All the people are offering to work these famine days, just for their keep. One day I would have work and the next two I would do nothing but hunt about for a job. The old woman and the girl went begging far away from home, but they got very little. No one had any bread. Still we managed to keep along somehow, hoping to pull through till the new crops. But when spring came no one would help us any more, and then sickness came. We were very bad then. One day we ate and two days we had nothing. Then we began to eat grass. Then my woman fell ill—whether it was from the grass or not I don't know. She couldn't move and I, also, have no strength left. And I don't know how we are going to be cured."

"I alone managed to keep up a little longer," said the old woman, "but I grew very weak without food and my strength failed. The girl also became very weak and frightened. I tried to send her to the neighbours, but she would not go. She got into a corner and we couldn't get her out. The other day one of our neighbours looked in but when she saw we were sick and hungry she turned and went out. It is true her husband has gone away and she has nothing to feed her children with ...And so we lay here, waiting for death."

Elisha listened to them and changed his mind about trying to join Yefim that day. He stopped the night, and the next morning he set to on the household work as if he had been the master. He made the fire and helped the old woman to mix the bread; then he took the girl and went to the neighbours to get the most needful things. There was nothing in the cottage, neither food nor clothing; everything had been eaten or sold. Elisha began to get the most necessary things together; some he made himself, others he bought.

So he lived there three days. The little boy got stronger and began to run about and to make friends with Elisha. The girl became quite bright again and helped Elisha with everything, and followed him about calling him "grandad." The old woman got well enough to go to her neighbours. The peasant himself could walk a little, holding on to the wall. Only the young woman was no better, but on the third day she came to herself and asked for food.

"Well," thought Elisha, "I must be going now. I never thought to waste so much time."

VI

The fourth day was the end of the summer fast from meat-eating, and Elisha thought. "I'll stay and break the fast with them and buy them something for the Saint's Day, and then I can start in the evening." So he went into the village and bought milk and lard and white flour, and helped the old woman to cook; and next morning he went to church, and came home, and ate the festival meal with them. The young woman got up that day and began to move about feebly. The man shaved, put on a clean shirt which the old woman had washed for him, and went into the village to a rich peasant to ask a favour. His corn and hay fields were mortgaged to this peasant, and now he went to ask whether he might have them till the new crops. In the evening he returned weeping and in despair. The rich peasant had refused. "Bring the money first," he said.

Elisha grew thoughtful again.

"How will they live now?" he thought. "People will be hay-making, and he will have nothing because his field is pawned. When the rye ripens and the men are reaping it (and what fine crops there will be too this year), he will have nothing because his three-acre is pledged to the rich peasant. If I go away they will soon be just as they were before.

So Elisha again changed his mind, and instead of leaving that evening he put it off till the morrow. Then he went to sleep in the yard. He prayed and lay down but he could not sleep. He wanted to go on with his journey; as it was he had spent much, both time and money; and yet he was sorry for the people. "You can't help everybody," he thought. "I wanted to give them a piece of bread each and get them some water, and now this is where I am! Now I must go and buy out their rye field and their grass land. And when I have done that, I must buy a cow for the children's milk and a horse for the man to cart his crops. You've got caught, friend Elisha. You've slipped your cable, and now you can just get out of it as best you can!"

Elisha sat up, pulled his kaftan (long cloth coat) from under his head, got out his snuff box and took a pinch, hoping to clear his mind. But it was of no use. He thought and thought, but could come to no decision. He must go, yet he was sorry to leave these people. What to do he did not know. So he rolled up his kaftan, put it under his head again, and lay down. He lay till dawn and cock-crowing, and was just falling asleep, when suddenly some one seemed to wake him. He dreamed that he was dressed for the journey, with his bag and his staff, and that he had to pass through the gate which was open only just wide enough to squeeze through. As he was slipping through his bag caught on one side, and while he was busy with this, his leg band caught on the other side, and became unfastened. He bent down to put that right, and then he saw that it was not the gate that held him, but the little girl, who clung to him crying: "Granddad, little granddad, bread!" He looked down and there was the boy clutching his foot, and the old woman and the man were looking out of the window. Elisha awoke and said to himself aloud: "To-morrow I will redeem the rye field and the grass land, and I'll buy a horse, and a cow for the children, and flour to last till the new crops. Else in going to look for Christ beyond the seas, I shall lose him in my own soul. I must help these people." Then he went to sleep till the morning.

He got up early—went to the rich peasant and redeemed the rye and grass fields. Then he bought a scythe—even that had been sold—and carried it to the cottage. He sent the man to mow his field, and he himself went back into the village. At last he found a horse and cart for sale at the inn, bargained for it, and paid the price; bought a sack of flour which he put into the cart, and went off to buy the cow. On his way he overtook two women who were talking together as they went. He heard what they said, and understood enough of the dialect to know that they were talking of him.

"At first they thought he was just an ordinary man. He said he had come in to get some water to drink. And then he stayed with them. The things he has bought for them! To-day I saw him buying a horse and cart for them at the innkeeper's. I have never seen such people in the world. It is a thing to wonder at."

Elisha understood that they were praising him and he decided not to buy the cow. So he turned back to the inn, paid for the horse, harnessed it and drove to the cottage. At the gate he stopped and got down. When the people saw the horse they were amazed, and though it seemed plain that he had bought it for them they hardly dared to think so. The man came to open the gate.

"Where did you get your horse, little father?" he asked.

"I bought it. It was going cheap. Better cut some grass to put in the manger for the night; and put the sack in the loft."

The man unharnessed the horse, took the sack, mowed some grass and put it into the manger. Then all the family lay down to sleep. Elisha lay down in the yard taking his own bag with him. When everyone was asleep he rose, put on his shoes and his haftan, slung his bag on his shoulders and went on his way to find Yefim.

VII

Elisha walked on about five versts (three miles); the dawn was beginning to break. He sat down under a tree, untied his bag and counted his money. He found he had only seventeen roubles and twenty kopecks left.

"Well," he thought, "I can't cross the sea with that. And if I begin to beg, I may fall into worse sin than before. Friend Yefim will have to get there alone, and he will burn a candle for me. As for me, I shall never be able to keep my vow, but thanks be to the Master, He is merciful; He will forgive me."

Elisha arose, put the bag on his shoulders, and turned homewards. Only he made a sweep in order to avoid the village, so that the people might not see him. He soon reached his home. The outward journey had seemed hard to him; at times he scarcely had been able to keep up with Yefim. But going back God gave him such strength that he knew no weariness. He walked along lightly, swinging his staff, and making seventy versts a day.

When he got home he found the harvests already gathered in. His family was delighted to have their old man back again, and questioned him eagerly as to his journey, and how he had lost his companion, and why he had given up his journey and returned home. Elisha however did not tell them how it all came about, but contented himself with saying:

"Well, God willed it so. I spent the money on the road, and then I lost my companion, and so I had to give it up. Forgive me, for Christ's sake."

He gave his old wife what remained of the money, and asked

about the household matters. All was well, everything had been done, there had been neither mistakes nor carelessness, and all were living in peace and concord.

Yefim's family heard about Elisha's return that very day, and came to ask him about their old man. He told them the same thing.

"Yefim was quite well," he said, "when we parted three days before St Peter's day. I wanted to catch him up, but then it so happened that I spent my money, and there was not enough left to go on with, so I came back."

The people wondered how a sensible man could do such a foolish thing—start on a journey and not finish it and lose all his money instead! They talked about it and then forgot it. And Elisha also forgot. He took up his house-work again, helped his son to store the wood for the winter and his women to grind the grain; he roofed the barns and hived the bees and gave the ten hives with their increase to the neighbour.

His old wife wanted to hide the number of young swarms, but Elisha knew very well which of the old hives were swarming and which were not, and he gave the neighbour seventeen instead of ten. When all was finished, Elisha sent his son away to work, and settled down at home for the winter, to plait bark shoes and to make bee-hives.

VIII

All that day while Elisha was in the hut with the starving peasants, Yefim was waiting for him. He went only a little way, and then he sat down. He waited and waited, and fell asleep and woke and waited again, but Elisha did not appear. He looked and looked till his eyes ached. The sun had sunk behind the trees, and still no Elisha came. "Perhaps he has passed me," he thought, "or perhaps someone gave him a lift and he did not see me while I was sleeping. And yet how could he have missed me? One sees far in the steppes. If I go back and he is in front we shall lose each other completely. I will go on; we are sure to meet at night."

He walked on to the next village and asked the Elder, if a little old man came, to send him to the same hut.

But Elisha did not come.

Yefim went further, and of every one he asked whether they

had seen a little bald old man. No one had seen him. Yefim wondered and went on his way alone.

"We shall meet in Odessa," he thought, "or on board ship," and he ceased to trouble about it.

On the way he met a pilgrim wearing a skull-cap, a cassock, and long hair; he had been to the monastery at Mount Athos and was now going a second time to Jerusalem. They met at a lodging place, fell into conversation, and went on together.

They reached Odessa, and waited there three days for a ship. Crowds of pilgrims from many lands were waiting there. Yefim again enquired about Elisha, but no one had seen him.

Yefim got a foreign passport, which cost him five roubles; then he paid forty roubles for the passage to Jerusalem and back, and bought bread and herrings for the journey.

The pilgrim tried to tell Yefim how he might get on the ship without paying, but Yefim would not listen. "No," he said, "I came prepared to pay, and I prefer to pay."

The ship was freighted and the pilgrims went on board, Yefim and his companion among them. The anchor was lifted and they started. The first day was fine, but towards evening a wind arose, the rain came down in torrents, and the ship was tossed about till the waves swept over the deck. The people were terrified; the women wailed and screamed, and some of the weaker men ran about looking for shelter.

Yefim also was frightened, only he would not show it; he sat on the deck without moving, on the spot he had chosen on coming aboard, among the Tambov pilgrims, and there he remained the whole night and all the next day. None of them spoke, but all sat holding their bags tightly all the time. On the third day the weather cleared up again, and on the fifth they came to Constantinople.

Some of the pilgrims landed and went to see the church of St Sophia, which is now in the hands of the Turks; but Yefim stayed on board, and only bought some white bread. They stayed there for a day, and then started again. They stopped at Smyrna and then at Alexandria, and at last reached Jaffa. At Jaffa all the pilgrims had to land, and thence to travel seventy versts on foot to Jerusalem. At the landing the pilgrims were greatly frightened. The ship was high, and the people had to jump down into the boats, which tossed to and fro so that you were as likely as not to fall into the water. Two pilgrims did get a wetting, but at last all were safely landed.

Then they continued their journey on foot, and on the third day, towards noon, they reached Jerusalem. They stopped outside the city, in the Russian quarter; had their passports examined; ate some food, and then went off to see the Holy places. But it was not the proper time for admittance to the grave of Christ.

So they went to the Patriarchal Monastery, where all the pilgrims were gathered together and the men separated from the women. Then they were told to take off their foot-gear and to sit in a circle. Then a monk appeared with a towel and began to wash their feet. He washed, wiped, and kissed the feet of each pilgrim in turn, and did the same to Yefim. Then the pilgrims attended vespers and matins, said their prayers, burned candles, and offered petitions for their relatives. Here they ate again, also, and wine was given them.

The next morning they went to the cell of Mary of Egypt where she had lived in penitence. There also they offered candles and paid for a *Te Deum*. Then they went to Abraham's Monastery and saw the garden of Jehovah, where Abraham nearly sacrificed his son to God. Afterwards they visited the spot where Christ appeared to Mary Magdalen, and to the church of James the brother of Christ.

All these places were pointed out to Yefim by the pilgrim, who also told him how much money was to be given everywhere.

They returned to their inn for dinner, and after they had eaten they were getting ready to go to bed, when suddenly the pilgrim began to cry out and to search among his clothes. "They have stolen my purse," he cried, "with twenty-three roubles. I had two ten rouble notes and three roubles in change." He groaned and mourned, but as there was nothing to be done, they all finally lay down to sleep.

IX

Yefim lay without sleeping, and temptation beset him. "No one has stolen his money," he thought; "he never had any. He did not give anywhere. He only told me to give and took a rouble from me."

Then Yefim began to blame himself for thinking such things. "Why do I judge the man?" he said to himself. "I am sinning. I will not think about it any more." But he soon forgot his resolution and remembered how greedy the pilgrim seemed about money and how unlikely it sounded when he said that his purse had been stolen. "He never had any money," thought Yefim. "It's only a trick."

They rose early to go to mass in the great Church of the Resurrection—the Lord's Sepulchre. The pilgrim stuck to Yefim and followed him about everywhere.

They reached the Church. There were crowds of pilgrims of all nations: Russians and Greeks and Armenians and Turks and Syrians. They all crowded to the Holy Gate. Then a monk came and guided them past the Turkish sentries to the spot where Christ's body had been taken from the cross and anointed, and where nine great candles were burning. The monk explained and showed everything, and Yefim placed a candle there.

Then the monks led him to the right up some steps to the hill of Golgotha, where the cross had stood, and Yefim prayed there. They showed him the hole in the earth where it had opened to its nethermost depths, and the spot where the hands and feet of Christ were nailed to the cross. They showed him Adam's grave, where the Lord's blood had fallen upon Adam's bones; the stone on which Christ had sat when he was crowned with the crown of thorns; the post to which he was bound when the soldiers scourged him; the stone with two holes for his feet.

The monks wanted to show something else, but the people were impatient and all hastened to the cave of the Lord's Sepulchre. The Latin mass was over, and the Orthodox (Greek) mass had just begun. Yefim went with the people into the cave.

He tried to get rid of the pilgrim, for in his thoughts he sinned against him all the time; but the pilgrim stayed by him and followed him everywhere,—to the mass, and to the Lord's Sepulchre. They tried to get to the front but were too late. The crowd was so packed that one could not move a step either forwards or backwards. So Yefim stood up, looking straight before him and praying and from time to time feeling for his purse. He was not quiet in his mind: on the one hand he thought that the pilgrim was lying to him, and on the other hand, that he might be speaking the truth, and then if the money had been really stolen from him, the same thing might happen to Yefim himself.

X

So he stood praying and looking before him into the shrine where the Tomb itself stood, with thirty-six lamps burning above it. And as he stood gazing over the heads before him he suddenly saw, standing just under the lamps where the sacred fire burns, and in front of all the people—a little old man in a gray kaftan, with his bald head shining in the light, just like Elisha Bodrov. "He looks like Elisha," thought Yefim, "but it cannot be. He could not have got here before me. The last ship started a week before ours. He could not have caught it, and I know he was not on ours, for I saw all the pilgrims."

Hardly had Yefim thought thus, when the old man began to pray, and bowed three times, first straight before him to God, and then to all the Christian brethren—to right and left. And when he turned his head, Yefim recognised him. It was Elisha himself: he could see his black, curly beard, with the gray hairs on the cheeks, his eyebrows and eyes and nose, and his whole face—it was Elisha without a doubt.

Yefim was delighted to have found his companion, and wondered how he had managed to arrive before him.

"There's a clever one," he thought; "he has got on in front of everybody! I suppose he found someone who helped him and brought him there. I will look for him when everyone goes up, and I will get rid of my pilgrim with the skull cap and go with Elisha. I daresay he will find a place for me too in front."

Yefim stood watching Elisha all the time, not to lose sight of him. When the mass was finished, the crowd surged forward, crushing each other in their haste to kiss the cross, and Yefim was pushed aside. Again fear seized him lest he should lose his purse. He clutched it with one hand and began shouldering his way through the crowd to get into the open. When at last he succeeded, he began to wander backwards and forwards, watching and looking for Elisha, both in the court and inside the church. In the cells surrounding the chapel he saw a great many people, some of them eating and drinking wine, and sleeping and reading. But nowhere could he see Elisha. And Yefim went back to the inn without finding him. That evening the pilgrim did not return. He disappeared, and Yefim's rouble with him. And Yefim was left alone.

The next day he again went to the Holy Sepulchre with an old Tambov peasant who had come on the same ship with him. He tried to get to the front, but was crushed back, so he stood against a pillar and began to pray. He looked forward, and there was Elisha again, standing right in front, beside the Tomb, under the lights, with his arms stretched out like the priest at the altar, and his bald head all shining. "Well," thought Yefim, "I shan't miss him this time." And he pushed his way to the front, but when he got there, Elisha had disappeared. Clearly, he had left his place. On the third day, while Yefim looked, there was Elisha again, standing in full sight on the most sacred spot, with his arms spread out and his face turned upwards, as though he saw something above him; and his bald head shone more than ever. "Well," thought Yefim, "I must catch him this time, I shall go and wait for him at the entrance. We can't miss each other there." So he went out and stood at the gate, and waited there half the day. All the people passed him, but there was no Elisha.

Yefim remained six weeks in Jerusalem and went everywhere: to Bethlehem and to Bethany and to the Jordan; and at the Holy Sepulchre he had a seal put on a new shirt, that he might be buried in it; and he took some water from the Jordan in a bottle, and sacred earth, and candles with the sacred flame, and he paid in eight places for prayers for the souls of his relatives, till all his money was spent and he had only just enough to get home with. At last he started on his way back. He reached Jaffa; got on board a ship that was sailing for Odessa, and thence started home on foot.

XI

Yefim followed the road by which he had gone. As he came nearer to his home he was again beset with anxieties as to how things had been going on during his absence. "Much water runs away in a year! It takes a life-time to build a home, but not long to destroy it. Has the son managed the business properly without me? How has the spring opened, and how have the cattle passed the winter, and how has the hut been finished?"

Yefim was now near the spot where he had parted with Elisha last year. The people were not to be recognised. Where last year they were starving, now they were living in plenty. The harvest had been good, and the people were better off and had forgotten their former misery.

One evening Yefim came to the place where Elisha had left him. As he entered the village, a little girl in a white smock ran out from behind one of the huts.

"Grandad, little grandad! Come to our house!"

Yefim wanted to pass on, but the little girl caught him by his kaftan and dragged him towards the hut, laughing. A woman with a small boy stood in the door-way and beckoned to him. "Come and have supper with us, little grandad; then you can spend the night."

Yefim entered. "I will just ask about Elisha," he thought. "I believe this was the very hut he went into for some water."

The woman took the bag from his shoulders, gave him some water to wash himself, and seated him at the table. Then she gave him milk, varénniki (curd dumplings) and gruel. Yefim thanked her, and praised her for being so hospitable to strangers.

The woman shook her head. "How can we help taking in strangers?" she said. "A stranger gave us life. We lived without remembering God, and God punished us so that we expected nothing but death. Last summer we were all lying in this hut, sick, and with nothing to eat. And we should have died, only God sent us an old man like yourself. He came in one day at noon to drink; and when he saw us he pitied us and stayed with us. He fed us and gave us drink, and helped us, and redeemed our land, and bought a horse and cart and left them with us."

Here an old woman entered the hut and interrupted the speaker.

"And up to this day," she said, "we don't know whether he was a man or an angel of God. He loved us all, and pitied us all, and then he went away without saying who he was; and we don't even know whom we should pray to God for. I can see it all now just so. There I lay waiting for death, when in comes a little old man with a bald head. He didn't seem anything much, and he asked for water. And I sinned and thought: 'What does he want here?' As soon as he saw us he took off his bag and placed it here and opened it."

"No, granny," said the little girl, "he put it first on the floor in the middle of the room and then he lifted it on to the bench."

So they disputed, calling to mind all his words and deeds: where he sat and slept, and what he did, and what he said to them.

Before the night the peasant came home in his cart, and he also began to talk of Elisha and what he had done for them.

"If he hadn't come to us," he said, "we should all have died in our sins. We were dying in despair, cursing God and man. But he brought us back to life, and through him we learned to know God and to believe in the goodness of men. Christ bless him! We lived like beasts before: and he made us men."

They gave food and drink to Yefim, and made a place for him to sleep in, and then lay down themselves.

Yefim lay awake, thinking of Elisha; his mind full of the three times he had seen him in the chapel at Jerusalem.

"So that is how he got a place before me," thought Yefim. "Whether God has accepted my labours or not I don't know. But God has certainly accepted his."

The next morning the people bade good-bye to Yefim, gave him patties for his journey and went to their work And Yefim took the road again.

XII

Yefim's pilgrimage had lasted a year. It was spring when he returned.

He reached home in the evening. His son was not at home, he was in the tavern, and when he did appear he was drunk. Yefim questioned him, and soon saw that his son had been making merry during his absence—had squandered all the money, and neglected all the work. Yefim began to upbraid him and he answered insolently: "Why didn't you stay yourself, instead of going off for a journey? You took all the money, and now you expect me to have some."

The old man grew angry and struck his son.

The next morning Yefim went off to the village headman to speak about his son. As he was passing Elisha's house, he saw Elisha's old wife standing in the doorway and beckoning to him.

"Good morning, friend," she said. "How did you make your journey?"

Yefim stopped. "Glory to God," he said, "all went well with me. I lost your old man, but I hear he has come home."

The old woman began to talk—she was always glad of a talk.

"Yes, he came back long ago, our breadwinner," she said. "He came home soon after the Assumption. And glad we were that God had brought him. We were lonesome enough when he wasn't with us. It's true he can't work much now, because his years are great; but still he is our master and we are glad. And how glad the boy was! 'Without him,' he says, 'it's as bad as without sunlight.' Ah! yes, desired friend, we were lonesome enough without him, and missed him very much, for we love him so."

"Well, then, is he at home now?"

"Yes, dear friend, he is at home, in the bee-garden; he is hiving the swarms. He says the bees are swarming finely this year. He says God gives us more than we deserve for our sins. The bees are so strong that he can't remember the like. Go, desired friend, he will be glad to see you."

Yefim passed through the passage into the yard and the bee-garden. And there stood Elisha in his gray kaftan, under the birch tree, without face-net or gloves, looking upwards, his arms stretched out, and his bald head shining, just as Yefim had seen him in Jerusalem. And above him through the birch branches, the sunshine gleamed like the sacred fire in the Holy Place, and round his head the golden bees had formed a halo and buzzed gently without stinging him. Yefim stood still.

The old woman called to Elisha.

"Gossip," she said, "our friend is here."

Elisha turned round, was glad, and went to meet him, plucking the bees gently out of his beard.

"God be with you, neighbour! God be with you, my dear friend! Well, and did you make your journey?"

"Yes, my feet made the journey. And I have brought you some holy water from the Jordan. Come home and get it. But I don't know if God has accepted my labour..."

"Well, well, glory to God, Christ save you!"

Yefim was silent.

"My feet were there," he said at last, "but whether my soul was there, or someone else's..."

"God's business, neighbour, God's business."

"I stopped on the way back at the cottage where you stayed behind..."

Elisha looked frightened and interrupted him hurriedly:

"God's business, neighbour, God's business. Well, come in and rest awhile, will you, and I will bring you some honey."

And Elisha changed the conversation and began to talk about household matters.

Yefim sighed and did not try again to speak about the people in the hut, or how he had seen Elisha in Jerusalem. But he now understood that the best way to keep one's vows to God and do His will is for each man to show loving-kindness and do good deeds unto others.

SWINBURNE

ALGERNON CHARLES SWINBURNE (1837–1909), the son of an English admiral, was born in London and educated at Eton and Oxford. Among his books of verse may be named *Atalanta in Calydon*, *Poems and Ballads*, *Songs before Sunrise*, and *Tristram of Lyonesse*. Swinburne, like Byron, was a good swimmer, and many of his poems refer to the sea. He has written, too, much about France and Italy and their stirring history. Swinburne's verse is as remarkable for its fulness of language as for its rhythm. The extract which follows is from *Tristram of Lyonesse*. Sir Tristram, the knight, is bringing the lovely princess Iseult from Ireland to be the bride of his uncle King Mark of Cornwall.

SIR TRISTRAM ROWS THE SHIP

And while they sat at speech as at a feast,
Came a light wind fast hardening forth of the east
And blackening till its might had marred the skies;
And the sea thrilled as with heart-sundering sighs
One after one drawn, with each breath it drew,
And the green hardened into iron blue,
And the soft light went out of all its face.
Then Tristram girt him for an oarsman's place
And took his oar and smote, and toiled with might
In the east wind's full face and the strong sea's spite
Labouring; and all the rowers rowed hard, but he

More mightily than any wearier three.
And Iseult watched him rowing with sinless eyes
That loved him but in holy girlish wise
For noble joy in his fair manliness
And trust and tender wonder; none the less
She thought if God had given her grace to be
Man, and make war on danger of earth and sea,
Even such a man she would be; for his stroke
Was mightiest as the mightier water broke,
And in sheer measure like strong music drave
Clean through the wet weight of the wallowing wave;
And as a tune before a great king played
For triumph was the tune their strong strokes made,
And sped the ship through with smooth strife of oars
Over the mid sea's grey foam-paven floors,
For all the loud breach of the waves at will.
So for an hour they fought the storm out still,
And the shorn foam spun from the blades, and high
The keel sprang from the wave-ridge, and the sky
Glared at them for a breath's space through the rain;
Then the bows with a sharp shock plunged again
Down, and the sea clashed on them, and so rose
The bright stem like one panting from swift blows,
And as a swimmer's joyous beaten head
Rears itself laughing, so in that sharp stead
The light ship lifted her long quivering bows
As might the man his buffeted strong brows
Out of the wave-breach; for with one stroke yet
Went all men's oars together, strongly set
As to loud music, and with hearts uplift
They smote their strong way through the drench and drift:
Till the keen hour had chafed itself to death
And the east wind fell fitfully, breath by breath,
Tired; and across the thin and slackening rain
Sprang the face southward of the sun again.
Then all they rested and were eased at heart;
And Iseult rose up where she sat apart,
And with her sweet soul deepening her deep eyes
Cast the furs from her and subtle embroideries

That wrapped her from the storming rain and spray,
And shining like all April in one day,
Hair, face, and throat dashed with the straying showers,
She stood the first of all the whole world's flowers,
And laughed on Tristram with her eyes, and said,
"I too have heart then, I was not afraid."

TENNYSON

ALFRED TENNYSON (1809–92) was the son of a Lincolnshire clergyman. His first poems were published at the age of seventeen before he went up to Trinity College, Cambridge, and other volumes of short pieces followed at intervals during the next sixteen years. His longer poems, *The Princess*, *In Memoriam*, *Maud* and *The Idylls of the King*, all published later, did not surpass the beauty of his earlier, shorter pieces Tennyson also wrote a few plays, one of which, *Becket*, was staged with much success by Henry Irving.

Sir Galahad, the subject of the first of the poems which follow, was the stainless knight of the Round Table, who achieved the Holy Grail, the Sacred Cup of our Lord which had fallen into the hands of the heathen.

Saint Agnes, the child martyr (celebrated on 21 January), is the maiden saint as Galahad is the pure knight.

SIR GALAHAD

My good blade carves the casques of men,
   My tough lance thrusteth sure,
My strength is as the strength of ten,
   Because my heart is pure.
The shattering trumpet shrilleth high,
   The hard brands shiver on the steel,
The splinter'd spear-shafts crack and fly,
   The horse and rider reel:
They reel, they roll in clanging lists,
   And when the tide of combat stands,
Perfume and flowers fall in showers,
   That lightly rain from ladies' hands

How sweet are looks that ladies bend
   On whom their favours fall!
For them I battle till the end,
   To save from shame and thrall

But all my heart is drawn above,
  My knees are bow'd in crypt and shrine:
I never felt the kiss of love,
  Nor maiden's hand in mine.
More bounteous aspects on me beam,
  Me mightier transports move and thrill;
So keep I fair thro' faith and prayer
  A virgin heart in work and will.

When down the stormy crescent goes,
  A light before me swims,
Between dark stems the forest glows,
  I hear a noise of hymns:
Then by some secret shrine I ride;
  I hear a voice, but none are there;
The stalls are void, the doors are wide,
  The tapers burning fair.
Fair gleams the snowy altar-cloth,
  The silver vessels sparkle clean,
The shrill bell rings, the censer swings,
  And solemn chaunts resound between.

Sometimes on lonely mountain-meres
  I find a magic bark,
I leap on board: no helmsman steers:
  I float till all is dark.
A gentle sound, an awful light!
  Three angels bear the holy Grail:
With folded feet, in stoles of white,
  On sleeping wings they sail.
Ah, blessed vision! blood of God!
  My spirit beats her mortal bars,
As down dark tides the glory slides,
  And star-like mingles with the stars.

When on my goodly charger borne
  Thro' dreaming towns I go,
The cock crows ere the Christmas morn,
  The streets are dumb with snow.

The tempest crackles on the leads,
  And, ringing, springs from brand and mail;
But o'er the dark a glory spreads,
  And gilds the driving hail.
I leave the plain, I climb the height;
  No branchy thicket shelter yields;
But blessed forms in whistling storms
  Fly o'er waste fens and windy fields.

A maiden knight—to me is given
  . Such hope, I know not fear;
I yearn to breathe the airs of heaven
  That often meet me here.
I muse on joy that will not cease,
  Pure spaces clothed in living beams,
Pure lilies of eternal peace,
  Whose odours haunt my dreams;
And, stricken by an angel's hand,
  This mortal armour that I wear,   ·
This weight and size, this heart and eyes,
  Are touched, are turned to finest air.

The clouds are broken in the sky,
  And thro' the mountain-walls
A rolling organ-harmony
  Swells up, and shakes and falls.
Then move the trees, the copses nod,
  Wings flutter, voices hover clear:
"O just and faithful knight of God!
  Ride on! the prize is near."
So pass I hostel, hall and grange;
  By bridge and ford, by park and pale,
All-armed I ride, whate'er betide,
  Until I find the holy Grail.

ST AGNES' EVE

Deep on the convent-roof the snows
  Are sparkling to the moon:
My breath to heaven like vapour goes:
  May my soul follow soon!
The shadows of the convent-towers
  Slant down the snowy sward,
Still creeping with the creeping hours
  That lead me to my Lord:
Make Thou my spirit pure and clear
  As are the frosty skies,
Or this first snowdrop of the year
  That in my bosom lies.

As these white robes are soil'd and dark,
  To yonder shining ground;
As this pale taper's earthly spark,
  To yonder argent round;
So shows my soul before the Lamb,
  My spirit before Thee;
So in mine earthly house I am,
  To that I hope to be.
Break up the heavens, O Lord! and far,
  Thro' all yon starlight keen,
Draw me, Thy bride, a glittering star,
  In raiment white and clean.

He lifts me to the golden doors;
  The flashes come and go;
All heaven bursts her starry floors,
  And strows her lights below,
And deepens on and up! the gates
  Roll back, and far within
For me the Heavenly Bridegroom waits,
  To make me pure of sin.
The sabbaths of Eternity,
  One sabbath deep and wide—
A light upon the shining sea—
  The Bridegroom with his bride!

CERVANTES

MIGUEL DE CERVANTES (1547–1616), the greatest of Spanish authors, who was born about 17 years before Shakespeare, wrote *Don Quixote* to ridicule grotesque and highflown romances about knights, magicians, giants and enchanted castles The book tells how, in La Mancha, a poor village of Spain, dwelt an elderly gentleman named Quixada or Quixana, who had read so many of these fabulous stories that his head became turned He imagined that he was called upon to become a knight like one of the heroes of the Round Table, and so he habited himself in rusty armour that had been hanging on the walls for generations, and, under the name of Don or Sir Quixote set out to find adventures and right the wrongs of the world. Don Quixote, with all his eccentricity, is a noble-minded gentleman, and his delicate good qualities form an excellent contrast to those of the fat, greedy, good-humoured peasant, Sancho Panza, whom the Don chose as his squire Don Quixote mounted on a lean and ancient horse (accompanied by Sancho riding on a donkey), and with his kind old head full of the fabulous incidents and elaborate courtesies of the ancient days of chivalry, rides forth into the commonplace, work-a-day world of carters and inn-keepers and country girls, who regard him just as English farm labourers of to-day would regard a tall, thin, grey-haired man in an old suit of armour who came riding over the hills among them, addressing them in elaborate language as noble knights, calling the dairymaids countesses and the cowsheds castles, and assuring them that he was Sir Lancelot or Sir Bedivere.   The translation is that of John Ormsby, first published in 1885

AN ADVENTURE OF DON QUIXOTE

Meanwhile Don Quixote worked upon a farm labourer, a neighbour of his, an honest man (if indeed that title can be given to him who is poor), but with very little wit in his pate. In a word, he so talked him over, and with such persuasions and promises, that the poor clown made up his mind to sally forth with him and serve him as esquire. Don Quixote, among other things, told him he ought to be ready to go with him gladly, because any moment an adventure might occur that might win an island in the twinkling of an eye and leave him governor of it On these and the like promises Sancho Panza (for so the labourer was called) left wife and children, and engaged himself as esquire to his neighbour. Don Quixote next set about getting some money; and selling one thing and pawning another, and making a bad bargain in every case, he got together a fair sum He provided himself with a buckler, which he begged as a loan from a friend, and, restoring his battered helmet as best he could, he warned his squire Sancho of the day and hour he meant to set out, that he might provide himself with what he thought most needful. Above all, he charged him to take alforjas[1] with him. The other said he would, and that he meant to take also a very good ass that he had, as he was not much given to going on foot. About the ass, Don Quixote hesitated a little, trying whether he could call to mind any knight-errant taking with him an esquire mounted on ass-back, but no instance occurred to his memory. For all that, however, he determined to take him, intending to furnish him with a more honourable mount when a chance of it presented itself, by appropriating the horse of the first discourteous knight he encountered. Himself he provided with shirts and such other things as he could, according to the advice the landlord had given him; all which being settled and done, without taking leave, Sancho Panza of his wife and children, or Don Quixote of his housekeeper and niece, they sallied forth, unseen by anybody, from the village one night, and made such good way in the course of it that by daylight they held themselves safe from discovery, even should search be made for them.

Sancho rode on his ass like a patriarch with his alforjas and bota[2], and longing to see himself soon governor of the island his master had promised him. Don Quixote decided upon taking the same route and road he had taken on his first journey, that over the Campo de Montiel, which he travelled with less discomfort than on the last occasion, for, as it was early morning and the rays of the sun fell on them obliquely, the heat did not distress them.

And now said Sancho Panza to his master, "Your worship will take care, Señor Knight-errant, not to forget about the island you have promised me, for be it ever so big I'll be equal to governing it."

To which Don Quixote replied, "Thou must know, friend Sancho Panza, that it was a practice very much in vogue with the knights-errant of old to make their squires governors of the islands or kingdoms they won, and I am determined that there shall be no failure on my part in so liberal a custom; on the contrary, I mean to improve upon it, for they sometimes, and

---

[1] saddlebags. [2] wine skin.

perhaps most frequently, waited until their squires were old, and then when they had had enough of service and hard days and worse nights, they gave them some title or other, of count, or at the most marquis, of some valley or province more or less; but if thou livest and I live, it may well be that before six days are over, I may have won some kingdom that has others dependent upon it, which will be just the thing to enable thee to be crowned king of one of them. Nor needst thou count this wonderful, for things and chances fall to the lot of such knights in ways so unexampled and unexpected that I might easily give thee even more than I promise thee."

"In that case," said Sancho Panza, "if I should become a king by one of those miracles your worship speaks of, even Juana Gutierrez, my old woman, would come to be queen and my children infantes."

"Well, who doubts it?" said Don Quixote

"I doubt it," replied Sancho Panza, "because for my part I am persuaded that if God was to shower down kingdoms upon earth, not one of them would fit the head of Mari Gutierrez. Let me tell you, señor, she is not worth two maravedis for a queen; countess will fit her better, and that only with God's help."

"Leave it to God, Sancho," returned Don Quixote, "for he will give her what suits her best, but do not undervalue thyself so much as to come to be content with anything less than being governor of a province."

"I will not, señor," answered Sancho, "especially as I have a man of such quality for a master in your worship, who will be able to give me all that will be suitable for me and that I can bear."

At this point they came in sight of thirty or forty windmills that there are on that plain, and as soon as Don Quixote saw them he said to his squire, "Fortune is arranging matters for us better than we could have shaped our desires ourselves, for look there, friend Sancho Panza, where thirty or more monstrous giants present themselves, all of whom I mean to engage in battle and slay, and with whose spoils we shall begin to make our fortunes; for this is righteous warfare, and it is God's good service to sweep so evil a breed from off the face of the earth."

"What giants?" said Sancho Panza.

"Those thou seest there," answered his master, "with the long arms, and some have them well-nigh two leagues long."

"Look, your worship," said Sancho; "what we see there are not giants but windmills, and what seem to be their arms are the sails that turned by the wind make the millstone go."

"It is easy to see," replied Don Quixote, "that thou art not used to this business of adventures; those are giants; and if thou art afraid, away with thee out of this and betake thyself to prayer while I engage them in fierce and unequal combat."

So saying, he gave the spur to his steed Rocinante, heedless of the cries his squire Sancho sent after him, warning him that most certainly they were windmills and not giants he was going to attack. He, however, was so positive they were giants that he neither heard the cries of Sancho, nor perceived, near as he was, what they were, but made at them shouting, "Fly not, cowards and vile beings, for it is a single knight that attacks you."

A slight breeze at this moment sprang up, and the great sails began to move, seeing which Don Quixote exclaimed, "Though ye flourish more arms than the giant Briareus, ye have to reckon with me."

So saying, and commending himself with all his heart to his lady Dulcinea, imploring her to support him in such a peril, with lance in rest and covered by his buckler, he charged at Rocinante's fullest gallop and fell upon the first mill that stood in front of him; but as he drove his lance-point into the sail the wind whirled it round with such force that it shivered the lance to pieces, sweeping with it horse and rider, who went rolling over on the plain, in a sorry plight. Sancho hastened to his assistance as fast as his ass could go, and when he reached him found him unable to move, with such a shock had Rocinante come down with him.

"God bless me!" said Sancho, "didn't I tell your worship to mind what you were about, for they were only windmills? and no one could have made any mistake about it but one who had something of the same kind in his head."

"Hush, friend Sancho," replied Don Quixote, "the fortunes of war more than any other are liable to frequent fluctuations; and moreover I think, and it is the truth, that that same sage Friston who carried off my study and books, has turned these giants into mills in order to rob me of the glory of vanquishing them, such is the enmity he bears me; but in the end his wicked arts will avail but little against my good sword."

"God order it as he may," said Sancho Panza, and helping him to rise got him up again on Rocinante, whose shoulder was half out; and then, discussing the late adventure, they followed the road to Puerto Lapice, for there, said Don Quixote, they could not fail to find adventures in abundance and variety, as it was a great thoroughfare. For all that, he was much grieved at the loss of his lance, and saying so to his squire, he added, "I remember having read how a Spanish knight, Diego Perez de Vargas by name, having broken his sword in battle, tore from an oak a ponderous bough or branch, and with it did such things that day, and pounded so many Moors, that he got the surname of Machuca, and he and his descendants from that day forth were called Vargas y Machuca. I mention this because from the first oak I see I mean to rend such another branch, large and stout like that, with which I am determined and resolved to do such deeds that thou mayest deem thyself very fortunate in being found worthy to come and see them, and be an eye-witness of things that will with difficulty be believed."

"Be that as God will," said Sancho; "I believe it all as your worship says it; but straighten yourself a little, for you seem all on one side, may be from the shaking of the fall."

"That is the truth," said Don Quixote, "and if I make no complaint of the pain it is because knights-errant are not permitted to complain of any wound, even though their bowels be coming out through it."

"If so," said Sancho, "I have nothing to say, but God knows I would rather your worship complained when anything ailed you. For my part, I confess I must complain however small the ache may be; unless indeed this rule about not complaining extends to the squires of knights-errant also."

Don Quixote could not help laughing at his squire's simplicity, and he assured him he might complain whenever and however he chose, just as he liked, for, so far, he had never read of anything to the contrary in the order of knighthood.

Sancho bade him remember it was dinner-time, to which his master answered that he wanted nothing himself just then, but that *he* might eat when he had a mind. With this permission

Sancho settled himself as comfortably as he could on his beast, and taking out of the alforjas what he had stowed away in them, he jogged along behind his master munching deliberately, and from time to time taking a pull at the bota with a relish that the thirstiest tapster in Malaga might have envied; and while he went on in this way, gulping down draught after draught, he never gave a thought to any of the promises his master had made him, nor did he rate it as hardship but rather as recreation going in quest of adventures, however dangerous they might be Finally they passed the night among some trees, from one of which Don Quixote plucked a dry branch to serve him after a fashion as a lance, and fixed on it the head he had removed from the broken one. All that night Don Quixote lay awake thinking of his lady Dulcinea, in order to conform to what he had read in his books, how many a night in the forests and deserts knights used to lie sleepless supported by the memory of their mistresses. Not so did Sancho Panza spend it, for having his stomach full of something stronger than chicory water he made but one sleep of it, and, if his master had not called him, neither the rays of the sun beating on his face nor all the cheery notes of the birds welcoming the approach of day would have had power to waken him. On getting up he tried the bota and found it somewhat less full than the night before, which grieved his heart because they did not seem to be on the way to remedy the deficiency readily. Don Quixote did not care to break his fast, for, as has been already said, he confined himself to savoury recollections for nourishment.

They returned to their former road, leading to Puerto Lapice, and at three in the afternoon they came in sight of it. "Here, brother Sancho Panza," said Don Quixote when he saw it, "we may plunge our hands up to the elbows in what they call adventures; but observe, even shouldst thou see me in the greatest danger in the world, thou must not put a hand to thy sword in my defence, unless indeed thou perceivest that those who assail me are rabble or base folk; for in that case thou mayest very properly aid me, but if they be knights it is on no account permitted or allowed thee by the laws of knighthood to help me until thou hast been dubbed a knight."

"Most certainly, señor," replied Sancho, "your worship shall be fully obeyed in this matter; all the more as of myself I am peaceful and no friend to mixing in strife and quarrels: it is true that as regards the defence of my own person I shall not give much heed to those laws, for laws human and divine allow each one to defend himself against any assailant whatever."

"That I grant," said Don Quixote, "but in this matter of aiding me against knights thou must hold in check thy natural impetuosity."

"I will do so, I promise you," answered Sancho, "and I will keep this precept as carefully as Sunday."

While they were thus talking there appeared on the road two friars of the order of St Benedict, mounted on two dromedaries, for not less tall were the two mules they rode on. They wore travelling spectacles and carried sunshades; and behind them came a coach attended by four or five persons on horseback and two muleteers on foot. In the coach there was, as afterwards appeared, a Biscay lady on her way to Seville, where her husband was about to take passage for the Indies with an appointment of high honour. The friars, though going the same road, were not in her company; but the moment Don Quixote perceived them he said to his squire, "Either I am mistaken, or this is going to be the most famous adventure that has ever been seen, for those black bodies we see there must be, and doubtless are, magicians who are carrying off some stolen princess in that coach, and with all my might I must undo this wrong."

"This will be worse than the windmills," said Sancho. "Look, señor; those are friars of St Benedict, and the coach plainly belongs to some travellers: mind, I tell you to mind well what you are about and don't let the devil mislead you."

"I have told thee already, Sancho," replied Don Quixote, "that on the subject of adventures thou knowest little. What I say is the truth, as thou shalt see presently."

So saying, he advanced and posted himself in the middle of the road along which the friars were coming, and as soon as he thought they had come near enough to hear what he said, he cried aloud, "Devilish and unnatural beings, release instantly the highborn princesses whom you are carrying off by force in this coach, else prepare to meet a speedy death as the just punishment of your evil deeds."

The friars drew rein and stood wondering at the appearance of

DON QUIXOTE'S FIGHT WITH YANGUESANS
William Strang

Don Quixote as well as at his words, to which they replied, "Señor Caballero, we are not devilish or unnatural, but two brothers of St Benedict following our road, nor do we know whether or not there are any captive princesses coming in this coach."

"No soft words with me, for I know you, lying rabble," said Don Quixote, and without waiting for a reply he spurred Rocinante and with levelled lance charged the first friar with such fury and determination, that, if the friar had not flung himself off the mule, he would have brought him to the ground against his will, and sore wounded, if not killed outright. The second brother, seeing how his comrade was treated, drove his heels into his castle of a mule and made off across the country faster than the wind.

Sancho Panza, when he saw the friar on the ground, dismounting briskly from his ass, rushed towards him and began to strip off his gown. At that instant the friars' muleteers came up and asked what he was stripping him for. Sancho answered them that this fell to him lawfully as spoil of the battle which his lord Don Quixote had won. The muleteers, who had no idea of a joke and did not understand all this about battles and spoils, seeing that Don Quixote was some distance off talking to the travellers in the coach, fell upon Sancho, knocked him down, and leaving hardly a hair in his beard, belaboured him with kicks and left him stretched breathless and senseless on the ground; and without any more delay helped the friar to mount, who, trembling, terrified, and pale, as soon as he found himself in the saddle, spurred after his companion, who was standing at a distance looking on, watching the result of the onslaught; then, not caring to wait for the end of the affair just begun, they pursued their journey making more crosses than if they had the devil after them.

Don Quixote was, as has been said, speaking to the lady in the coach: "Your beauty, lady mine," said he, "may now dispose of your person as may be most in accordance with your pleasure, for the pride of your ravishers lies prostrate on the ground through this strong arm of mine; and lest you should be pining to know the name of your deliverer, know that I am called Don Quixote of La Mancha, knight-errant and adventurer, and captive to the peerless and beautiful lady Dulcinea del Toboso: and in return for the service you have received of me I ask no more than that you should return to El Toboso, and on my behalf present yourself before that lady and tell her what I have done to set you free."

One of the squires in attendance upon the coach, a Biscayan, was listening to all Don Quixote was saying, and, perceiving that he would not allow the coach to go on, but was saying it must return at once to El Toboso, he made at him, and seizing his lance addressed him in bad Castilian and worse Biscayan after this fashion, "Begone, caballero, and ill go with thee; by the God that made me, unless thou quittest coach, slayest thee as art here a Biscayan."

Don Quixote understood him quite well, and answered him very quietly, "If thou wert a knight, as thou art none, I should have already chastised thy folly and rashness, miserable creature." To which the Biscayan returned, "I no gentleman!—I swear to God thou liest as I am Christian: if thou droppest lance and drawest sword, soon shalt thou see thou art carrying water to the cat: Biscayan on land, hidalgo at sea, hidalgo at the devil, and look, if thou sayest otherwise thou liest."

"You will see presently," replied Don Quixote; and throwing his lance on the ground he drew his sword, braced his buckler on his arm, and attacked the Biscayan, bent upon taking his life

The Biscayan, when he saw him coming on, though he wished to dismount from his mule, in which, being one of those sorry ones let out for hire, he had no confidence, had no choice but to draw his sword; it was lucky for him, however, that he was near the coach, from which he was able to snatch a cushion that served him for a shield, and then they went at one another as if they had been two mortal enemies. The others strove to make peace between them, but could not, for the Biscayan declared in his disjointed phrase that if they did not let him finish his battle he would kill his mistress and everyone that strove to prevent him. The lady in the coach, amazed and terrified at what she saw, ordered the coachman to draw aside a little, and set herself to watch this severe struggle, in the course of which the Biscayan smote Don Quixote a mighty stroke on the shoulder over the top of his buckler, which, given to one without armour, would have cleft him to the waist Don Quixote, feeling the weight of this prodigious blow, cried aloud, saying, "O lady of my soul, Dulcinea, flower of beauty, come to the aid of this your knight, who, in fulfilling his obligations to your beauty, finds himself in this extreme peril " To say this, to lift his sword, to shelter himself well behind his buckler, and to assail the Biscayan was the work of an instant, determined as he was to put all to the venture of a single blow. The Biscayan, seeing him come on in this way, was convinced of his courage by his spirited bearing, and resolved to follow his example, so he waited for him keeping well under cover of his cushion, being unable to execute any sort of manœuvre with his mule, which, dead tired and never meant for this kind of game, could not stir a step.

On, then, as aforesaid, came Don Quixote against the wary Biscayan, with uplifted sword and a firm intention of splitting him in half, while on his side the Biscayan waited for him sword in hand, and under the protection of his cushion; and all present stood trembling, waiting in suspense the result of blows such as threatened to fall, and the lady in the coach and the rest of her following were making a thousand vows and offerings to all the images and shrines of Spain, that God might deliver her squire and all of them from this great peril in which they found themselves.

With trenchant swords upraised and poised on high, it seemed as though the two valiant and wrathful combatants stood threatening heaven, and earth, and hell, with such resolution and determination did they bear themselves. The fiery Biscayan was the first to strike a blow, which was delivered with such force and fury that had not the sword turned in its course, that single stroke would have sufficed to put an end to the bitter struggle and to all the adventures of our knight; but that good fortune which reserved him for greater things, turned aside the sword of his adversary, so that, although it smote him upon the left shoulder, it did him no more harm than to strip all that side of its armour, carrying away a great part of his helmet with half of his ear, all which with fearful ruin fell to the ground, leaving him in a sorry plight.

Good God! Who is there that could properly describe the rage that filled the heart of our Manchegan when he saw himself dealt with in this fashion? All that can be said is, it was such that he again raised himself in his stirrups, and, grasping his sword more firmly with both hands, he came down on the Biscayan with such fury, smiting him full over the cushion and over the head, that—

even so good a shield proving useless—as if a mountain had fallen on him, he began to bleed from nose, mouth, and ears, reeling as if about to fall backwards from his mule, as no doubt he would have done had he not flung his arms about its neck, at the same time, however, he slipped his feet out of the stirrups and then unclasped his arms, and the mule, taking fright at the terrible blow, made off across the plain, and with a few plunges flung its master to the ground. Don Quixote stood looking on very calmly, and, when he saw him fall, leaped from his horse and with great briskness ran to him, and, presenting the point of his sword to his eyes, bade him surrender, or he would cut his head off. The Biscayan was so bewildered that he was unable to answer a word, and it would have gone hard with him, so blind was Don Quixote, had not the ladies in the coach, who had hitherto been watching the combat in great terror, hastened to where he stood and implored him with earnest entreaties to grant them the great grace and favour of sparing their squire's life; to which Don Quixote replied with much gravity and dignity, "In truth, fair ladies, I am well content to do what you ask of me; but it must be on one condition and understanding, which is that this knight promise me to go to the village of El Toboso, and on my part present himself before the peerless lady Dulcinea, that she deal with him as shall be most pleasing to her."

The terrified and disconsolate ladies, without discussing Don Quixote's demand or asking who Dulcinea might be, promised that their squire should do all that had been commanded on his part.

"Then, on the faith of that promise," said Don Quixote, "I shall do him no further harm, though he well deserves it of me."

Now by this time Sancho had risen, rather the worse for the handling of the friars' muleteers, and stood watching the battle of his master, Don Quixote, and praying to God in his heart that it might be his will to grant him the victory, and that he might thereby win some island to make him governor of, as he had promised. Seeing, therefore, that the struggle was now over, and that his master was returning to mount Rocinante, he approached to hold the stirrup for him, and, before he could mount, he went on his knees before him, and taking his hand. kissed it saying, "May it please your worship, Señor Don Quixote, to give me the government of that island which has been won in this hard fight, for be it ever so big I feel myself in sufficient force to be able to govern it as much and as well as anyone in the world who has ever governed islands."

To which Don Quixote replied, "You must know, brother Sancho, that this adventure and those like it are not adventures of islands, but of cross-roads, in which nothing is got except a broken head or an ear the less: have patience, for adventures will present themselves from which I may make you, not only a governor, but something more."

Sancho gave him many thanks, and again kissing his hand and the skirt of his hauberk, helped him to mount Rocinante, and mounting his ass himself, proceeded to follow his master, who at a brisk pace, without taking leave, or saying anything further to the ladies belonging to the coach, turned into a wood that was hard by. Sancho followed him at his ass's best trot, but Rocinante stepped out so that, seeing himself left behind, he was forced to call to his master to wait for him. Don Quixote did so, reining in Rocinante until his weary squire came up, who on reaching him said, "It seems to me, señor, it would be prudent in us to go and take refuge in some church, for, seeing how mauled he with whom you fought has been left, it will be no wonder if they give information of the affair to the Holy Brotherhood and arrest us, and, faith, if they do, before we come out of gaol we shall have to sweat for it."

"Peace," said Don Quixote; "where hast thou ever seen or heard that a knight-errant has been arraigned before a court of justice, however many homicides he may have committed?"

"I know nothing about omecils," answered Sancho, "nor in my life have had anything to do with one; I only know that the Holy Brotherhood looks after those who fight in the fields, and in that other matter I do not meddle."

"Then thou needst have no uneasiness, my friend," said Don Quixote, "for I will deliver thee out of the hands of the Chaldeans, much more out of those of the Brotherhood. But tell me, as thou livest, hast thou seen a more valiant knight than I in all the known world; hast thou read in history of any who has or had higher mettle in attack, more spirit in maintaining it, more dexterity in wounding or skill in overthrowing?"

"The truth is," answered Sancho, "that I have never read any history, for I can neither read nor write, but what I will venture to bet is that a more daring master than your worship I have never served in all the days of my life, and God grant that this daring be not paid for where I have said; what I beg of your worship is to dress your wound, for a great deal of blood flows from that ear, and I have here some lint and a little white ointment in the alforjas."

"All that might be well dispensed with," said Don Quixote, "if I had remembered to make a vial of the balsam of Fierabras, for time and medicine are saved by one single drop."

"What vial and what balsam is that?" said Sancho Panza

"It is a balsam," answered Don Quixote, "the receipt of which I have in my memory, with which one need have no fear of death, or dread dying of any wound; and so when I make it and give it to thee thou hast nothing to do when in some battle thou seest they have cut me in half through the middle of the body—as is wont to happen frequently—but neatly and with great nicety, ere the blood congeal, to place that portion of the body which shall have fallen to the ground upon the other half which remains in the saddle, taking care to fit it on evenly and exactly Then thou shalt give me to drink but two drops of the balsam I have mentioned, and thou shalt see me become sounder than an apple."

"If that be so," said Panza, "I renounce henceforth the government of the promised island, and desire nothing more in payment of my many and faithful services than that your worship give me the receipt of this supreme liquor, for I am persuaded it will be worth more than two reals an ounce anywhere, and I want no more to pass the rest of my life in ease and honour, but it remains to be told if it costs much to make it.'

"With less than three reals six quarts of it may be made," said Don Quixote.

"Sinner that I am!" said Sancho, "then why does your worship put off making it and teaching it to me?"

"Peace, friend," answered Don Quixote; "greater secrets I mean to teach thee and greater favours to bestow upon thee; and for the present let us see to the dressing, for my ear pains me more than I could wish."

Sancho took out some lint and ointment from the alforjas; but when Don Quixote came to see his helmet shattered, he was like to lose his senses, and clapping his hand upon his sword and raising his eyes to heaven, he said, "I swear by the Creator of all things and the four Gospels in their fullest extent, to do as the great Marquis of Mantua did when he swore to avenge the death of his nephew Baldwin (and that was not to eat bread from a table-cloth, nor embrace his wife, and other points which, though I cannot now call them to mind, I here grant as expressed), until I take complete vengeance upon him who has committed such an offence against me."

Hearing this, Sancho said to him, "Your worship should bear in mind, Señor Don Quixote, that if the knight has done what was commanded him in going to present himself before my lady Dulcinea del Toboso, he will have done all that he was bound to do, and does not deserve further punishment unless he commits some new offence."

"Thou hast said well and hit the point," answered Don Quixote; "and so I recall the oath in so far as relates to taking fresh vengeance on him, but I make and confirm it anew to lead the life I have said until such time as I take by force from some knight another helmet such as this and as good; and think not, Sancho, that I am raising smoke with straw in doing so, for I have one to imitate in the matter, since the very same thing to a hair happened in the case of Mambrino's helmet, which cost Sacripante so dear."

"Señor," said Sancho, "to the devil with all such oaths, for they are very pernicious to salvation and hurtful to the conscience; just tell me now, if for several days to come we fall in with no man armed with a helmet, what are we to do? Is the oath to be observed in spite of all the inconvenience and discomfort it will be to sleep in your clothes, and not to sleep in a house, and a thousand other mortifications contained in the oath of that old fool the Marquis of Mantua, which your worship is now wanting to revive? Mind you there are no men in armour travelling on any of these roads, nothing but carriers and carters, who not only do not wear helmets, but perhaps never heard tell of them all their lives."

"Thou art wrong there," said Don Quixote, "for we shall not have been two hours among these cross-roads before we see more men in armour than came to Albracca to win the fair Angelica."

"Enough," said Sancho; "so be it then, and God grant us

success, and that the time for winning that island which is costing me so dear may soon come, and then let me die."

"I have already told thee, Sancho," said Don Quixote, "not to be uneasy on that score; for if an island should fail, there is the kingdom of Denmark, or of Sobradisa, which will fit thee as ring the finger, and all the more that being on *terra firma* thou wilt all the better enjoy thyself. But let us leave that to its own time; see if thou hast anything for us to eat in those alforjas, because we must presently go in quest of some castle where we may lodge to-night and make the balsam I told thee of, for I swear to thee by God, this ear is giving me great pain."

"I have here an onion and a little cheese and a few scraps of bread," said Sancho, "but they are not victuals fit for a valiant knight like your worship."

"How little thou knowest about it," answered Don Quixote; "I would have thee to know, Sancho, that it is the glory of knights-errant to go without eating for a month, and even when they do eat, that it should be of what comes first to hand; and this would have been clear to thee hadst thou read as many histories as I have, for, though they are very many, among them all I have found no mention made of knights-errant eating, unless by accident or at some sumptuous banquets prepared for them, and the rest of the time they passed in dalliance. And though it is plain they could not do without eating and performing all the other natural functions, because, in fact, they were men like ourselves, it is plain too that, wandering as they did the most part of their lives through woods and wilds and without a cook, their most usual fare would be rustic viands such as those thou dost now offer me; so that, friend Sancho, let not that distress thee which pleases me, and do not seek to make a new world or pervert knight-errantry."

"Pardon me, your worship," said Sancho, "for, as I cannot read or write, as I said just now, I neither know nor comprehend the rules of the profession of chivalry: henceforward I will stock the alforjas with every kind of dry fruit for your worship, as you are a knight; and for myself, as I am not one, I will furnish them with poultry and other things more substantial."

"I do not say, Sancho," replied Don Quixote, "that it is imperative on knights-errant not to eat anything else but the fruits thou speakest of; only that their more usual diet must be those, and certain herbs they found in the fields which they knew and I know too"

"A good thing it is," answered Sancho, "to know those herbs, for to my thinking it will be needful some day to put that knowledge into practice."

And here taking out what he said he had brought, the pair made their repast peaceably and sociably. But anxious to find quarters for the night, they quickly despatched their poor dry fare, mounted at once, and made haste to reach some habitation before night set in; but daylight and the hope of succeeding in their object failed them close by the huts of some goatherds, so they determined to pass the night there, and it was as much to Sancho's discontent not to have reached a house, as it was to his master's satisfaction to sleep under the open heaven, for he fancied that each time this happened to him he performed an act of ownership that helped to prove his chivalry.

THOMAS LOVE PEACOCK

THOMAS LOVE PEACOCK (1785-1866) was born at Weymouth. His life was passed in easy, quiet circumstances. He held an important post under the East India Company, and gave his leisure to literature. He was a friend of Shelley (of whose life he wrote a short sketch) and he himself wrote verse—the best of it appearing as songs in his half-humorous, half-satirical novels, with their curious names, *Headlong Hall*, *Nightmare Abbey*, *Crotchet Castle* and *Gryll Grange*. He wrote two "historical" tales, *The Misfortunes of Elphin* and *Maid Marian*. The extract which follows is taken from the last named book.

A RESCUE BY ROBIN HOOD

[The outlawed Earl of Huntingdon lived in Sherwood Forest under the name of Robin Hood. He loved Matilda, daughter of the fiery old Baron Fitzwater, and they were about to be wedded when the ceremony was interrupted by the entry of Sir Ralph Montfaucon who had been sent to arrest the Earl. Robin escaped to the forest, and the parted lovers were enabled to meet by the jovial old Brother Michael of Rubygill Abbey. Sir Ralph spent many days searching for Robin Hood.]

I

An autumn and a winter had passed away, when the course of his perlustrations brought him one day to a beautiful sylvan valley, where he found a number of young women weaving garlands of flowers, and singing over their pleasant occupation. He approached them, and courteously inquired the way to the nearest town

"There is no town within several miles," was the answer.

"A village, then, if it be but large enough to furnish an inn?"

"There is Gamwell just by, but there is no inn nearer than the nearest town."

"An abbey, then?"

"There is no abbey nearer than the nearest inn."

"A house, then, or a cottage, where I may obtain hospitality for the night?"

"Hospitality!" said one of the young women; "you have not far to seek for that. Do you not know that you are in the neighbourhood of Gamwell Hall?"

"So far from it," said the knight, "that I never heard the name of Gamwell Hall before."

"Never heard of Gamwell Hall!" exclaimed all the young women together, who could as soon have dreamed of his never having heard of the sky.

"Indeed, no!" said Sir Ralph; "but I shall be very happy to get rid of my ignorance."

"And so shall I," said his squire; "for it seems that in this case knowledge will for once be a cure for hunger, wherewith I am grievously afflicted."

"And why are you so busy, my pretty damsels, weaving these garlands?" said the knight.

"Why, do you not know, sir," said one of the young women, "that to-morrow is Gamwell feast?"

The knight was again obliged, with all humility, to confess his ignorance.

"Oh! sir," said his informant, "then you will have something to see, that I can tell you; for we shall choose a Queen of the May, and we shall crown her with flowers, and place her in a chariot of flowers, and draw it with lines of flowers, and we shall hang all the trees with flowers, and we shall strew all the ground with flowers, and we shall dance with flowers, and in flowers, and on flowers, and we shall be all flowers."

"That you will," said the knight; "and the sweetest and

brightest of all the flowers of the May, my pretty damsels." On which all the pretty damsels smiled at him and each other.

"And there will be all sorts of May-games, and there will be prizes for archery, and there will be the knight's ale, and the foresters' venison, and there will be Kit Scrapesqueak with his fiddle, and little Tom Whistlerap with his fife and tabor, and Sam Trumtwang with his harp, and Peter Muggledrone with his bagpipe, and how I shall dance with Will Whitethorn!" added the girl, clapping her hands as she spoke, and bounding from the ground with the pleasure of the anticipation.

A tall, athletic young man approached, to whom the rustic maidens courtesied with great respect; and one of them informed Sir Ralph that it was young Master William Gamwell. The young gentleman invited and conducted the knight to the hall, where he introduced him to the old knight, his father, and to the old lady, his mother, and to the young lady, his sister, and to a number of bold yeomen, who were laying siege to beef, brawn, and plum pie, around a ponderous table, and taking copious draughts of old October. A motto was inscribed over the interior door—

EAT, DRINK, AND BE MERRY:

an injunction which Sir Ralph and his squire showed remarkable alacrity in obeying. Old Sir Guy of Gamwell gave Sir Ralph a very cordial welcome, and entertained him during supper with several of his best stories, enforced with an occasional slap on the back, and pointed with a peg in the ribs, a species of vivacious eloquence in which the old gentleman excelled, and which is supposed by many of that pleasant variety of the human species, known by the name of choice fellows, and comical dogs, to be the genuine tangible shape of the cream of a good joke.

II

What! shall we have incision? shall we imbrue?
Henry IV.

Old Sir Guy of Gamwell, and young William Gamwell, and fair Alice Gamwell, and Sir Ralph Montfaucon and his squire, rode together the next morning to the scene of the feast. They arrived on a village-green, surrounded with cottages peeping from among the trees by which the green was completely encircled. The whole circle was hung round with one continuous garland of flowers, depending in irregular festoons from the branches. In the centre of the green was a May-pole hidden in boughs and garlands; and a multitude of round-faced bumpkins and cherry-cheeked lasses were dancing around it, to the quadruple melody of Scrapesqueak, Whistlerap, Trumtwang, and Muggledrone: harmony we must not call it; for, though they had agreed to a partnership in point of time, each, like a true painstaking man, seemed determined to have his time to himself: Muggledrone played *allegretto*, Trumtwang *allegro*, Whistlerap *presto*, and Scrapesqueak *prestissimo*. There was a kind of mathematical proportion in their discrepancy: while Muggledrone played the tune four times, Trumtwang played it five, Whistlerap six, and Scrapesqueak eight; for the latter completely distanced all his competitors, and indeed worked his elbow so nimbly that its outline was scarcely distinguishable through the mistiness of its rapid vibration.

While the knight was delighting his eyes and ears with these pleasant sights and sounds, all eyes were turned in one direction; and Sir Ralph, looking round, saw a fair lady in green and gold come riding through the trees, accompanied by a portly friar in gray, and several fair damsels and gallant grooms. On their nearer approach, he recognized the Lady Matilda and her ghostly adviser, Brother Michael. A party of foresters arrived from another direction, and then ensued cordial interchanges of greeting, and collisions of hands and lips, among the Gamwells and the new-comers—"How does my fair coz, Mawd?" and "How does my sweet coz, Mawd?" and "How does my wild coz, Mawd?" And "Eh! jolly friar, your hand, old boy": and "Here, honest friar": and "To me, merry friar": and "By your favour, Mistress Alice": and "Hey! Cousin Robin": and "Hey! Cousin Will": and "Od's life! merry Sir Guy, you grow younger every year,"— as the old knight shook them all in turn with one hand, and slapped them on the back with the other, in token of his affection. A number of young men and women advanced, some drawing, and others dancing round, a floral car; and having placed a crown of flowers on Matilda's head, and saluted her Queen of the May, they drew her to the place appointed for the rural sports.

A hogshead of ale was abroach under an oak, and a fire was blazing in an open space before the trees to roast the fat deer which the foresters brought. The sports commenced; and, after an agreeable series of bowling, quoiting, pitching, hurling, racing, leaping, grinning, wrestling or friendly dislocation of joints, and cudgel-playing or amicable cracking of skulls, the trial of archery ensued. The conqueror was to be rewarded with a golden arrow from the hand of the Queen of the May, who was to be his partner in the dance till the close of the feast. This stimulated the knight's emulation: young Gamwell supplied him with a bow and arrow, and he took his station among the foresters, but had the mortification to be outshot by them all, and to see one of them lodge the point of his arrow in the golden ring of the centre, and receive the prize from the hand of the beautiful Matilda, who smiled on him with particular grace The jealous knight scrutinized the successful champion with great attention, and surely thought he had seen that face before. In the meantime the forester led the lady to the station. The luckless Sir Ralph drank deep draughts of love from the matchless grace of her attitudes, as, taking the bow in her left hand, and adjusting the arrow with her right, advancing her left foot, and gently curving her beautiful figure with a slight motion of her head that waved her black feathers and her ringleted hair, she drew the arrow to its head, and loosed it from her open fingers. The arrow struck within the ring of gold, so close to that of the victorious forester that the points were in contact, and the feathers were intermingled. Great acclamations succeeded, and the forester led Matilda to the dance Sir Ralph gazed on her fascinating motions till the torments of baffled love and jealous rage became unendurable; and approaching young Gamwell, he asked him if he knew the name of that forester who was leading the dance with the Queen of the May?

"Robin, I believe," said young Gamwell carelessly; "I think they call him Robin."

"Is that all you know of him?" said Sir Ralph.

"What more should I know of him?" said young Gamwell.

"Then I can tell you," said Sir Ralph, "he is the outlawed Earl of Huntingdon, on whose head is set so large a price"

"Ay, is he?" said young Gamwell, in the same careless manner.

"He is a prize worth the taking," said Sir Ralph.

"No doubt," said young Gamwell.

"How think you?" said Sir Ralph: "are the foresters his adherents?"

"I cannot say," said young Gamwell.

"Is your peasantry loyal and well-disposed?" said Sir Ralph.

"Passing loyal," said young Gamwell

"If I should call on them in the king's name," said Sir Ralph, "think you they would aid and assist?"

"Most likely they would," said young Gamwell, "one side or the other."

"Ay, but which side?" said the knight

"That remains to be tried," said young Gamwell

"I have King Henry's commission," said the knight, "to apprehend this earl that was. How would you advise me to act, being, as you see, without attendant force?"

"I would advise you," said young Gamwell, "to take yourself off without delay, unless you would relish the taste of a volley of arrows, a shower of stones, and a hailstorm of cudgel-blows, which would not be turned aside by a God save King Henry."

Sir Ralph's squire no sooner heard this, and saw by the looks of the speaker that he was not likely to prove a false prophet, than he clapped spurs to his horse and galloped off with might and main. This gave the knight a good excuse to pursue him, which he did with great celerity, calling, "Stop, you rascal." When the squire fancied himself safe out of the reach of pursuit, he checked his speed, and allowed the knight to come up with him. They rode on several miles in silence, till they discovered the towers and spires of Nottingham, where the knight introduced himself to the sheriff, and demanded an armed force to assist in the apprehension of the outlawed Earl of Huntingdon The sheriff, who was willing to have his share of the prize, determined to accompany the knight in person, and regaled him and his man with good store of the best; after which they, with a stout retinue of fifty men, took the way to Gamwell feast.

"God's my life," said the sheriff, as they rode along, "I had as lief you would tell me of a service of plate. I much doubt if this outlawed earl, this forester Robin, be not the man they call Robin Hood, who has quartered himself in Sherwood Forest, and whom, in endeavouring to apprehend, I have fallen divers times into disasters He has gotten together a band of disinherited prodigals, outlawed debtors, excommunicated heretics, elder sons that have spent all they had, and younger sons that never had anything to spend; and with these he kills the king's deer, and plunders wealthy travellers of five-sixths of their money; but if they be abbots or bishops, them he despoils utterly."

The sheriff then proceeded to relate to his companion the adventure of the Abbot of Doubleflask (which some grave historians have related of the Abbot of Saint Mary's, and others of the Bishop of Hereford): how the abbot, returning to his abbey in company with his high selerer, who carried in his portmanteau the rents of the abbey-lands, and with a numerous train of attendants, came upon four seeming peasants, who were roasting the king's venison by the king's highway: how, in just indignation at this flagrant infringement of the forest laws, he asked them what they meant, and they answered that they meant to dine: how he ordered them to be seized and bound, and led captive to Nottingham, that they might know wild-flesh to have been destined by Providence for licensed and privileged appetites, and not for the base hunger of unqualified knaves: how they prayed for mercy, and how the abbot swore by Saint Charity that he would show them none: how one of them thereupon drew a bugle-horn from under his smock-frock and blew three blasts, on which the abbot and his train were instantly surrounded by sixty bowmen in green: how they tied him to a tree, and made him say mass for their sins: how they unbound him, and sate him down with them to dinner, and gave him venison and wild-fowl and wine, and made him pay for his fare all the money in his high selerer's portmanteau, and enforced him to sleep all night under a tree in his cloak, and to leave the cloak behind him in the morning: how the abbot, light in pocket, and heavy in heart, raised the country upon Robin Hood, for so he had heard the chief forester called by his men, and hunted him into an old woman's cottage: how Robin changed dresses with the old woman, and how the abbot rode in great triumph into Nottingham, having in custody an old woman in a green doublet and breeches: how the old woman discovered herself: how the merry men of Nottingham laughed at the abbot: how the abbot railed at the old woman, and how the old woman out-railed the abbot, telling him that Robin had given her food and firing through the winter, which no abbot would ever do, but would rather take it from her for what he called the good of the Church, by which he meant his own laziness and gluttony; and that she knew a true man from a false thief, and a free forester from a greedy abbot.

"Thus you see," added the sheriff, "how this villain perverts the deluded people by making them believe that those who tithe and toll upon them for their spiritual and temporal benefit are not their best friends and fatherly guardians; for he holds that in giving to boors and old women what he takes from priests and peers, he does but restore to the former what the latter had taken from them; and this the impudent varlet calls distributive justice. Judge now if any loyal subject can be safe in such neighbourhood."

While the sheriff was thus enlightening his companion concerning the offenders, and whetting his own indignation against them, the sun was fast sinking to the west. They rode on till they came in view of a bridge, which they saw a party approaching from the opposite side, and the knight presently discovered that the party consisted of the Lady Matilda and Friar Michael, young Gamwell, Cousin Robin, and about half-a-dozen foresters. The knight pointed out the earl to the sheriff, who exclaimed, "Here, then, we have him an easy prey"; and they rode on manfully towards the bridge, on which the other party made halt.

"Who be these," said the friar, "that come riding so fast this way? Now, as God shall judge me, it is that false knight Sir Ralph Montfaucon and the Sheriff of Nottingham, with a posse of men. We must make good our post, and let them dislodge us if they may."

The two parties were now near enough to parley; and the sheriff and the knight, advancing in the front of the cavalcade, called on the lady, the friar, young Gamwell, and the foresters, to deliver up that false traitor, Robert, formerly Earl of Huntingdon. Robert himself made answer by letting fly an arrow that struck the ground between the fore-feet of the sheriff's horse. The horse reared up from the whizzing, and lodged the sheriff in the dust, and, at the same time, the fair Matilda favoured the knight with an arrow in his right arm, that compelled him to withdraw from the affray. His men lifted the sheriff carefully up, and replaced him on his horse, whom he immediately, with great rage and zeal, urged on to the assault, with his fifty men at his heels, some of whom were intercepted in their advance by the arrows of the foresters and Matilda; while the friar, with an eight-foot staff, dislodged the sheriff a second time, and laid on him with all the vigour of the Church militant on earth, in spite of his ejaculations of "Hey, Friar Michael! What means this, honest friar? Hold, ghostly friar! Hold, holy friar!"—till Matilda interposed, and delivered the battered sheriff to the care of the foresters. The friar continued flourishing his staff among the sheriff's men, knocking down one, breaking the ribs of another, dislocating the shoulder of a third, flattening the nose of a fourth, cracking the skull of a fifth, and pitching a sixth into the river, till the few who were lucky enough to escape with whole bones, clapped spurs to their horses and fled for their lives, under a farewell volley of arrows

Sir Ralph's squire, meanwhile, was glad of the excuse of attending his master's wound, to absent himself from the battle; and put the poor knight to a great deal of unnecessary pain by making as long a business as possible of extracting the arrow, which he had not accomplished, when Matilda approaching, extracted it with great facility, and bound up the wound with her scarf, saying, "I reclaim my arrow, sir knight, which struck where I aimed it, to admonish you to desist from your enterprise. I could as easily have lodged it in your heart."

"It did not need," said the knight, with rueful gallantry; "you have lodged one there already."

"If you mean to say that you love me," said Matilda, "it is more than I ever shall you· but if you will show your love by no further interfering with mine, you will at least merit my gratitude"

The knight made a wry face under the double pain of heart and body caused at the same moment by the material or martial, and the metaphorical or erotic arrow, of which the latter was thus barbed by a declaration more candid than flattering; but he did not choose to put in any such claim to the lady's gratitude as would bar all hopes of her love: he therefore remained silent; and the lady and her escort, leaving him and the sheriff to the care of the squire, rode on till they came in sight of Arlingford Castle, when they parted in several directions. The friar rode off alone;

and after the foresters had lost sight of him, they heard his voice
through the twilight, singing—

> " A staff, a staff, of a young oak graff,
>   That is both stoure and stiff,
> Is all a good friar can needs desire
>   To shrive a proud sheriffe.
> And thou, fine fellôwe, who has tasted so
>   Of the forester's greenwood game,
> Wilt be in no haste thy time to waste
>   In seeking more taste of the same:
> Or this can I read thee, and riddle thee well,
> Thou hadst better by far be the devil in hell,
>   Than the Sheriff of Nottinghãme."

III

> Now, master sheriff, what's your will with me?
>   *Henry IV.*

Matilda had carried her point with the baron of ranging at
liberty whithersoever she would, under her positive promise to
return home, she was a sort of prisoner on parole she had obtained
this indulgence by means of an obsolete habit of always telling
the truth and keeping her word, which our enlightened age has
discarded with other barbarisms, but which had the effect of
giving her father so much confidence in her that he could not
help considering her word a better security than locks and
bars.

The baron had been one of the last to hear of the rumours of
the new outlaws of Sherwood, as Matilda had taken all possible
precautions to keep those rumours from his knowledge, fearing
that they might cause the interruption of her greenwood liberty,
and it was only during her absence at Gamwell feast, that the
butler, being thrown off his guard by liquor, forgot her injunctions,
and regaled the baron with a long story of the right merry adventure
of Robin Hood and the Abbot of Doubleflask.

The baron was one morning, as usual, cutting his way valorously
through a rampart of cold provision, when his ears were suddenly
assailed by a tremendous alarum, and sallying forth, and looking

from his castle wall, he perceived a large party of armed men on the other side of the moat, who were calling on the warder, in the king's name, to lower the drawbridge and raise the portcullis, which had both been secured by Matilda's order. The baron walked along the battlement till he came opposite to these unexpected visitors, who, as soon as they saw him, called out, "Lower the drawbridge, in the king's name."

"For what, in the devil's name?" said the baron.

"The Sheriff of Nottingham," said one, "lies in bed grievously bruised, and many of his men are wounded, and several of them slain; and Sir Ralph Montfaucon, knight, is sore wounded in the arm; and we are charged to apprehend William Gamwell the younger, of Gamwell Hall, and Father Michael, of Rubygill Abbey, and Matilda Fitzwater, of Arlingford Castle, as agents and accomplices in the said breach of the king's peace."

"Breach of the king's fiddle-stick!" answered the baron. "What do you mean by coming here with your cock and bull stories of my daughter grievously bruising the Sheriff of Nottingham? You are a set of vagabond rascals in disguise, and I hear, by-the-by, there is a gang of thieves that has just set up business in Sherwood Forest: a pretty pretence, indeed, to get into my castle with force and arms, and make a famine in my buttery, and a drought in my cellar, and a void in my strong box, and a vacuum in my silver scullery."

"Lord Fitzwater," cried one, "take heed how you resist lawful authority: we will prove ourselves——"

"You will prove yourselves arrant knaves I doubt not," answered the baron; "but, villains, you shall be more grievously bruised by me than ever was the sheriff by my daughter (a pretty tale truly!), if you do not forthwith avoid my territory."

By this time the baron's men had flocked to the battlements, with long-bows and cross-bows, slings and stones, and Matilda, with her bow and quiver, at their head The assailants, finding the castle so well defended, deemed it expedient to withdraw till they could return in greater force, and rode off to Rubygill Abbey, where they made known their errand to the father abbot, who, having satisfied himself of their legitimacy, and conned over the allegations, said that doubtless Brother Michael had heinously offended; but it was not for the civil law to take cognizance of the misdoings of a holy friar, that he would summon a chapter of monks, and pass on the offender a sentence proportionate to his offence. The ministers of civil justice said that would not do. The abbot said it would do and should; and bade them not provoke the meekness of his catholic charity to lay them under the curse of Rome. This threat had its effect, and the party rode off to Gamwell Hall, where they found the Gamwells and their men just sitting down to dinner, which they saved them the trouble of eating by consuming it in the king's name themselves, having first seized and bound young Gamwell; all which they accomplished by dint of superior numbers, in despite of a most vigorous stand made by the Gamwellites in defence of their young master and their provisions

The baron, meanwhile, after the ministers of justice had departed, interrogated Matilda concerning the alleged fact of the grievous bruising of the Sheriff of Nottingham. Matilda told him the whole history of Gamwell feast, and of their battle on the bridge, which had its origin in a design of the Sheriff of Nottingham to take one of the foresters into custody.

"Ay! ay!" said the baron, "and I guess who that forester was; but truly this friar is a desperate fellow. I did not think there could have been so much valour under a gray frock. And so you wounded the knight in the arm. You are a wild girl, Mawd,— a chip of the old block, Mawd A wild girl, and a wild friar, and three or four foresters, wild lads all, to keep a bridge against a tame knight, and a tame sheriff, and fifty tame varlets: by this light, the like was never heard! But do you know, Mawd, you must not go about so any more, sweet Mawd: you must stay at home, you must ensconce; for there is your tame sheriff on the one hand, that will take you perforce; and there is your wild forester on the other hand, that will take you without any force at all, Mawd · your wild forester, Robin, Cousin Robin, Robin Hood of Sherwood Forest, that beats and binds bishops, spreads nets for archbishops, and hunts a fat abbot as if he were a buck: excellent game, no doubt, but you must hunt no more in such company. I see it now: truly I might have guessed before that the bold outlaw Robin, the most courteous Robin, the new thief of Sherwood Forest, was your lover, the earl that has been: I might have guessed it before, and what led you so much to the woods; but you hunt no more in such company. No more May games and Gamwell feasts. My lands and castle would be the forfeit of a few more such pranks; and I think they are as well in my hands as the king's, quite as well."

"You know, father," said Matilda, "the condition of keeping me at home: I get out if I can, and not on parole."

"Ay! ay!" said the baron, "if you can; very true: watch and ward, Mawd, watch and ward is my word: if you can, is yours. The mark is set, and so start fair."

The baron would have gone on in this way for an hour; but the friar made his appearance with a long oak staff in his hand, singing,—

> " Drink and sing, and eat and laugh,
>   And so go forth to battle
> For the top of a skull and the end of a staff
>   Do make a ghostly rattle."

"Ho! ho! friar!" said the baron—"singing friar, laughing friar, roaring friar, fighting friar, hacking friar, thwacking friar; cracking, cracking, cracking friar; joke-cracking, bottle-cracking, skull-cracking friar!"

"And ho! ho!" said the friar—"bold baron, old baron, sturdy baron, wordy baron, long baron, strong baron, mighty baron, flighty baron, mazed baron, crazed baron, hacked baron, thwacked baron, cracked, cracked, cracked baron; bone-cracked, sconce-cracked, brain-cracked baron!"

"What do you mean," said the baron, "bully friar, by calling me hacked and thwacked?"

"Were you not in the wars," said the friar, "where he who escapes unhacked does more credit to his heels than his arms? I pay· tribute to your valour in calling you hacked and thwacked."

"I never was thwacked in my life," said the baron, "I stood my ground manfully, and covered my body with my sword. If I had had the luck to meet with a fighting friar, indeed, I might have been thwacked, and soundly, too; but I hold myself a match for any two laymen; it takes nine fighting laymen to make a fighting friar."

"Whence come you now, holy father?" asked Matilda.

"From Rubygill Abbey," said the friar, "whither I never return

> For I must seek some hermit cell,
> Where I alone my beads may tell,
> And on the wight who that way fares
> Levy a toll for my ghostly pray'rs,
>   Levy a toll, levy a toll,
>   Levy a toll for my ghostly pray'rs."

"What is the matter then, father?" said Matilda.

"This is the matter," said the friar: "my holy brethren have held a chapter on me, and sentenced me to seven years' privation of wine. I therefore deemed it fitting to take my departure, which they would fain have prohibited. I was enforced to clear the way with my staff. I have grievously beaten my dearly beloved brethren: I grieve thereat; but they enforced me thereto. I have beaten them much; I mowed them down to the right and to the left, and left them like an ill-reaped field of wheat, ear and straw pointing all ways, scattered in singleness and jumbled in masses; and so bade them farewell, saying, Peace be with you. But I must not tarry, lest danger be in my rear: therefore, farewell, sweet Matilda: and farewell, noble baron: and farewell, sweet Matilda, again, the alpha and omega of Father Michael, the first and the last."

"Farewell, father," said the baron, a little softened, "and God send you be never assailed by more than fifty men at a time."

"Amen," said the friar, "to that good wish."

"And we shall meet again, father, I trust," said Matilda.

"When the storm is blown over," said the baron.

"Doubt it not," said the friar, "though flooded Trent were between us, and fifty devils guarded the bridge."

He kissed Matilda's forehead, and walked away without a song.

IV

Let gallows gape for dog: let man go free.—Henry V.

A page had been brought up in Gamwell Hall, who, while he was little, had been called Little John, and continued to be so called after he had grown to be a foot taller than any other man in the house. He was full seven feet high. His latitude was worthy of his longitude, and his strength was worthy of both; and though an honest man by profession, he had practised archery on the king's deer for the benefit of his master's household, and for the improvement of his own eye and hand, till his aim had become infallible within the range of two miles. He had fought manfully in defence of his young master, took his captivity exceedingly to heart, and fell into bitter grief and boundless rage when he heard that he had been tried in Nottingham, and sentenced to die. Alice Gamwell, at Little John's request, wrote three letters of one tenour; and Little John, having attached them to three blunt arrows, saddled the fleetest steed in old Sir Guy of Gamwell's stables, mounted, and rode first to Ailingford Castle, where he shot one of the three arrows over the battlements; then to Rubygill Abbey, where he shot the second into the abbey garden; then back past Gamwell Hall to the borders of Sherwood Forest, where he shot the third into the wood. Now the first of these arrows lighted in the nape of the neck of Lord Fitzwater, and lodged itself firmly between his skin and his collar; the second rebounded with the hollow vibration of a drumstick from the shaven sconce of the Abbot of Rubygill; and the third pitched perpendicularly into the centre of a venison pasty in which Robin Hood was making incision.

Matilda ran up to her father in the court of Arlingford Castle, seized the arrow, drew off the letter, and concealed it in her bosom before the baron had time to look round, which he did with many expressions of rage against the impudent villain who had shot a blunt arrow into the nape of his neck.

"But you know, father," said Matilda, "a sharp arrow in the same place would have killed you; therefore the sending a blunt one was very considerate."

"Considerate, with a vengeance!" said the baron. "Where was the consideration of sending it at all? This is some of your forester's pranks. He has missed you in the forest, since I have kept watch and ward over you, and by way of a love-token and a remembrance to you takes a random shot at me."

The Abbot of Rubygill picked up the missive-missile or messenger arrow, which had rebounded from his shaven crown, with a very unghostly malediction on the sender, which he suddenly checked with a pious and consolatory reflection on the goodness of Providence in having blessed him with such a thickness of skull, to which he was now indebted for temporal preservation, as he had before been for spiritual promotion. He opened the letter which was addressed to Father Michael; and found it to contain an intimation that William Gamwell was to be hanged on Monday at Nottingham.

"And I wish," said the abbot, "Father Michael were to be hanged with him: an ungrateful monster, after I had rescued him from the fangs of civil justice, to reward my lenity by not leaving a bone unbruised among the holy brotherhood of Rubygill "

Robin Hood extracted from his venison pasty a similar intimation of the evil destiny of his cousin, whom he determined, if possible, to rescue from the jaws of Cerberus

The Sheriff of Nottingham, though still sore with his bruises, was so intent on revenge, that he raised himself from his bed to attend the execution of William Gamwell He rode to the august structure of retributive Themis, as the French call a gallows, in all the pride and pomp of shrievalty, and with a splendid retinue of well-equipped knaves and varlets, as our ancestors called honest serving-men

Young Gamwell was brought forth with his arms pinioned behind him; his sister Alice and his father, Sir Guy, attending him in a disconsolate mood He had rejected the confessor provided by the sheriff, and had insisted on the privilege of choosing his own, whom Little John had promised to bring. Little John, however, had not made his appearance when the fatal procession had begun its march; but when they reached the place of execution, Little John appeared, accompanied by a ghostly friar.

"Sheriff," said young Gamwell, "let me not die with my hands pinioned· give me a sword, and set any odds of your men against me, and let me die the death of a man, like the descendant of a noble house, which has never yet been stained with ignominy."

"No, no," said the sheriff; "I have had enough of setting odds against you. I have sworn you shall be hanged, and hanged you shall be."

"Then God have mercy on me," said young Gamwell; "and now, holy friar, shrive my sinful soul "

The friar approached

"Let me see this friar," said the sheriff: "if he be the friar of the bridge, I had as lief have the devil in Nottingham; but he shall find me too much for him here."

"The friar of the bridge," said Little John, "as you very well know, sheriff, was Father Michael of Rubygill Abbey, and you may easily see that this is not the man."

"I see it," said the sheriff, "and God be thanked for his absence."

Young Gamwell stood at the foot of the ladder. The friar approached him, opened his book, groaned, turned up the whites of his eyes, tossed up his arms in the air, and said "*Dominus vobiscum.*" He then crossed both his hands on his breast under the folds of his holy robes, and stood a few moments as if in inward prayer. A deep silence among the attendant crowd accompanied this action of the friar; interrupted only by the hollow tone of the death-bell, at long and dreary intervals. Suddenly the friar threw off his holy robes, and appeared a forester clothed in green, with a sword in his right hand and a horn in his left. With the sword he cut the bonds of William Gamwell, who instantly snatched a sword from one of the sheriff's men; and with the horn he blew a loud blast, which was answered at once by four bugles from the quarters of the four winds, and from each quarter came five and twenty bowmen running all on a row.

"Treason! treason!" cried the sheriff. Old Sir Guy sprung to his son's side, and so did Little John; and the four setting back to back, kept the sheriff and his men at bay till the bowmen came within shot and let fly their arrows among the sheriff's men, who, after a brief resistance, fled in all directions. The forester who had personated the friar sent an arrow after the flying sheriff, calling with a strong voice, "To the sheriff's left arm, as a keepsake from Robin Hood." The arrow reached its destiny; the sheriff redoubled his speed, and, with the one arrow in his arm, did not stop to breathe till he was out of reach of another.

The foresters did not waste time in Nottingham, but were soon at a distance from its walls. Sir Guy returned with Alice to Gamwell Hall; but thinking he should not be safe there, from the share he had had in his son's rescue, they only remained long enough to supply themselves with clothes and money, and departed, under the escort of Little John, to another seat of the Gamwells in Yorkshire. Young Gamwell, taking it for granted that his offence was past remission, determined on joining Robin Hood, and accompanied him to the forest, where it was deemed expedient that he should change his name; and he was rechristened without a priest, and with wine instead of water, by the immortal name of Scarlet.

THE WAR SONG OF DINAS VAWR

[This song occurs in *The Misfortunes of Elphin*, the scene of which is laid in ancient Wales. The song is sung by the noisy warriors of King Melvas in the castle hall of Dinas Vawr.]

The mountain sheep are sweeter,
But the valley sheep are fatter;
We therefore deemed it meeter
To carry off the latter.
We made an expedition;
We met a host, and quelled it,
We forced a strong position,
And killed the men who held it.

On Dyfed's richest valley,
Where herds of kine were browsing,
We made a mighty sally,
To furnish our carousing.
Fierce warriors rushed to meet us;
We met them, and o'erthrew them:
They struggled hard to beat us;
But we conquered them, and slew them.

As we drove our prize at leisure,
The king marched forth to catch us:
His rage surpassed all measure,
But his people could not match us.
He fled to his hall-pillars;
And, ere our force we led off,
Some sacked his house and cellars,
While others cut his head off.

We there, in strife bewild'ring,
Spilt blood enough to swim in:
We orphaned many children,
And widowed many women.
The eagles and the ravens
We glutted with our foemen;
The heroes and the cravens,
The spearmen and the bowmen.

We brought away from battle,
And much their land bemoaned them,
Two thousand head of cattle,
And the head of him who owned them:
Ednyfed, King of Dyfed,
His head was borne before us;
His wine and beasts supplied our feasts,
And his overthrow, our chorus.

HILAIRE BELLOC

HILAIRE BELLOC (b. 1870) is partly French by birth and has served in the
French artillery. He was educated at the Oratory School and Oxford.
His numerous works include poems, novels, essays, historical sketches and
books of travel, the best of them being *The Path to Rome*.

THE SOUTH COUNTRY

When I am living in the Midlands
    That are sodden and unkind,
I light my lamp in the evening:
    My work is left behind;
And the great hills in the South Country
    Come back into my mind.

The great hills of the South Country
    They stand along the sea:
And it's there walking in the high woods
    That I could wish to be,
And the men that were boys when I was a boy
    Walking along with me.

The men that live in North England
 I saw them for a day:
Their hearts are set upon the waste fells,
 Their skies are fast and grey:
From their castle-walls a man may see
 The mountains far away.

The men that live in West England
 They see the Severn strong,
A-rolling on rough water brown
 Light aspen leaves along
They have the secret of the Rocks,
 And the oldest kind of song.

But the men that live in the South Country
 Are the kindest and most wise,
They get their laughter from the loud surf,
 And the faith in their happy eyes
Comes surely from our Sister the Spring
 When over the sea she flies;
The violets suddenly bloom at her feet,
 She blesses us with surprise.

I never get between the pines,
 But I smell the Sussex air;
Nor I never come on a belt of sand
 But my home is there;
And along the sky the line of the Downs
 So noble and so bare.

A lost thing could I never find,
 Nor a broken thing mend;
And I fear I shall be all alone
 When I get towards the end
Who will there be to comfort me,
 Or who will be my friend?

I will gather and carefully make my friends
   Of the men of the Sussex Weald,
They watch the stars from silent folds,
   They stiffly plough the field
By them and the God of the South Country
   My poor soul shall be healed.

If I ever become a rich man,
   Or if ever I grow to be old,
I will build a house with deep thatch
   To shelter me from the cold,
And there shall the Sussex songs be sung
   And the story of Sussex told.

I will hold my house in the high wood
   Within a walk of the sea,
And the men that were boys when I was a boy
   Shall sit and drink with me.

THE ENGLISH BIBLE

In the time of Queen Elizabeth there existed several translations of the Bible or parts of the Bible into English The oldest was made by friends and followers of John Wyclif at the end of the fourteenth century; then came Tyndale's (1525-34), next Coverdale's—the *Great Bible* (1539), next the version made by English reformers settled at Geneva—the *Geneva Bible* (1559-60), and then a translation made by certain bishops in Elizabeth's reign—the *Bishops' Bible* (1568). The Book of Psalms as it appears in the Church of England Prayer Book is, in the main, the work of Coverdale.

Early in the seventeenth century, King James ordered a new translation of the Bible to be made, it was published in 1611, and has been known ever since as the Authorised Version An amended form of this translation published in 1881-5 is popularly called the Revised Version.

The Bible of 1611 found its way to the hearts of the English people, and its splendid language has influenced English thought and speech for over three hundred years. Two supreme glories of the English tongue are two great books published in the reign of James I—the Bible of 1611 and *Mr William Shakespeare's Comedies, Histories & Tragedies* of 1623

BELSHAZZAR'S FEAST

Belshazzar the king made a great feast to a thousand of his lords, and drank wine before the thousand. Belshazzar, whiles he tasted the wine, commanded to bring the golden and silver vessels which his father Nebuchadnezzar had taken out of the temple which was in Jerusalem, that the king, and his princes, his wives, and his concubines, might drink therein. Then they brought the golden vessels that were taken out of the temple of the house of God which was at Jerusalem; and the king, and his princes, his wives, and his concubines, drank in them. They drank wine, and praised the gods of gold, and of silver, of brass, of iron, of wood, and of stone.

In the same hour came forth fingers of a man's hand, and wrote over against the candlestick upon the plaister of the wall of the king's palace: and the king saw the part of the hand that wrote. Then the king's countenance was changed, and his thoughts troubled him, so that the joints of his loins were loosed, and his knees smote one against another. The king cried aloud to bring in the astrologers, the Chaldeans, and the soothsayers. And the king spake, and said to the wise men of Babylon, Whosoever shall read this writing, and shew me the interpretation thereof, shall be clothed with scarlet, and have a chain of gold about his neck, and shall be the third ruler in the kingdom. Then came in all the king's wise men: but they could not read the writing, nor make knowen to the king the interpretation thereof. Then was king Belshazzar greatly troubled, and his countenance was changed in him, and his lords were astonied.

Now the queen, by reason of the words of the king and his lords, came into the banquet house: and the queen spake and said, O king, live for ever· let not thy thoughts trouble thee, nor let thy countenance be changed: there is a man in thy kingdom, in whom is the spirit of the holy gods; and in the days of thy father light and understanding and wisdom, like the wisdom of the gods, was found in him; whom the king Nebuchadnezzar thy father, the king, I say, thy father, made master of the magicians, astrologers, Chaldeans, and soothsayers; forasmuch as an excellent spirit, and knowledge, and understanding, interpreting of dreams, and shewing of hard sentences, and dissolving of doubts, were

found in the same Daniel, whom the king named Belteshazzar·
now let Daniel be called, and he will shew the interpretation.
Then was Daniel brought in before the king, and the king spake
and said unto Daniel, Art thou that Daniel, which art of the
children of the captivity of Judah, whom the king my father
brought out of Jewry? I have even heard of thee, that the spirit
of the gods is in thee, and that light and understanding and
excellent wisdom is found in thee And now the wise men, the
astrologers, have been brought in before me, that they should
read this writing, and make knowen unto me the interpretation
thereof: but they could not shew the interpretation of the thing.
And I have heard of thee, that thou canst make interpretations,
and dissolve doubts: now if thou canst read the writing, and make
knowen to me the interpretation thereof, thou shalt be clothed with
scarlet, and have a chain of gold about thy neck, and shalt be the
third ruler in the kingdom.

Then Daniel answered and said before the king, Let thy gifts
be to thyself, and give thy rewards to another; yet I will read the
writing unto the king, and make knowen to him the interpretation.
O thou king, the most high God gave Nebuchadnezzar thy father
a kingdom, and majesty, and glory, and honour. And for the
majesty that he gave him, all people, nations, and languages,
trembled and feared before him: whom he would he slew; and
whom he would he kept alive; and whom he would he set up;
and whom he would he put down. But when his heart was lifted
up, and his mind hardened in pride, he was deposed from his
kingly throne, and they took his glory from him. And he was
driven from the sons of men; and his heart was made like the
beasts, and his dwelling was with the wild asses· they fed him
with grass like oxen, and his body was wet with the dew of heaven,
till he knew that the most high God ruled in the kingdom of men,
and that he appointeth over it whomsoever he will. And thou
his son, O Belshazzar, hast not humbled thine heart, though thou
knewest all this; but hast lifted up thyself against the Lord of
heaven; and they have brought the vessels of his house before
thee, and thou, and thy lords, thy wives, and thy concubines,
have drunk wine in them; and thou hast praised the gods of
silver, and gold, of brass, iron, wood, and stone, which see not,
nor hear, nor know: and the God in whose hand thy breath is,

and whose are all thy ways, hast thou not glorified: then was the part of the hand sent from him; and this writing was written.

And this is the writing that was written, MENE, MENE, TEKEL, UPHARSIN. This is the interpretation of the thing: MENE; God hath numbered thy kingdom, and finished it. TEKEL; Thou art weighed in the balances, and art found wanting. PERES; Thy kingdom is divided, and given to the Medes and Persians. Then commanded Belshazzar, and they clothed Daniel with scarlet, and put a chain of gold about his neck, and made a proclamation concerning him, that he should be the third ruler in the kingdom.

In that night was Belshazzar the king of the Chaldeans slain. And Darius the Median took the kingdom.

GEORGE BORROW

GEORGE BORROW (1803–81) was born at East Dereham, Norfolk, the son of a militia officer The boy's family changed their place of abode frequently during his early years, but settled finally at Norwich. He began very early to gain a knowledge of several little known languages, including Romany, the language of the Gipsies, and this knowledge led to his being employed by the Bible Society in the circulation of the Scriptures in Russia, Portugal and Spain. His chief books, mainly accounts of his own life and adventures, are *The Bible in Spain*, *Lavengro*, *The Romany Rye* and *Wild Wales*. He died at Oulton, near Lowestoft The passage that follows is from *The Bible in Spain*. Antonio is a Spanish gipsy whom Borrow met in Badajoz, and with whom he travelled for some part of his wanderings. Of the many foreign words that occur in the passage a few are Spanish but most are Romany.

A GIPSY OF SPAIN

Nothing further of any account occurred in the gipsy house. The next day Antonio and myself were again in the saddle. We travelled at least thirteen leagues before we reached the Venta[1], where we passed the night We rose early in the morning, my guide informing me that we had a long day's journey to make. "Where are we bound to?" I demanded. "To Trujillo," he replied

[1] inn.

When the sun arose, which it did gloomily and amidst threatening rain-clouds, we found ourselves in the neighbourhood of a
range of mountains which lay on our left, and which Antonio
informed me were called the Sierra of San Selvan. Our route,
however, lay over wide plains, scantily clothed with brushwood,
with here and there a melancholy village, with its old and dilapidated church. Throughout the greater part of the day a drizzling
rain was falling, which turned the dust of the roads into mud and
mire, considerably impeding our progress Towards evening we
reached a moor, a wild place enough, strewn with enormous stones
and rocks Before us, at some distance, rose a strange conical
hill, rough and shaggy, which appeared to be neither more nor
less than an immense assemblage of the same kind of rocks which
lay upon the moor. The rain had now ceased, but a strong wind
rose and howled at our backs. Throughout the journey, I had
experienced considerable difficulty in keeping up with the mule
of Antonio The walk of the horse was slow, and I could discover
no vestige of the spirit which the gipsy had assured me lurked
within him. We were now upon a tolerably clear spot of the moor.
"I am about to see," I said, "whether this horse has any of the
quality which you have described." "Do so," said Antonio, and
spurred his beast onward, speedily leaving me far behind I
jerked the horse with the bit, endeavouring to arouse his dormant
spirit; whereupon he stopped, reared, and refused to proceed.
"Hold the bridle loose and touch him with your whip," shouted
Antonio from before I obeyed, and forthwith the animal set off
at a trot, which gradually increased in swiftness till it became a
downright furious, speedy trot. His limbs were now thoroughly
lithy, and he brandished his four legs in a manner perfectly
wondrous The mule of Antonio, which was a spirited animal of
excellent paces, would fain have competed with him, but was
passed in a twinkling This tremendous trot endured for about a
mile, when the animal, becoming yet more heated, broke suddenly
into a gallop. Hurrah ¹ no hare ever ran so wildly or blindly; it
was literally *ventre à terre*; and I had considerable difficulty in
keeping him clear of rocks, against which he would have
rushed in his savage fury, and dashed himself and rider to
atoms
This race brought me to the foot of the hill, where I waited till

the gipsy rejoined me. We left the hill, which seemed quite inaccessible on our right, passing through a small and wretched village. The sun went down, and dark night presently came upon us. We proceeded on, however, for nearly three hours, until we heard the barking of dogs and perceived a light or two in the distance. "That is Trujillo," said Antonio, who had not spoken for a long time. "I am glad of it," I replied. "I am thoroughly tired; I shall sleep soundly in Trujillo." "That is as it may be," said the gipsy, and spurred his mule to a brisker pace. We soon entered the town, which appeared dark and gloomy enough. I followed close behind the gipsy, who led the way I knew not whither, through dismal streets and dark places, where cats were squalling. "Here is the house," said he at last, dismounting before a low, mean hut. He knocked—no answer was returned; he knocked again, but still there was no reply; he shook the door and essayed to open it, but it appeared firmly locked and bolted. "Caramba[1]!" said he, "they are out; I feared it might be so. Now, what are we to do?"

"There can be no difficulty," said I, "with respect to what we have to do. If your friends have gone out, it is easy enough to go to a posada[2]."

"You know not what you say," replied the gipsy. "I dare not go to the mesuna[2], nor enter any house in Trujillo save this, and this is shut. Well, there is no remedy—we must move on; and between ourselves, the sooner we leave this place the better. My own planoró[3] was garroted at Trujillo."

He lighted a cigar by means of a steel and yesca[4], sprang on his mule, and proceeded through streets and lanes equally dismal as those which we had already traversed, till we again found ourselves out of the town.

I confess I did not much like this decision of the gipsy. I felt very slight inclination to leave the town behind and to venture into unknown places in the dark night, amidst rain and mist; for the wind had now dropped, and the rain began again to fall briskly. I was, moreover, much fatigued, and wished for nothing better than to deposit myself in some comfortable manger, where I might sink to sleep, lulled by the pleasant sound of horses and

[1] An exclamation, or oath. [2] inn.
[3] brother. [4] tinder.

mules dispatching their provender. I had, however, put myself under the direction of the gipsy, and I was too old a traveller to quarrel with my guide under the present circumstances. I therefore followed close at his crupper, our only light being the glow emitted from the gipsy's cigar. At last he flung it from his mouth into a puddle, and we were then in darkness.

We proceeded in this manner for a long time. The gipsy was silent; I myself was equally so; the rain descended more and more. I sometimes thought I heard doleful noises, something like the hooting of owls. "This is a strange night to be wandering abroad in," I at length said to Antonio.

"It is, brother," said he; "but I would sooner be abroad in such a night, and in such places, than in the estaripel[1] of Trujillo."

We wandered at least a league farther, and appeared now to be near a wood, for I could occasionally distinguish the trunks of immense trees. Suddenly Antonio stopped his mule. "Look, brother," said he, "to the left, and tell me if you do not see a light; your eyes are sharper than mine." I did as he commanded me. At first I could see nothing, but moving a little farther on, I plainly saw a large light at some distance, seemingly amongst the trees. "Yonder cannot be a lamp or candle," said I; "it is more like the blaze of a fire." "Very likely," said Antonio. "There are no queres[2] in this place. It is doubtless a fire made by durotunes[3]. Let us go and join them, for, as you say, it is doleful work wandering about at night amidst rain and mire."

We dismounted, and entered what I now saw was a forest, leading the animals cautiously amongst the trees and brushwood. In about five minutes we reached a small open space, at the farther side of which, at the foot of a large cork tree, a fire was burning, and by it stood or sat two or three figures. They had heard our approach, and one of them now exclaimed, "*Quien vive?*"[4] "I know that voice," said Antonio, and leaving the horse with me, rapidly advanced towards the fire. Presently I heard an Ola! and a laugh, and soon the voice of Antonio summoned me to advance. On reaching the fire, I found two dark lads, and a still darker woman of about forty—the latter seated on what appeared to be horse or mule furniture. I likewise saw a horse and two

[1] prison.   [2] houses.   [3] shepherds.   [4] Who goes there?

donkeys tethered to the neighbouring trees. It was, in fact, a gipsy bivouac ..."Come forward, brother, and show yourself," said Antonio to me "You are amongst friends These are of the Errate[1]—the very people whom I expected to find at Trujillo, and in whose house we should have slept."

"And what," said I, "could have induced them to leave their house in Trujillo and come into this dark forest, in the midst of wind and rain, to pass the night?"

"They come on business of Egypt, brother, doubtless," replied Antonio, "and that business is none of ours. Calla boca![2] It is lucky we have found them here, else we should have had no supper and our horses no corn "

"My ro[3] is prisoner at the village yonder," said the woman, pointing with her hand in a particular direction. "He is prisoner yonder for choring a mailla[4]. We are come to see what we can do on his behalf; and where can we lodge better than in this forest, where there is nothing to pay? It is not the first time, I trow, that Caloré[1] have slept at the root of a tree."

One of the striplings now gave us barley for our animals in a large bag, into which we successively introduced their heads, allowing the famished creatures to regale themselves till we conceived that they had satisfied their hunger. There was a puchero[5] simmering at the fire, half full of bacon, garbanzos[6], and other provisions. This was emptied into a large wooden platter, and out of this Antonio and myself supped; the other gipsies refused to join us, giving us to understand that they had eaten before our arrival. They all, however, did justice to the leathern bottle of Antonio, which, before his departure from Merida, he had the precaution to fill.

I was by this time completely overcome with fatigue and sleep. Antonio flung me an immense horse-cloth, of which he bore more than one beneath the huge cushion on which he rode In this I wrapped myself, and placing my head upon a bundle, and my feet as near as possible to the fire, I lay down.

Antonio and the other gipsies remained seated by the fire conversing I listened for a moment to what they said, but I did not perfectly understand it, and what I did understand by no means

[1] gipsies   [2] Hold your tongue!   [3] husband.
[4] stealing a donkey   [5] stew-pot.   [6] peas.

interested me. The rain still drizzled, but I heeded it not, and was soon asleep

The sun was just appearing as I awoke. I made several efforts before I could rise from the ground. My limbs were quite stiff, and my hair was covered with rime; for the rain had ceased, and a rather severe frost set in. I looked around me, but could see neither Antonio nor the gipsies; the animals of the latter had likewise disappeared, so had the horse which I had hitherto rode. The mule, however, of Antonio still remained fastened to the tree. This latter circumstance quieted some apprehensions which were beginning to arise in my mind. "They are gone on some business of Egypt," I said to myself, "and will return anon." I gathered together the embers of the fire, and heaping upon them sticks and branches, soon succeeded in calling forth a blaze, beside which I again placed the puchero, with what remained of the provision of last night. I waited for a considerable time in expectation of the return of my companions; but as they did not appear, I sat down and breakfasted. Before I had well finished I heard the noise of a horse approaching rapidly, and presently Antonio made his appearance amongst the trees with some agitation in his countenance. He sprang from the horse, and instantly proceeded to untie the mule.

"Mount, brother, mount!" said he, pointing to the horse. "I went with the Callee[1] and her chabés[2] to the village where the ro is in trouble. The chinobaro[3], however, seized them at once with their cattle, and would have laid hands also on me; but I set spurs to the grasti[4], gave him the bridle, and was soon far away. Mount, brother, mount! or we shall have the whole rustic canaille upon us in a twinkling."

I did as he commanded. We were presently in the road which we had left the night before. Along this we hurried at a great rate, the horse displaying his best speedy trot; whilst the mule, with its ears pricked up, galloped gallantly at his side. "What place is that on the hill yonder?" said I to Antonio, at the expiration of an hour, as we prepared to descend a deep valley.

"That is Jaraicejo," said Antonio. "A bad place it is, and a bad place it has ever been for the Calo people."

---

[1] gipsy (fem).   [2] boys.   [3] chief officer.   [4] horse.

"If it is such a bad place," said I, "I hope we shall not have to pass through it."

"We must pass through it," said Antonio, "for more reasons than one: first, forasmuch as the road lies through Jaraicejo; and second, forasmuch as it will be necessary to purchase provisions there, both for ourselves and horses. On the other side of Jaraicejo there is a wild desert, a despoblado[1], where we shall find nothing."

We crossed the valley, and ascended the hill, and as we drew near to the town the gipsy said, "Brother, we had best pass through that town singly. I will go in advance; follow slowly, and when there purchase bread and barley; you have nothing to fear. I will await you on the despoblado."

Without waiting for my answer, he hastened forward, and was speedily out of sight.

I followed slowly behind, and entered the gate of the town—an old dilapidated place, consisting of little more than one street. Along this street I was advancing, when a man with a dirty foraging-cap on his head, and holding a gun in his hand, came running up to me. "Who are you?" said he, in rather rough accents; "from whence do you come?"

"From Badajoz and Trujillo," I replied. "Why do you ask?"

"I am one of the National Guard," said the man, "and am placed here to inspect strangers. I am told that a gipsy fellow just now rode through the town. It is well for him that I had stepped into my house. Do you come in his company?"

"Do I look like a person," said I, "likely to keep company with gipsies?"

The National measured me from top to toe, and then looked me full in the face with an expression which seemed to say, "Likely enough." In fact, my appearance was by no means calculated to prepossess people in my favour. Upon my head I wore an old Andalusian hat, which, from its condition, appeared to have been trodden underfoot; a rusty cloak, which had perhaps served half a dozen generations, enwrapped my body; my nether garments were by no means of the finest description, and as far as could be seen were covered with mud, with which my face was likewise plentifully bespattered, and upon my chin was a beard of a week's growth.

[1] waste land

"Have you a passport?" at length demanded the National.

I remembered having read that the best way to win a Spaniard's heart is to treat him with ceremonious civility I therefore dismounted, and taking off my hat, made a low bow to the constitutional soldier, saying, "Señor Nacional, you must know that I am an English gentleman travelling in this country for my pleasure. I bear a passport, which on inspecting you will find to be perfectly regular. It was given me by the great Lord Palmerston, minister of England, whom you of course have heard of here. At the bottom you will see his own handwriting Look at it and rejoice, perhaps you will never have another opportunity. As I put unbounded confidence in the honour of every gentleman, I leave the passport in your hands whilst I repair to the posada to refresh myself. When you have inspected it, you will perhaps oblige me so far as to bring it to me. Cavalier, I kiss your hands."

I then made him another low bow, which he returned with one still lower, and leaving him now staring at the passport and now looking at myself, I went into a posada, to which I was directed by a beggar whom I met.

I fed the horse, and procured some bread and barley, as the gipsy had directed me. I likewise purchased three fine partridges of a fowler, who was drinking wine in the posada. He was satisfied with the price I gave him, and offered to treat me with a copita[1], to which I made no objection. As we sat discoursing at the table, the National entered with the passport in his hand, and sat down by us.

National. Caballero, I return you your passport; it is quite in form I rejoice much to have made your acquaintance I have no doubt that you can give me some information respecting the present war.

Myself. I shall be very happy to afford so polite and honourable a gentleman any information in my power.

National What is England doing? Is she about to afford any assistance to this country? If she pleased she could put down the war in three months.

Myself. Be under no apprehension, Señor Nacional; the war will be put down, don't doubt. You have heard of the English

---

[1] small glass.

legion which my Lord Palmerston has sent over? Leave the
matter in their hands, and you will soon see the result.

National. It appears to me that this Caballero Balmerson
must be a very honest man

Myself There can be no doubt of it.

National. I have heard that he is a great general.

Myself There can be no doubt of it. In some things neither
Napoleon nor the Sawyer[1] would stand a chance with him for a
moment. *Es mucho hombre*[2].

National. I am glad to hear it. Does he intend to head the
legion himself?

Myself. I believe not, but he has sent over, to head the
fighting-men, a friend of his, who is thought to be nearly as much
versed in military matters as himself

National. I am rejoiced to hear it. I see that the war will soon
be over. Caballero, I thank you for your politeness, and for the
information which you have afforded me I hope you will have a
pleasant journey. I confess that I am surprised to see a gentleman
of your country travelling alone, and in this manner, through
such regions as these. The roads are at present very bad. There
have of late been many accidents, and more than two deaths in
this neighbourhood. The despoblado out yonder has a particularly
evil name, be on your guard, Caballero I am sorry that gipsy
was permitted to pass Should you meet him and not like his
looks, shoot him at once, stab him, or ride him down. He is a
well-known thief, contrabandista, and murderer, and has committed more assassinations than he has fingers on his hands.
Caballero, if you please, we will allow you a guard to the other
side of the pass You do not wish it? Then farewell. Stay; before
I go I should wish to see once more the signature of the Caballero
Balmerson.

I showed him the signature, which he looked upon with profound reverence, uncovering his head for a moment, we then
embraced and parted

I mounted the horse and rode from the town, at first proceeding
very slowly. I had no sooner, however, reached the moor, than

[1] El Serrador, a Carlist partisan, who about this period was much talked
of in Spain.

[2] He is very much a man.

I put the animal to his speedy trot, and proceeded at a tremendous rate for some time, expecting every moment to overtake the gipsy. I, however, saw nothing of him, nor did I meet with a single human being. The road along which I sped was narrow and sandy, winding amidst thickets of broom and brushwood, with which the despoblado was overgrown, and which in some places were as high as a man's head. Across the moor, in the direction in which I was proceeding, rose a lofty eminence, naked and bare. The moor extended for at least three leagues. I had nearly crossed it, and reached the foot of the ascent. I was becoming very uneasy, conceiving that I might have passed the gipsy amongst the thickets, when I suddenly heard his well-known Ola! and his black savage head and staring eyes suddenly appeared from amidst a clump of broom.

"You have tarried long, brother," said he; "I almost thought you had played me false."

He bade me dismount, and then proceeded to lead the horse behind the thicket, where I found the mule picketed to the ground. I gave him the barley and provisions, and then proceeded to relate to him my adventure with the National.

"I would I had him here," said the gipsy, on hearing the epithets which the former had lavished upon him—"I would I had him here; then should my chuli[1] and his carlo[2] become better acquainted."

"And what are you doing here yourself," I demanded, "in this wild place, amidst these thickets?"

"I am expecting a messenger down yon pass," said the gipsy, "and till that messenger arrive I can neither go forward nor return. It is on business of Egypt, brother, that I am here."

As he invariably used this last expression when he wished to evade my inquiries, I held my peace and said no more. The animals were fed, and we proceeded to make a frugal repast on bread and wine.

"Why do you not cook the game which I brought?" I demanded. "In this place there is plenty of materials for a fire."

"The smoke might discover us, brother," said Antonio. "I am desirous of lying escondido[3] in this place until the arrival of the messenger."

[1] knife.   [2] heart.   [3] hidden.

It was now considerably past noon. The gipsy lay behind the thicket, raising himself up occasionally and looking anxiously towards the hill which lay over against us. At last, with an exclamation of disappointment and impatience, he flung himself on the ground, where he lay a considerable time, apparently ruminating; at last he lifted up his head and looked me in the face.

Antonio. Brother, I cannot imagine what business brought you to this country.

Myself. Perhaps the same which brings you to this moor—business of Egypt.

Antonio. Not so, brother. You speak the language of Egypt, it is true, but your ways and words are neither those of the Calés nor of the Busné[1].

Myself. Did you not hear me speak in the foros about God and Tebleque[2]? It was to declare His glory to the Cales and Gentiles that I came to the land of Spain.

Antonio. And who sent you on this errand?

Myself. You would scarcely understand me were I to inform you. Know, however, that there are many in foreign lands who lament the darkness which envelops Spain, and the scenes of cruelty, robbery, and murder which deform it.

Antonio. Are they Caloré or Busné?

Myself. What matters it? Both Caloré and Busné are sons of the same God.

Antonio. You lie, brother: they are not of one father nor of one Errate[3]. You speak of robbery, cruelty, and murder. There are too many Busné, brother; if there were no Busné there would be neither robbery nor murder. The Caloré neither rob nor murder each other—the Busné do; nor are they cruel to their animals—their law forbids them. When I was a child I was beating a burra[4]; but my father stopped my hand, and chided me. "Hurt not the animal," said he, "for within it is the soul of your own sister!"

Myself. And do you believe in this wild doctrine, O Antonio?

Antonio. Sometimes I do, sometimes I do not. There are some who believe in nothing—not even that they live! Long since,

---

[1] Gentiles, those not Calés or gipsies. [2] the Saviour.
[3] race. [4] donkey.

I knew an old Caloro—he was old, very old, upwards of a hundred years—and I once heard him say that all we thought we saw was a lie; that there was no world, no men nor women, no horses nor mules, no olive trees. But whither are we straying? I asked what induced you to come to this country; you tell me the glory of God and Tebleque. Disparáte!¹ Tell that to the Busné. You have good reasons for coming, no doubt, else you would not be here. Some say you are a spy of the Londoné; perhaps you are—I care not. Rise, brother, and tell me whether any one is coming down the pass.

"I see a distant object," I replied, "like a speck on the side of the hill."

The gipsy started up, and we both fixed our eyes on the object. The distance was so great that it was at first with difficulty that we could distinguish whether it moved or not. A quarter of an hour, however, dispelled all doubts, for within this time it had nearly reached the bottom of the hill, and we could descry a figure seated on an animal of some kind.

"It is a woman," said I at length, "mounted on a gray donkey."

"Then it is my messenger," said Antonio, "for it can be no other."

The woman and the donkey were now upon the plain, and for some time were concealed from us by the copse and brushwood which intervened. They were not long, however, in making their appearance at the distance of about a hundred yards. The donkey was a beautiful creature of a silver gray, and came frisking along, swinging her tail, and moving her feet so quick that they scarcely seemed·to touch the ground. The animal no sooner perceived us than she stopped short, turned round, and attempted to escape by the way she had come. Her rider, however, detained her; whereupon the donkey kicked violently, and would probably have flung the former, had she not sprung nimbly to the ground. The form of the woman was entirely concealed by the large wrapping man's cloak which she wore. I ran to assist her, when she turned her face full upon me, and I instantly recognised the sharp, clever features of Antonia, whom I had seen at Badajoz, the daughter of my guide. She said nothing to me, but advancing to her father, addressed something to him in a low voice which I

¹ Nonsense!

did not hear. He started back and vociferated "*Todos[1]!*" "Yes," said she in a louder tone, probably repeating the words which I had not caught before, "all are captured."

The gipsy remained for some time like one astounded, and unwilling to listen to their discourse, which I imagined might relate to business of Egypt, I walked away amidst the thickets. I was absent for some time, but could occasionally hear passionate expressions and oaths. In about half an hour I returned. They had left the road, but I found them behind the broom-clump, where the animals stood. Both were seated on the ground. The features of the gipsy were peculiarly dark and grim. He held his unsheathed knife in his hand, which he would occasionally plunge into the earth, exclaiming, "*Todos! Todos!*"

"Brother," said he at last, "I can go no farther with you; the business which carried me to Castumba[2] is settled: you must now travel by yourself and trust to your baji[3]."

"I trust in Undevel[4]," I replied, "who wrote my fortune long ago. But how am I to journey? I have no horse, for you doubtless want your own."

The gipsy appeared to reflect. "I want the horse, it is true, brother," he said, "and likewise the macho[5]. But you shall not go *en pindré*[6]; you shall purchase the burra of Antonia, which I presented her when I sent her upon this expedition."

"The burra," I replied, "appears both savage and vicious."

"She is both, brother, and on that account I bought her: a savage and vicious beast has generally four excellent legs. You are a Caló, brother, and can manage her. You shall therefore purchase the savage burra, giving my daughter Antonia a baria[7] of gold. If you think fit you can sell the beast at Talavera or Madrid, for Estremenian bestis[8] are highly considered in Castumba."

In less than an hour I was on the other side of the pass, mounted on the savage burra.

[1] All!   [2] Castile   [3] fortune.   [4] God.
[5] mule.   [6] on foot.   [7] ounce.   [8] animals.

WILLIAM BLAKE

TO THE EVENING STAR

Thou fair-hair'd angel of the evening,
Now, whilst the sun rests on the mountains, light
Thy bright torch of love: thy radiant crown
Put on, and smile upon our evening bed!
Smile on our loves, and while thou drawest the
Blue curtains of the sky, scatter thy silver dew
On every flower that shuts its sweet eyes
In timely sleep. Let thy west wind sleep on
The lake, speak silence with thy glimmering eyes,
And wash the dusk with silver.—Soon, full soon,
Dost thou withdraw; then the wolf rages wide,
And the lion glares through the dun forest:
The fleeces of our flocks are cover'd with
Thy sacred dew: protect them with thine influence

MILTON

EVENING

(From *Paradise Lost*)

Now came still evening on, and twilight gray
Had in her sober livery all things clad;
Silence accompanied; for beast and bird,
They to their grassy couch, these to their nests
Were slunk, all but the wakeful nightingale;
She all night long her amorous descant sung.
Silence was pleased. Now glow'd the firmament
With living sapphires; Hesperus, that led
The starry host, rode brightest, till the moon,
Rising in clouded majesty, at length
Apparent queen, unveil'd her peerless light,
And o'er the dark her silver mantle threw.

OLIVER GOLDSMITH

OLIVER GOLDSMITH (1728–74) was born at Pallas, Co. Longford, Ireland, the son of a clergyman; he was educated at several schools and at Trinity College, Dublin. He was somewhat weak and thriftless in character. After being rejected for the church, and failing to make progress in law, he attempted to qualify as a doctor. He went to Edinburgh to study medicine, wandered about Europe and returned to England, where, in South London, he obtained some humble employment. He was given work to do as a writer and translator His writings began to attract notice and for the rest of his days he lived by his pen. He earned very little, much less than he spent; so he was generally in difficulties He became acquainted with Dr Johnson, who liked him for his kind-hearted, gentle simplicity. Goldsmith died in the Temple, where he is buried. His best works are *She Stoops to Conquer* (a play), *The Deserted Village* (a poem), *The Vicar of Wakefield* (a novel) and *The Citizen of the World* (a collection of essays). The passage that follows is Letter cxiv from the last-named book.

CITY NIGHT PIECE

The clock just struck two, the expiring taper rises and sinks in the socket, the watchman forgets the hour in slumber, the laborious and the happy are at rest, and nothing wakes but meditation, guilt, revelry, and despair. The drunkard once more fills the destroying bowl, the robber walks his midnight round, and the suicide lifts his guilty arm against his own sacred person.

Let me no longer waste the night over the page of antiquity, or the sallies of co-temporary genius, but pursue the solitary walk, where vanity, ever changing, but a few hours past, walked before me, where she kept up the pageant, and now, like a froward child, seems hushed with her own importunities.

What a gloom hangs all around; the dying lamp feebly emits a yellow gleam, no sound is heard but of the chiming clock, or the distant watch-dog All the bustle of human pride is forgotten, an hour like this may well display the emptiness of human vanity.

There will come a time, when this temporary solitude may be made continual, and the city itself, like its inhabitants, fade away, and leave a desert in its room.

What cities, as great as this, have once triumphed in existence, had their victories as great, joy as just, and as unbounded, and with short sighted presumption, promised themselves immortality.

Posterity can hardly trace the situation of some. The sorrowful traveller wanders over the awful ruins of others; and as he beholds, he learns wisdom, and feels the transience of every sublunary possession.

Here, he cries, stood their citadel, now grown over with weeds; there their senate-house, but now the haunt of every noxious reptile; temples and theatres stood here, now only an undistinguished heap of ruin. They are fallen, for luxury and avarice first made them feeble. The rewards of state were conferred on amusing, and not on useful, members of society. Their riches and opulence invited the invaders, who, though at first repulsed, returned again, conquered by perseverance, and at last swept the defendants into undistinguished destruction.

How few appear in those streets, which but some few hours ago were crowded; and those who appear, now no longer wear their daily mask, nor attempt to hide their lewdness or their misery.

But who are those who make the streets their couch, and find a short repose from wretchedness at the doors of the opulent? These are strangers, wanderers, and orphans, whose circumstances are too humble to expect redress, and whose distresses are too great even for pity. Their wretchedness excites rather horror than pity. Some are without the covering even of rags, and others emaciated with disease; the world has disclaimed them; society turns its back upon their distress, and has given them up to nakedness and hunger.

Why, why was I born a man, and yet see the suffering of wretches I cannot relieve! Poor houseless creatures! the world will give you reproaches, but will not give you relief. The slightest misfortunes of the great, the most imaginary uneasinesses of the rich, are aggravated with all the power of eloquence, and held up to engage our attention and sympathetic sorrow. The poor weep unheeded, persecuted by every subordinate species of tyranny; and every law, which gives others security, becomes an enemy to them.

Why was this heart of mine formed with so much sensibility! or why was not my fortune adapted to its impulse! Tenderness, without a capacity of relieving, only makes the man who feels it more wretched than the object which sues for assistance. Adieu.

BEN JONSON

BEN JONSON (1573–1637), dramatist and poet, author of some beautiful short poems and of several fine plays including *Every Man in his Humour* and *The Alchemist*. The following hymn to the moon is one of his finest poems. "Drink to me only with thine eyes" is even more familiar from its musical setting. He wrote a beautiful poem on the death of a child actor called Salathiel Pavy.

HYMN TO DIANA

Queen and Huntress, cháste and fair,
   Now the sun is laid to sleep,
Seated in thy silver chair
   State in wonted manner keep:
      Hesperus entreats thy light,
      Goddess excellently bright.

Earth, let not thy envious shade
   Dare itself to interpose;
Cynthia's shining orb was made
   Heaven to clear when day did close:
      Bless us then with wishéd sight,
      Goddess excellently bright.

Lay thy bow of pearl apart
   And thy crystal-shining quiver;
Give unto the flying hart
   Space to breathe, how short soever:
      Thou that mak'st a day of night,
      Goddess excellently bright!

SALISBURY
Constable

GEORGE HERBERT

GEORGE HERBERT (1593–1633), sweetest of English religious poets, was born in Montgomery Castle. He was educated at Westminster and Trinity College, Cambridge, and intended to enter public life at the court of James I; but he was gradually drawn towards the Church. He became vicar of Bemerton (near Salisbury) where he died. His chief book is a volume of religious poems called *The Temple*. A charming life of Herbert was written by Izaak Walton, author of *The Compleat Angler*.

THE PULLEY

When God at first made man,
Having a glass of blessings standing by;
Let us (said he) pour on him all we can:
Let the world's riches, which dispersèd lie,
Contract into a span.

So strength first made a way;
Then beauty flow'd, then wisdom, honour, pleasure:
When almost all was out, God made a stay,
Perceiving that alone, of all his treasure,
Rest in the bottom lay.

For if I should (said he)
Bestow this jewel also on my creature,
He would adore my gifts instead of me,
And rest in Nature, not the God of Nature:
So both should losers be.

Yet let him keep the rest,
But keep them with repining restlessness:
Let him be rich and weary, that at least,
If goodness lead him not, yet weariness
May toss him to my breast.

KEATS

John Keats (1795–1821) was the son of the head ostler in a livery stable at the sign of the Swan and Hoop, Finsbury He was born there in October, 1795, and educated at an Enfield school It was intended that he should be a doctor, and he became a student at Guy's and St Thomas's Hospital. He was drawn, however, to literature, and, encouraged by admiring friends, he wrote and published a volume of verses in 1817 This was followed in the next year by *Endymion*, a long poem, and in 1820 appeared a volume containing his best work, *Lamia, Isabella, The Eve of St Agnes,* the *Ode to a Nightingale* and other poems Keats fell ill with consumption and left England to seek health in Italy He died in Rome at the age of twenty-five. His work had been unfairly attacked by certain reviewers, and Shelley, his friend and fellow-poet, was inspired to write in his defence a noble poem called *Adonais,* which will for ever unite the names of the young poets.

TO AUTUMN

I

Season of mists and mellow fruitfulness,
  Close bosom-friend of the maturing sun;
Conspiring with him how to load and bless
  With fruit the vines that round the thatch-eaves run;
To bend with apples the moss'd cottage-trees,
  And fill all fruit with ripeness to the core;
    To swell the gourd, and plump the hazel shells
With a sweet kernel; to set budding more,
And still more, later flowers for the bees,
  Until they think warm days will never cease,
    For Summer has o'erbrimm'd their clammy cells.

II

Who hath not seen thee oft amid thy store?
  Sometimes whoever seeks abroad may find
Thee sitting careless on a granary floor,
  Thy hair soft-lifted by the winnowing wind;
Or on a half-reap'd furrow sound asleep,
  Drows'd with the fume of poppies, while thy hook

Spares the next swath and all its twined flowers:
And sometimes like a gleaner thou dost keep
  Steady thy laden head across a brook;
  Or by a cyder-press, with patient look,
Thou watchest the last oozings hours by hours

III

Where are the songs of Spring? Ay, where are they?
  Think not of them, thou hast thy music too—
While barréd clouds bloom the soft-dying day,
  And touch the stubble-plains with rosy hue;
Then in a wailful choir the small gnats mourn
  Among the river sallows, borne aloft
  Or sinking as the light wind lives or dies;
And full-grown lambs loud bleat from hilly bourn;
  Hedge-crickets sing; and now with treble soft
  The redbreast whistles from a garden-croft;
  And gathering swallows twitter in the skies.

SHELLEY

Percy Bysshe Shelley (1792–1822) was born near Horsham in Sussex,
the son of a county gentleman. He was educated at Eton and at Oxford,
whence he was sent down after a year. He wrote verses and romances at
an early age, and his pen was always busy with poems, and with pamphlets
in favour of social reform. Like Byron, with whom he was on terms of
friendship, Shelley lived much in Italy, where he wrote some of his best
poems and several delightful descriptive letters Among his works in verse
may be named *Prometheus Unbound, Hellas, Adonais, The Witch of Atlas,*
the *Ode to the West Wind* and *To a Skylark* His shorter poems include
some of the loveliest lyrics in our language Shelley was drowned when
his schooner, the *Ariel,* was wrecked by a sudden storm in the bay of
Spezzia His body was washed ashore, and burnt in the presence of Byron
and Leigh Hunt; the ashes were buried at Rome in the cemetery where
lies the body of Keats

THE CLOUD

I bring fresh showers for the thirsting flowers,
  From the seas and the streams;
I bear light shade for the leaves when laid
  In their noonday dreams.

From my wings are shaken the dews that waken
  The sweet buds every one,
When rocked to rest on their mother's breast,
  As she dances about the sun.
I wield the flail of the lashing hail,
  And whiten the green plains under,
And then again I dissolve it in rain,
  And laugh as I pass in thunder.

I sift the snow on the mountains below,
  And their great pines groan aghast;
And all the night 'tis my pillow white,
  While I sleep in the arms of the blast.
Sublime on the towers of my skiey bowers,
  Lightning my pilot sits;
In a cavern under is fettered the thunder,
  It struggles and howls at fits;
Over earth and ocean, with gentle motion,
  This pilot is guiding me,
Lured by the love of the genii that move
  In the depths of the purple sea;
Over the rills, and the crags, and the hills,
  Over the lakes and the plains,
Wherever he dream, under mountain or stream,
  The Spirit he loves remains;
And I all the while bask in Heaven's blue smile,
  Whilst he is dissolving in rains.

The sanguine Sunrise, with his meteor eyes,
  And his burning plumes outspread,
Leaps on the back of my sailing rack,
  When the morning star shines dead;
As on the jag of a mountain crag,
  Which an earthquake rocks and swings,
An eagle alit one moment may sit
  In the light of its golden wings.

And when Sunset may breathe, from the lit sea beneath,
    Its ardours of rest and of love,
And the crimson pall of eve may fall
    From the depth of Heaven above,
With wings folded I rest on mine aery nest,
    As still as a brooding dove.

That orbéd maiden with white fire laden,
    Whom mortals call the Moon,
Glides glimmering o'er my fleece-like floor,
    By the midnight breezes strewn;
And wherever the beat of her unseen feet,
    Which only the angels hear,
May have broken the woof of my tent's thin roof,
    The stars peep behind her and peer;
And I laugh to see them whirl and flee,
    Like a swarm of golden bees,
When I widen the rent in my wind-built tent,
    Till the calm rivers, lakes, and seas,
Like strips of the sky fallen through me on high,
    Are each paved with the moon and these.

I bind the Sun's throne with a burning zone,
    And the Moon's with a girdle of pearl,
The volcanoes are dim, and the stars reel and swim,
    When the whirlwinds my banner unfurl.
From cape to cape, with a bridge-like shape,
    Over a torrent sea,
Sunbeam-proof, I hang like a roof,—
    The mountains its columns be.
The triumphal arch through which I march
    With hurricane, fire, and snow,
When the Powers of the air are chained to my chair,
    Is the million-coloured bow;
The sphere-fire above its soft colours wove,
    While the moist Earth was laughing below.

I am the daughter of Earth and Water,
    And the nursling of the Sky;
I pass through the pores of the ocean and shores;
    I change, but I cannot die.
For after the rain, when with never a stain
    The pavilion of Heaven is bare,
And the winds and sunbeams with their convex gleams
    Build up the blue dome of air,
I silently laugh at my own cenotaph,
    And out of the caverns of rain,
Like a child from the womb, like a ghost from the tomb,
    I arise and unbuild it again.

J. A. FROUDE

JAMES ANTHONY FROUDE (1818–94), the son of a clergyman, was born in Devonshire, and educated at Westminster and Oxford. His writings are mainly historical Among them may be named a *History of England* during part of the Tudor period, *Short Studies on Great Subjects* (a collection of essays) and *Oceana*, an account of his visit to Australia and New Zealand. The passage that follows is taken from his *History*. The court at Dunstable referred to at the beginning is the court that decreed a divorce between Henry VIII and his first wife Catherine of Aragon

THE CORONATION OF ANNE BOLEYN

In anticipation of the timely close of the proceedings at Dunstable, notice had been given in the city early in May, that preparations should be made for the coronation on the first of the following month Queen Anne was at Greenwich, but, according to custom, the few preceding days were to be spent at the Tower; and on the 19th of May, she was conducted thither in state by the lord mayor and the city companies, with one of those splendid exhibitions upon the water which in the days when the silver Thames deserved its name, and the sun could shine down upon it out of the blue summer sky, were spectacles scarcely rivalled in gorgeousness by the world-famous wedding of the Adriatic. The river was crowded with boats, the banks and the ships in the pool swarmed with people; and fifty great barges formed the procession, all blazing with gold and banners. The queen herself was in her own barge, close to that of the lord mayor, and in keeping with the fantastic genius of the time, she was preceded up the water by "a foyst or wafter full of ordnance, in which was a great diagon continually moving and casting wildfire, and round about the foyst stood terrible monsters and wild men, casting fire and making hideous noise." So, with trumpets blowing, cannon pealing, the Tower guns answering the guns of the ships, in a blaze of fireworks and splendour, Anne Boleyn was borne along to the great archway of the Tower, where the king was waiting on the stairs to receive her.

And now let us suppose eleven days to have elapsed, the welcome news to have arrived at length from Dunstable, and the fair summer morning of life dawning in treacherous beauty after the long night of expectation. No bridal ceremonial had been possible; the marriage had been huddled over like a stolen love-match, and the marriage feast had been eaten in vexation and disappointment. These past mortifications were to be atoned for by a coronation pageant which the art and the wealth of the richest city in Europe should be poured out in the most lavish profusion to adorn

On the morning of the 31st of May, the families of the London citizens were stirring early in all houses. From Temple Bar to the Tower, the streets were fresh strewed with gravel, the footpaths were railed off along the whole distance, and occupied on one side by the guilds, their workmen, and apprentices, on the other by the city constables and officials in their gaudy uniforms, "with their staves in hand for to cause the people to keep good room and order." Cornhill and Gracechurch Street had dressed their fronts in scarlet and crimson, in arras and tapestry, and the rich carpet-work from Persia and the East. Cheapside, to outshine her rivals, was draped even more splendidly in cloth of gold, and tissue, and velvet. The sheriffs were pacing up and down on their great Flemish horses, hung with liveries, and all the windows were thronged with ladies crowding to see the procession pass. At length the Tower guns opened, the grim gates rolled back, and under the archway in the bright May sunshine, the long column began slowly to defile. Two states only permitted their representatives to grace the scene with their presence—Venice and France. It was, perhaps, to make the most of this isolated countenance,

that the French ambassador's train formed the van of the cavalcade.
Twelve French knights came riding foremost in surcoats of blue
velvet with sleeves of yellow silk, their horses trapped in blue,
with white crosses powdered on their hangings. After them followed
a troop of English gentlemen, two and two, and then the Knights
of the Bath, "in gowns of violet, with hoods purfled with miniver
like doctors." Next, perhaps at a little interval, the abbots passed
on, mitred, in their robes; the barons followed in crimson velvet,
the bishops then, and then the earls and marquises, the dresses
of each order increasing in elaborate gorgeousness All these
rode on in pairs. Then came alone Audeley, lord-chancellor, and
behind him the Venetian ambassador and the Archbishop of
York; the Archbishop of Canterbury, and Du Bellay, Bishop of
Bayonne and of Paris, not now with bugle and hunting-frock,
but solemn with stole and crozier. Next, the lord mayor, with the
city mace in hand, the Garter in his coat of arms, and then Lord
William Howard—Belted Will Howard, of the Scottish Border,
Marshal of England. The officers of the queen's household succeeded the marshal in scarlet and gold, and the van of the procession was closed by the Duke of Suffolk, as high constable, with
his silver wand. It is no easy matter to picture to ourselves the
blazing trail of splendour which in such a pageant must have
drawn along the London streets,—those streets which now we
know so black and smoke-grimed, themselves then radiant with
masses of colour, gold, and crimson, and violet. Yet there it was,
and there the sun could shine upon it, and tens of thousands of
eyes were gazing on the scene out of the crowded lattices.

Glorious as the spectacle was, perhaps however, it passed
unheeded Those eyes were watching all for another object, which
now drew near In an open space behind the constable there was
seen approaching "a white chariot," drawn by two palfreys in
white damask which swept the ground, a golden canopy borne
above it making music with silver bells. and in the chariot sat
the observed of all observers, the beautiful occasion of all this
glittering homage; fortune's plaything of the hour, the Queen of
England—queen at last—borne along upon the waves of this sea
of glory, breathing the perfumed incense of greatness which she
had risked her fair name, her delicacy, her honour, her self-respect,
to win; and she had won it.

There she sat, dressed in white tissue robes, her fair hair flowing loose over her shoulders, and her temples circled with a light coronet of gold and diamonds—most beautiful—loveliest—most favoured perhaps, as she seemed at that hour, of all England's daughters. Alas! "within the hollow round" of that coronet—

> Kept death his court, and there the antick sate,
> Scoffing her state and grinning at her pomp.
> Allowing her a little breath, a little scene
> To monarchise, be feared, and kill with looks,
> Infusing her with self and vain conceit,
> As if the flesh which walled about her life
> Were brass impregnable , and humoured thus,
> Bored through her castle walls; and farewell, Queen.

Fatal gift of greatness! so dangerous ever! so more than dangerous in those tremendous times when the fountains are broken loose of the great deeps of thought; and nations are in the throes of revolution,—when ancient order and law and tradition are splitting in the social earthquake, and as the opposing forces wrestle to and fro, those unhappy ones who stand out above the crowd become the symbols of the struggle, and fall the victims of its alternating fortunes. And what if into an unsteady heart and brain, intoxicated with splendour, the outward chaos should find its way, converting the poor silly soul into an image of the same confusion,—if conscience should be deposed from her high place, and the Pandora box be broken loose of passions and sensualities and follies; and at length there be nothing left of all which man or woman ought to value, save hope of God's forgiveness

Three short years have yet to pass, and again, on a summer morning, Queen Anne Boleyn will leave the Tower of London—not radiant then with beauty on a gay errand of coronation, but a poor wandering ghost, on a sad tragic errand, from which she will never more return, passing away out of an earth where she may stay no longer, into a presence where, nevertheless, we know that all is well—for all of us—and therefore for her.

But let us not cloud her shortlived sunshine with the shadow of the future. She went on in her loveliness, the peeresses following in their carriages, with the royal guard in their rear. In Fenchurch Street she was met by the children of the city schools, and at the corner of Gracechurch Street a masterpiece had been prepared of the pseudo-classic art, then so fashionable, by the merchants of the Styll Yard. A Mount Parnassus had been constructed, and a Helicon fountain upon it playing into a basin with four jets of Rhenish wine. On the top of the mountain sat Apollo with Calliope at his feet, and on either side the remaining Muses, holding lutes or harps, and singing each of them some "posy" or epigram in praise of the queen, which was presented, after it had been sung, written in letters of gold.

From Gracechurch Street, the procession passed to Leadenhall, where there was a spectacle in better taste, of the old English Catholic kind, quaint perhaps and forced, but truly and even beautifully emblematic. There was again a "little mountain," which was hung with red and white roses; a gold ring was placed on the summit, on which, as the queen appeared, a white falcon was made to "descend as out of the sky"—"and then incontinent came down an angel with great melody, and set a close crown of gold upon the falcon's head; and in the same pageant sat Saint Anne with all her issue beneath her; and Mary Cleophas with her four children, of the which children one made a goodly oration to the queen, of the fruitfulness of St Anne, trusting that like fruit should come of her."

With such "pretty conceits," at that time the honest tokens of an English welcome, the new queen was received by the citizens of London. These scenes must be multiplied by the number of the streets, where some fresh fancy met her at every turn. To preserve the festivities from flagging, every fountain and conduit within the walls ran all day with wine; the bells of every steeple were ringing; children lay in wait with song, and ladies with posies, in which all the resources of fantastic extravagance were exhausted; and thus in an unbroken triumph—and to outward appearance received with the warmest affection—she passed under Temple Bar, down the Strand by Charing Cross to Westminster Hall. The king was not with her throughout the day; nor did he intend to be with her in any part of the ceremony. She was to reign without a rival, the undisputed sovereign of the hour.

Saturday being passed in showing herself to the people, she retired for the night to "the king's manour house at Westminster," where she slept. On the following morning, between eight and nine o'clock, she returned to the hall, where the lord mayor, the city council, and the peers were again assembled, and took her place on the high dais at the top of the stairs under the cloth of state; while the bishops, the abbots, and the monks of the abbey formed in the area. A railed way had been laid with carpets across Palace Yard and the Sanctuary to the abbey gates, and when all was ready, preceded by the peers in their robes of parliament, the Knights of the Garter in the dress of the order, she swept out under her canopy, the bishops and the monks "solemnly singing." The train was borne by the old Duchess of Norfolk her aunt, the Bishops of London and Winchester on either side "bearing up the lappets of her robe." The Earl of Oxford carried the crown on its cushion immediately before her. She was dressed in purple velvet furred with ermine, her hair escaping loose, as she usually wore it, under a wreath of diamonds.

On entering the abbey, she was led to the coronation chair where she sat while the train fell into their places, and the pre-liminaries of the ceremonial were despatched. Then she was conducted up to the high altar, and anointed Queen of England, and she received from the hands of Cranmer, fresh come in haste from Dunstable, with the last words of his sentence upon Catherine scarcely silent upon his lips, the golden sceptre, and St Edward's crown.

Did any twinge of remorse, any pang of painful recollection, pierce at that moment the incense of glory which she was inhaling? Did any vision flit across her of a sad mourning figure which once had stood where she was standing, now desolate, neglected, sinking into the darkening twilight of a life cut short by sorrow? Who can tell? At such a time, that figure would have weighed heavily upon a noble mind, and a wise mind would have been taught by the thought of it, that although life be fleeting as a dream, it is long enough to experience strange vicissitudes of fortune. But Anne Boleyn was not noble and was not wise,—too probably she felt nothing but the delicious, all-absorbing, all-intoxicating present, and if that plain, suffering face presented itself to her memory at all, we may fear that it was rather as a foil to her own surpassing loveliness. Two years later, she was able to exult

over Catherine's death; she is not likely to have thought of her
with gentler feelings in the first glow and flush of triumph

We may now leave these scenes. They concluded in the usual
English style, with a banquet in the great hall, and with all
outward signs of enjoyment and pleasure. There must have been
but few persons present however who did not feel that the sunshine
of such a day might not last for ever, and that over so dubious a
marriage no Englishman could exult with more than half a heart.

AUSTIN DOBSON

HENRY AUSTIN DOBSON, b. 1840, writer of much delightful verse and of
Eighteenth Century Vignettes, a series of papers on persons and places of that
period.

A BALLADE TO QUEEN ELIZABETH

King Philip had vaunted his claims;
  He had sworn for a year he would sack us;
With an army of heathenish names
  He was coming to fagot and stack us;
  Like the thieves of the sea he would track us,
And shatter our ships on the main;
  But we had bold Neptune to back us,—
And where are the galleons of Spain?

His carackes were christened of dames
  To the kirtles whereof he would tack us;
With his saints and his gilded stern-frames,
  He had thought like an egg-shell to crack us;
  Now Howard may get to his Flaccus,
And Drake to his Devon again,
  And Hawkins bowl rubbers to Bacchus,—
For where are the galleons of Spain?

Let his Majesty hang to St James
  The axe that he whetted to hack us;
He must play at some lustier games
  Or at sea he can hope to out-thwack us;

QUEEN ELIZABETH: DESIGN FOR A GREAT
SEAL OF IRELAND
Nicholas Hilliard

To his mines of Peru he would pack us
To tug at his bullet and chain;
   Alas that his Greatness should lack us!—
But where are the galleons of Spain?

Envoy

Gloriana!—the Don may attack us
Whenever his stomach be fain;
   He must reach us before he can rack us,...
And where are the galleons of Spain?

MICHAEL DRAYTON

MICHAEL DRAYTON (1563–1631) wrote many works in verse, among them
being *Polyolbion*, a long description of various parts of England, and
Nymphidia, a fairy poem.

AGINCOURT

Fair stood the wind for France,
When we our sails advance;
Nor now to prove our chance
   Longer will tarry.
But putting to the main,
At Caux, the mouth of Seine,
With all his martial train,
   Landed King HARRY.

And taking many a fort
Furnished in warlike sort,
Marcheth towards Agincourt
   In happy hour;
Skirmishing, day by day,
With those that stopp'd his way,
Where the French Gen'ral lay
   With all his power.

Which, in his height of pride,
King HENRY to deride;
His ransom to provide,
   To the King sending.

Which he neglects the while,
As from a nation vile,
Yet, with an angry smile,
    Their fall portending

And turning to his men,
Quoth our brave HENRY then:
"Though they to one be ten
    Be not amazéd!
Yet have we well begun:
Battles so bravely won
Have ever to the sun
    By Fame been raiséd!"

"And for myself," quoth he,
"This my full rest shall be:
England ne'er mourn for me,
    Nor more esteem me!
Victor I will remain,
Or on this earth lie slain·
Never shall She sustain
    Loss to redeem me!

"Poitiers and Cressy tell,
When most their pride did swell,
Under our swords they fell.
    No less our skill is,
Than when our Grandsire great,
Claiming the regal seat,
By many a warlike feat
    Lopped the French lilies."

The Duke of YORK so dread
The eager vaward led;
With the Main, HENRY sped
    Amongst his henchmen:
EXETER had the Rear,
A braver man not there!
O Lord, how hot they were
    On the false Frenchmen!

They now to fight are gone;
Armour on armour shone,
Drum now to drum did groan:
    To hear, was wonder.
That, with the cries they make,
The very earth did shake;
Trumpet, to trumpet spake;
    Thunder, to thunder.

Well it thine age became,
O noble ERPINGHAM!
Which didst the signal aim
    To our hid forces:
When, from a meadow by,
Like a storm suddenly,
The English Archery
    Stuck the French horses.

With Spanish yew so strong;
Arrows a cloth-yard long,
That like to serpents stung,
    Piercing the weather.
None from his fellow starts;
But, playing manly parts,
And like true English hearts,
    Stuck close together.

When down their bows they threw;
And forth their bilbowes[1] drew
And on the French they flew:
    Not one was tardy.
Arms were from shoulders sent,
Scalps to the teeth were rent,
Down the French peasants went:
    Our men were hardy.

This while our noble King,
His broad sword brandishing,
Down the French host did ding
    As to o'erwhelm it.

    [1] swords.

And many a deep wound lent;
His arms with blood besprent,
And many a cruel dent
    Bruiséd his helmet.

GLOUCESTER that Duke so good,
Next of the royal blood,
For famous England stood
    With his brave brother.
CLARENCE, in steel so bright,
Though but a Maiden Knight;
Yet in that furious fight,
    Scarce such another!

WARWICK, in blood did wade,
OXFORD, the foe invade,
And cruel slaughter made,
    Still as they ran up.
SUFFOLK his axe did ply;
BEAUMONT and WILLOUGHBY
Bare them right doughtily:
    FERRERS, and FANHOPE.

Upon Saint CRISPIN's Day,
Fought was this noble Fray;
Which Fame did not delay
    To England to carry.
O when shall English men
With such acts fill a pen?
Or England breed again
    Such a King HARRY?

BENJAMIN FRANKLIN

BENJAMIN FRANKLIN (1706–90) was born at Boston, in America, and appren-
ticed, while still a child, to the trade of printing He worked steadily, not
only at his trade but at his own education. He came to England and
followed his calling for nearly two years. On his return to America, he took
a leading part in the politics of Pennsylvania, the state in which he had
settled. He studied electricity, proved that lightning is a form of electricity
and first suggested the use of lightning-conductors for the protection of
tall buildings He came to England again as representative of his State;

and he made a third visit to try to settle the dangerous troubles that had arisen between England and the American Colonies. He was treated with haughtiness by some members of the government and when next he came to Europe it was to seek help from France against England. In this he was successful; and when American independence had been won, Franklin became the United States ambassador to Paris. He wrote much, the best of his books being his *Autobiography* from which the passage that follows is taken

FRANKLIN'S EARLY YEARS

From a child I was fond of reading, and all the little money that came into my hands was ever laid out in books. Pleased with the *Pilgrim's Progress*, my first collection was of John Bunyan's works in separate little volumes. I afterward sold them to enable me to buy R Burton's *Historical Collections*; they were small chapmen's books, and cheap, 40 or 50 in all. My father's little library consisted chiefly of books in polemic divinity, most of which I read, and have since often regretted that, at a time when I had such a thirst for knowledge, more proper books had not fallen in my way, since it was now resolved I should not be a clergyman. Plutarch's Lives there was in which I read abundantly, and I still think that time spent to great advantage. There was also a book of De Foe's, called an *Essay on Projects*, and another of Dr Mather's, called *Essays to do Good*, which perhaps gave me a turn of thinking that had an influence on some of the principal future events of my life.

This bookish inclination at length determined my father to make me a printer, though he had already one son (James) of that profession. In 1717 my brother James returned from England with a press and letters to set up his business in Boston. I liked it much better than that of my father, but still had a hankering for the sea. To prevent the apprehended effect of such an inclination, my father was impatient to have me bound to my brother. I stood out some time, but at last was persuaded, and signed the indentures when I was yet but twelve years old. I was to serve as an apprentice till I was twenty-one years of age, only I was to be allowed journeyman's wages during the last year. In a little time I made great proficiency in the business, and became a useful hand to my brother. I now had access to better books. An acquaintance with the apprentices of booksellers enabled me sometimes to borrow a small one, which I was careful to return soon and clean. Often I sat up in my room reading the gieatest part of the night, when the book was borrowed in the evening and to be returned early in the morning, lest it should be missed or wanted.

And after some time an ingenious tradesman, Mr Matthew Adams, who had a pretty collection of books, and who frequented our printing-house, took notice of me, invited me to his library, and very kindly lent me such books as I chose to read. I now took a fancy to poetry, and made some little pieces; my brother, thinking it might turn to account, encouraged me, and put me on composing occasional ballads. One was called *The Lighthouse Tragedy*, and contained an account of the drowning of Captain Worthilake, with his two daughters: the other was a sailor's song, on the taking of *Teach* (or Blackbeard) the pirate. They were wretched stuff, in the Grub-street-ballad style; and when they were printed he sent me about the town to sell them. The first sold wonderfully, the event being recent, having made a great noise. This flattered my vanity; but my father discouraged me by ridiculing my performances, and telling me verse-makers were generally beggars. So I escaped being a poet, most probably a very bad one; but as prose writing has been of great use to me in the course of my life, and was a principal means of my advancement, I shall tell you how, in such a situation, I acquired what little ability I have in that way.

There was another bookish lad in the town, John Collins by name, with whom I was intimately acquainted. We sometimes disputed, and very fond we were of argument, and very desirous of confuting one another, which disputatious turn, by the way, is apt to become a very bad habit, making people often extremely disagreeable in company by the contradiction that is necessary to bring it into practice; and thence, besides souring and spoiling the conversation, is productive of disgusts and, perhaps, enmities where you may have occasion for friendship. I had caught it by reading my father's books of dispute about religion. Persons of good sense, I have since observed, seldom fall into it, except lawyers, university men, and men of all sorts that have been bred at Edinburgh.

A question was once, somehow or other, started between Collins and me, of the propriety of educating the female sex in learning, and their abilities for study. He was of opinion that it was improper, and that they were naturally unequal to it. I took the contrary side, perhaps a little for dispute's sake. He was naturally more eloquent, had a ready plenty of words; and sometimes, as I thought, bore me down more by his fluency than by the strength of his reasons. As we parted without settling the point, and were not to see one another again for some time, I sat down to put my arguments in writing, which I copied fair and sent to him. He answered, and I replied. Three or four letters of a side had passed, when my father happened to find my papers and read them. Without entering into the discussion, he took occasion to talk to me about the manner of my writing; observed that, though I had the advantage of my antagonist in correct spelling and pointing (which I owed to the printing-house), I fell far short in elegance of expression, in method and in perspicuity, of which he convinced me by several instances. I saw the justice of his remarks, and thence grew more attentive to the manner in writing, and determined to endeavour at improvement.

About this time I met with an odd volume of the *Spectator* It was the third. I had never before seen any of them. I bought it, read it over and over, and was much delighted with it. I thought the writing excellent, and wished, if possible, to imitate it. With this view I took some of the papers, and, making short hints of the sentiment in each sentence, laid them by a few days, and then, without looking at the book, tried to complete the papers again, by expressing each hinted sentiment at length, and as fully as it had been expressed before, in any suitable words that should come to hand. Then I compared my *Spectator* with the original, discovered some of my faults, and corrected them. But I found I wanted a stock of words, or a readiness in recollecting and using them, which I thought I should have acquired before that time if I had gone on making verses; since the continual occasion for words of the same import, but of different length, to suit the measure, or of different sound for the rhyme, would have laid me under a constant necessity of searching for variety, and also have tended to fix that variety in my mind, and make me master of it. Therefore I took some of the tales and turned them into verse; and, after a time, when I had pretty well forgotten the prose, turned them back again. I also sometimes jumbled my collections of hints into confusion, and after some weeks endeavoured to reduce them into the best order, before I began to form the full sentences and complete the paper. This was to teach me method in the arrangement of thoughts By comparing my work afterwards with the original, I discovered many faults and amended them; but I sometimes had the pleasure of fancying that, in certain particulars of small import, I had been lucky enough to improve the method or the language, and this encouraged me to think I might possibly in time come to be a tolerable English writer, of which I was extremely ambitious. My time for these exercises and for reading was at night, after work or before it began in the morning, or on Sundays, when I contrived to be in the printing-house alone, evading as much as I could the common attendance on public worship which my father used to exact on me when I was under his care, and which indeed I still thought a duty, though I could not, as it seemed to me, afford time to practise it.

When about 16 years of age I happened to meet with a book, written by one Tryon, recommending a vegetable diet. I determined to go into it. My brother, being yet unmarried, did not keep house, but boarded himself and his apprentices in another family. My refusing to eat flesh occasioned an inconveniency, and I was frequently chid for my singularity. I made myself acquainted with Tryon's manner of preparing some of his dishes, such as boiling potatoes or rice, making hasty pudding, and a few others, and then proposed to my brother, that if he would give me, weekly, half the money he paid for my board, I would board myself. He instantly agreed to it, and I presently found that I could save half what he paid me This was an additional fund for buying books. But I had another advantage in it. My brother and the rest going from the printing-house to their meals, I remained there alone, and, despatching presently my light repast, which often was no more than a biscuit or a slice of bread, a handful of raisins or a tart from the pastry-cook's, and a glass of water, had the rest of the time till their return for study, in which I made the greater progress, from that greater clearness of head and quicker apprehension which usually attend temperance in eating and drinking

And now it was that, being on some occasion made ashamed of

my ignorance in figures, which I had twice failed in learning when at school, I took Cocker's book of Arithmetic, and went through the whole by myself with great ease. I also read Seller's and Shermy's books of Navigation, and became acquainted with the little geometry they contain; but never proceeded far in that science And I read about this time Locke *On Human Understanding*, and the *Art of Thinking*, by Messrs du Port Royal.

While I was intent on improving my language, I met with an English grammar (I think it was Greenwood's), at the end of which there were two little sketches of the arts of rhetoric and logic, the latter finishing with a specimen of a dispute in the Socratic method; and soon after I procured Xenophon's *Memorable Things of Socrates*, wherein there are many instances of the same method. I was charmed with it, adopted it, dropped my abrupt contradiction and positive argumentation, and put on the humble inquirer and doubter. And being then, from reading Shaftesbury and Collins, become a real doubter in many points of our religious doctrine, I found this method safest for myself and very embarrassing to those against whom I used it; therefore I took a delight in it, practised it continually, and grew very artful and expert in drawing people, even of superior knowledge, into concessions, the consequences of which they did not foresee, entangling them in difficulties out of which they could not extricate themselves, and so obtaining victories that neither myself nor my cause always deserved I continued this method some few years, but gradually left it, retaining only the habit of expressing myself in terms of modest diffidence; never using, when I advanced anything that may possibly be disputed, the words *certainly, undoubtedly*, or any others that give the air of positiveness to an opinion; but rather say, *I conceive* or *apprehend a thing to be so and so, it appears to me*, or *I should think it so or so*, for such and such reasons, or *I imagine it to be so*, or *it is so, if I am not mistaken*. This habit, I believe, has been of great advantage to me when I have had occasion to inculcate my opinions, and persuade men into measures that I have been from time to time engaged in promoting; and, as the chief ends of conversation are to *inform* or to be *informed*, to *please* or to *persuade*, I wish well-meaning, sensible men would not lessen their power of doing good by a positive, assuming manner, that seldom fails to disgust, tends to create opposition, and to defeat every one of those purposes for which speech was given to us, to wit, giving or receiving information or pleasure For, if you would inform, a positive and dogmatical manner in advancing your sentiments may provoke contradiction and prevent a candid attention. If you wish information and improvement from the knowledge of others, and yet at the same time express yourself as firmly fixed in your present opinions, modest, sensible men, who do not love disputation, will probably leave you undisturbed in the possession of your error. And by such a manner, you can seldom hope to recommend yourself in *pleasing* your hearers, or to persuade those whose concurrence you desire. Pope says, judiciously:

> *Men should be taught as if you taught them not,*
> *And things unknown propos'd as things forgot;*

farther recommending to us

> To speak, tho' sure, with seeming diffidence.

And he might have coupled with this line that which he has coupled with another, I think, less properly,

> For want of modesty is want of sense.

If you ask, Why less properly? I must repeat the lines,

> Immodest words admit of no defence,
> For want of modesty is want of sense.

Now, is not *want of sense* (where a man is so unfortunate as to want it) some apology for his *want of modesty*? and would not the lines stand more justly thus?

> Immodest words admit *but* this defence,
> That want of modesty is want of sense.

This, however, I should submit to better judgments.

My brother had, in 1720 or 1721, begun to print a newspaper. It was the second that appeared in America, and was called the *New England Courant*. The only one before it was the *Boston News-Letter*. I remember his being dissuaded by some of his friends from the undertaking, as not likely to succeed, one newspaper being, in their judgment, enough for America. At this time (1771) there are not less than five-and-twenty. He went on, however, with the undertaking, and after having worked in composing the types and printing off the sheets, I was employed to carry the papers through the streets to the customers

He had some ingenious men among his friends, who amused themselves by writing little pieces for this paper, which gained it credit and made it more in demand, and these gentlemen often visited us Hearing their conversations, and their accounts of the approbation their papers were received with, I was excited to try my hand among them, but, being still a boy, and suspecting that my brother would object to printing anything of mine in his paper if he knew it to be mine, I contrived to disguise my hand, and, writing an anonymous paper, I put it in at night under the door of the printing-house. It was found in the morning, and communicated to his writing friends when they called in as usual. They read it, commented on it in my hearing, and I had the exquisite pleasure of finding it met with their approbation, and that, in their different guesses at the author, none were named but men of some character among us for learning and ingenuity. I suppose now that I was rather lucky in my judges, and that perhaps they were not really so very good ones as I then esteemed them.

Encouraged, however, by this, I wrote and conveyed in the same way to the press several more papers which were equally approved; and I kept my secret till my small fund of sense for such performances was pretty well exhausted, and then I discovered it, when I began to be considered a little more by my brother's acquaintance, and in a manner that did not quite please him, as he thought, probably with reason, that it tended to make me too vain. And, perhaps, this might be one occasion of the differences that we began to have about this time. Though a brother, he considered himself as my master, and me as his apprentice, and, accordingly, expected the same services from me as he would from another, while I thought he demeaned me too much in some he required of me, who from a brother expected more indulgence. Our disputes were often brought before our father, and I fancy I was either generally in the right, or else a better pleader, because the judgment was generally in my favour. But my brother was passionate, and had often beaten me, which I took extremely amiss; and, thinking my apprenticeship very tedious, I was continually wishing for some opportunity of shortening it, which at length offered in a manner unexpected[1].

One of the pieces in our newspaper on some political point, which I have now forgotten, gave offence to the Assembly. He was taken up, censured, and imprisoned for a month, by the speaker's warrant, I suppose, because he would not discover his author. I too was taken up and examined before the council; but, though I did not give them any satisfaction, they contented themselves with admonishing me, and dismissed me, considering me, perhaps, as an apprentice, who was bound to keep his master's secrets.

During my brother's confinement, which I resented a good deal, notwithstanding our private differences, I had the management of the paper; and I made bold to give our rulers some rubs in it, which my brother took very kindly, while others began to consider me in an unfavourable light, as a young genius that had a turn for libelling and satire. My brother's discharge was accompanied with an order of the House (a very odd one), that *"James Franklin should no longer print the paper called the New England Courant."*

There was a consultation held in our printing-house among his friends, what he should do in this case. Some proposed to evade the order by changing the name of the paper; but my brother, seeing inconveniences in that, it was finally concluded on as a better way, to let it be printed for the future under the name of BENJAMIN FRANKLIN; and to avoid the censure of the Assembly, that might fall on him as still printing it by his apprentice, the contrivance was that my old indenture should be returned to me, with a full discharge on the back of it, to be shown on occasion, but to secure to him the benefit of my service, I was to sign new indentures for the remainder of the term, which were to be kept private. A very flimsy scheme it was; however, it was immediately executed, and the paper went on accordingly, under my name for several months.

At length, a fresh difference arising between my brother and me, I took upon me to assert my freedom, presuming that he

[1] I fancy his harsh and tyrannical treatment of me might be a means of impressing me with that aversion to arbitrary power that has stuck to me through my whole life.

would not venture to produce the new indentures. It was not fair in me to take this advantage, and this I therefore reckon one of the first errata of my life; but the unfairness of it weighed little with me, when under the impressions of resentment for the blows his passion too often urged him to bestow upon me, though he was otherwise not an ill-natured man: perhaps I was too saucy and provoking.

When he found I would leave him, he took care to prevent my getting employment in any other printing-house of the town, by going round and speaking to every master, who accordingly refused to give me work I then thought of going to New York, as the nearest place where there was a printer, and I was rather inclined to leave Boston when I reflected that I had already made myself a little obnoxious to the governing party, and, from the arbitrary proceedings of the Assembly in my brother's case, it was likely I might, if I stayed, soon bring myself into scrapes; and farther, that my indiscreet disputations began to make me pointed at with horror by good people. I determined on the point, but my father now siding with my brother, I was sensible that, if I attempted to go openly, means would be used to prevent me. My friend Collins, therefore, undertook to manage a little for me. He agreed with the captain of a New York sloop for my passage, under the notion of my being a young acquaintance of his, that had got into trouble, and therefore I could not appear or come away publicly. So I sold some of my books to raise a little money, was taken on board privately, and as we had a fair wind, in three days I found myself in New York, near 300 miles from home, a boy of but 17, without the least recommendation to, or knowledge of any person in the place, and with very little money in my pocket.

MOIRA O'NEILL

An Irish lady, who has written a volume called *Songs of the Glens of Antrim*. The poem which follows is one of these songs

CORRYMEELA

Over here in England I'm helpin' wi' the hay,
An' I wisht I was in Ireland the livelong day;
Weary on the English hay, an' sorra take the wheat!
Och! Corrymeela an' the blue sky over it

There's a deep dumb river flowin' by beyont the heavy trees,
This livin' air is moithered wi' the bummin' o' the bees;
I wisht I'd hear the Claddagh burn go runnin' through the heat
Past Corrymeela, wi' the blue sky over it.

The people that's in England is richer nor the Jews,
There's not the smallest young gossoon but thravels in his shoes!
I'd give the pipe between me teeth to see a barefut child,
Och ! Corrymeela an' the low south wind

Here's hands so full o' money an' hearts so full o' care,
By the luck o' love! I'd still go light for all I did go bare.
"God save ye, *colleen dhas*," I said: the girl she thought me wild
Far Corrymeela, an' the low south wind

D'ye mind me now, the song at night is mortial hard to raise,
The girls are heavy goin' here, the boys are ill to plase;
When one'st I'm out this workin' hive, 'tis I'll be back again—
Ay, Corrymeela, in the same soft rain.

The puff of smoke from one ould roof before an English town!
For a *shaugh* wid Andy Feelan here I'd give a silver crown,
For a curl o' hair like Mollie's ye'll ask the like in vain,
Sweet Corrymeela, an' the same soft rain.

W. B. YEATS

WILLIAM BUTLER YEATS, born in Dublin in 1865, an Irish poet and play-wright, author of *Deirdre, On Baile's Strand, The Shadowy Waters, Kathleen Ni Houlihan* and other *Plays for an Irish Theatre.*

THE LAKE ISLE OF INNISFREE

I will arise and go now, and go to Innisfree,
And a small cabin build there, of clay and wattles made;
Nine bean rows will I have there, a hive for the honey bee,
And live alone in the bee-loud glade.

And I shall have some peace there, for peace comes dropping slow,
Dropping from the veils of the morning to where the cricket sings;
There midnight's all a glimmer, and noon a purple glow,
And evening full of the linnet's wings.

I will arise and go now, for always night and day
I hear lake water lapping with low sounds by the shore;
While I stand on the roadway, or on the pavements gray,
I hear it in the deep heart's core.

ROBERT BURNS

ROBERT BURNS (1759–96) was born at Alloway, near Ayr, the son of a small
farmer. He was much influenced by popular Scottish songs and ballads,
and most of his finest poems are written in the language of his native land.
Some of the very best of these he wrote to fit the music of old Scottish airs.
The life of the poet was not prosperous. He failed to succeed as a farmer,
and received, at the age of thirty, a small government post as an exciseman.
It is difficult to think of any other national writer so beloved as Burns is
by his countrymen.

AULD LANG SYNE

Should auld acquaintance be forgot,
   And never brought to mind?
Should auld acquaintance be forgot,
   And auld lang syne?

For auld lang syne, my dear,
   For auld lang syne,
We'll tak a cup o' kindness yet,
   For auld lang syne.

And surely ye'll be[1] your pint stowp!
   And surely I'll be mine!
And we'll tak a cup o' kindness yet,
   For auld lang syne.

We twa hae run about the braes,
   And pou'd the gowans[2] fine,
But we've wander'd monie a weary fit,
   Sin' auld lang syne.

We twa hae paidl'd in the burn,
   Frae morning sun till dine;
But seas between us braid hae roar'd
   Sin' auld lang syne.

[1] pay for.   [2] daisies.

And there's a hand, my trusty fiere[1]!
   And gie's a hand o' thine!
And we'll tak a right guid-willie waught[2],
   For auld lang syne.

FOR A' THAT

Is there for honest poverty
   That hings his head, an' a' that?
The coward slave—we pass him by,
   We dare be poor for a' that!
For a' that, an' a' that,
   Our toils obscure an' a' that,
The rank is but the guinea's stamp,
   The man's the gowd for a' that.

What though on hamely fare we dine,
   Wear hoddin grey, an' a' that?
Gie fools their silks, and knaves their wine,
   A man's a man for a' that.
For a' that, an' a' that,
   Their tinsel show, an' a' that,
The honest man, tho' e'er sae poor,
   Is king o' men for a' that.

Ye see yon birkie[3] ca'd a lord,
   Wha struts, an' stares, an' a' that;
Tho' hundreds worship at his word,
   He's but a cuif[4] for a' that.
For a' that, an' a' that,
   His ribband, star, an' a' that,
The man o' independent mind
   He looks an' laughs at a' that.

A prince can mak a belted knight,
   A marquis, duke, an' a' that;
But an honest man's aboon his might,
   Gude faith, he maunna fa'[5] that!

---

[1] friend.   [2] goodwill drink.   [3] fellow.   [4] booby.   [5] claim.

For a' that, an' a' that,
  Their dignities an' a' that,
The pith o' sense an' pride o' worth
  Are higher rank than a' that.

Then let us pray that come it may,
  (As come it will for a' that),
That sense and worth, o'er a' the earth,
  Shall bear the gree, an' a' that!
For a' that, an' a' that,
  It's coming yet for a' that,
That man to man, the world o'er,
  Shall brithers be for a' that

BONIE DOON

Ye flowery banks o' bonie Doon,
  How can ye blume sae fair?
How can ye chant, ye little birds,
  And I sae fu' o' care?

Thou'll break my heart, thou bonie bird,
  That sings upon the bough:
Thou minds me o' the happy days
  When my fause Luve was true!

Thou'll break my heart, thou bonie bird,
  That sings beside thy mate:
For sae I sat, and sae I sang,
  And wist na o' my fate!

Aft hae I rov'd by bonie Doon
  To see the woodbine twine,
And ilka bird sang o' its luve,
  And sae did I o' mine.

Wi' lightsome heart I pu'd a rose
  Frae aff its thorny tree,
And my fause luver staw my rose,
  But left the thorn wi' me.

ANONYMOUS

FAIR HELEN

I wish I were where Helen lies,
Night and day on me she cries;
O that I were where Helen lies,
    On fair Kirconnell Lee!

Curst be the heart that thought the thought,
And curst the hand that fired the shot,
When in my arms burd Helen dropt,
    And died to succour me!

O think na ye my heart was sair,
When my love dropt down and spak nae mair!
There did she swoon wi' meikle care,
    On fair Kirconnell Lee.

As I went down the water-side,
None but my foe to be my guide,
None but my foe to be my guide,
    On fair Kirconnell Lee;

I lighted down my sword to draw,
I hackéd him in pieces sma',
I hackéd him in pieces sma',
    For her sake that died for me.

O Helen fair, beyond compare!
I'll make a garland of thy hair,
Shall bind my heart for evermair,
    Until the day I die.

O that I were where Helen lies!
Night and day on me she cries;
Out of my bed she bids me rise,
    Says, "Haste and come to me!"

O Helen fair! O Helen chaste!
If I were with thee, I were blest,
Where thou lies low and takes thy rest
    On fair Kirconnell Lee.

I wish my grave were growing green,
A winding-sheet drawn ower my een,
And I in Helen's arms lying,
    On fair Kirconnell Lee.

I wish I were where Helen lies!
Night and day on me she cries,
And I am weary of the skies,
    For her sake that died for me.

EDGAR ALLAN POE

EDGAR ALLAN POE (1809-49), a great American writer, was born at Boston
Part of his boyhood was spent in England, and he attended a school in the
north of London His career as a student at the university of Virginia and
as a cadet at West Point was unsuccessful owing to his dissipated habits
He published his first poems at the age of eighteen, and added to them at
intervals His best known verses are *Annabel Lee, The Haunted Palace,
The Bells* and the poem which follows. More widely known are his many
tales—some very horrible, and some very fine in their wild, imaginative
way He wrote three of the earliest and best of detective stories (*The
Murders in the Rue Morgue, The Mystery of Marie Roget* and *The Purloined
Letter*), and a fine story *The Gold Bug*, combining the excitements of a
cryptogram and buried treasure. Much of his life was passed in misery and
poverty, due partly to bad luck and partly to his intemperate habits.

THE RAVEN

Once upon a midnight dreary, while I pondered, weak and weary,
Over many a quaint and curious volume of forgotten lore,
While I nodded, nearly napping, suddenly there came a tapping,
As of some one gently rapping, rapping at my chamber door.
"'Tis some visitor," I muttered, "tapping at my chamber door—
    Only this, and nothing more."

Ah, distinctly I remember, it was in the bleak December,
And each separate dying ember wrought its ghost upon the floor.
Eagerly I wished the morrow;—vainly I had sought to borrow
From my books surcease of sorrow—sorrow for the lost Lenore—
For the rare and radiant maiden whom the angels name Lenore—
    Nameless here for evermore.

And the silken sad uncertain rustling of each purple curtain
Thrilled me—filled me with fantastic terrors never felt before;
So that now, to still the beating of my heart, I stood repeating
"'Tis some visitor entreating entrance at my chamber door—
Some late visitor entreating entrance at my chamber door;—
          This it is, and nothing more."

Presently my soul grew stronger; hesitating then no longer,
"Sir," said I, "or Madam, truly your forgiveness I implore;
But the fact is I was napping, and so gently you came rapping,
And so faintly you came tapping, tapping at my chamber door,
That I scarce was sure I heard you"—here I opened wide the
     door.—
          Darkness there, and nothing more.

Deep into that darkness peering, long I stood there wondering,
     fearing,
Doubting, dreaming dreams no mortal ever dared to dream before;
But the silence was unbroken, and the stillness gave no token,
And the only word there spoken was the whispered word,
     "Lenore!"
This I whispered, and an echo murmured back the word,
     "Lenore!"
          Merely this, and nothing more.

Back into the chamber turning, all my soul within me burning,
Soon again I heard a tapping somewhat louder than before.
"Surely," said I, "surely that is something at my window lattice;
Let me see, then, what thereat is, and this mystery explore—
Let my heart be still a moment and this mystery explore,—
          'Tis the wind, and nothing more."

Open here I flung the shutter, when, with many a flirt and flutter,
In there stepped a stately raven of the saintly days of yore.
Not the least obeisance made he; not a minute stopped or stayed
     he;
But, with mien of lord or lady, perched above my chamber door—
Perched upon a bust of Pallas just above my chamber door—
          Perched, and sat, and nothing more.

Then this ebony bird beguiling my sad fancy into smiling,
By the grave and stern decorum of the countenance it wore,
"Though thy crest be shorn and shaven, thou," I said, "art sure
    no craven,
Ghastly grim and ancient raven wandering from the Nightly
    shore—
Tell me what thy lordly name is on the Night's Plutonian shore!"
        Quoth the raven, "Nevermore."

Much I marvelled this ungainly fowl to hear discourse so plainly,
Though its answer little meaning—little relevancy bore;
For we cannot help agreeing that no living human being
Ever yet was blest with seeing bird above his chamber door—
Bird or beast upon the sculptured bust above his chamber door,
        With such name as "Nevermore."

But the raven, sitting lonely on the placid bust, spoke only
That one word, as if his soul in that one word he did outpour.
Nothing further then he uttered—not a feather then he fluttered—
Till I scarcely more than muttered, "Other friends have flown
    before—
On the morrow *he* will leave me, as my hopes have flown before."
        Then the bird said, "Nevermore."

Startled at the stillness broken by reply so aptly spoken,
"Doubtless," said I, "what it utters is its only stock and store,
Caught from some unhappy master whom unmerciful Disaster
Followed fast and followed faster till his songs one burden bore,—
Till the dirges of his Hope that melancholy burden bore
        Of 'Never—nevermore.'"

But the raven still beguiling all my fancy into smiling,
Straight I wheeled a cushioned seat in front of bird and bust and
    door;
Then, upon the velvet sinking, I betook myself to linking
Fancy unto fancy, thinking what this ominous bird of yore—
What this grim, ungainly, ghastly, gaunt, and ominous bird of
    yore
        Meant in croaking "Nevermore."

This I sat engaged in guessing, but no syllable expressing
To the fowl whose fiery eyes now burned into my bosom's core;
This and more I sat divining, with my head at ease reclining
On the cushion's velvet lining that the lamplight gloated o'er,
But whose velvet violet lining with the lamplight gloating o'er
    She shall press, ah, nevermore!

Then, methought, the air grew denser, perfumed from an unseen
    censer
Swung by Seraphim whose footfalls tinkled on the tufted floor.
"Wretch," I cried, "thy God hath lent thee—by these angels
    He hath sent thee
Respite—respite and nepenthe from thy memories of Lenore!
Quaff, oh, quaff this kind nepenthe, and forget this lost Lenore!"
    Quoth the raven, "Nevermore."

"Prophet!" said I, "thing of evil!—prophet still, if bird or devil!—
Whether Tempter sent, or whether tempest tossed thee here
    ashore,
Desolate, yet all undaunted, on this desert land enchanted—
On this home by Horror haunted—tell me truly, I implore,—
Is there,—*is* there balm in Gilead?—tell me—tell me, I implore!"
    Quoth the raven, "Nevermore."

"Prophet!" said I, "thing of evil!—prophet still, if bird or devil!
By that Heaven that bends above us—by that God we both adore—
Tell this soul with sorrow laden if, within the distant Aidenn,
It shall clasp a sainted maiden whom the angels name Lenore—
Clasp a rare and radiant maiden whom the angels name Lenore"
    Quoth the raven, "Nevermore."

"Be that word our sign of parting, bird or fiend!" I shrieked,
    upstarting,—
"Get thee back into the tempest and the Night's Plutonian shore!
Leave no black plume as a token of that lie thy soul hath spoken!
Leave my loneliness unbroken!—quit the bust above my door!
Take thy beak from out my heart, and take thy form from off my
    door!"
    Quoth the raven, "Nevermore."

And the raven, never flitting, still is sitting, still is sitting
On the pallid bust of Pallas just above my chamber door;
And his eyes have all the seeming of a demon's that is dreaming,
And the lamplight o'er him streaming throws his shadow on the floor;
And my soul from out that shadow that lies floating on the floor
    Shall be lifted—nevermore!

VOLTAIRE

FRANÇOIS MARIE AROUET DE VOLTAIRE (1694–1778), one of the greatest writers of the world, was born in Paris He was educated for the law, but he took a dislike to that profession He began very early to write satirical poems, some against the crimes of very important personages, and for one of these poems he was imprisoned in the Bastile. He was thrown into that famous prison a second time for an attack on a prominent noble, and was liberated on condition of exile to England In this country he met the poet Pope and the statesman Bolingbroke, and he gained some acquaintance with English literature He saw, too, the difference between the liberty of thought and government in England and the state of tyranny that prevailed in France In all his many writings he courageously attacked the abuses of government and religion, and his work prepared the way for the French Revolution He wrote poems, tragedies, histories and treatises of various kinds, as well as some tales in the eastern manner, the best of which is *Zadig*, from which the following passages are taken. His fame spread throughout Europe He was admired by the empress of Russia and was invited to the court of Frederic the Great He spent nearly three years in Berlin; but, in the end, he and his royal admirer quarrelled bitterly Much of his life was passed at Ferney near Geneva where he wrote a great deal and managed his affairs in a business-like manner His mocking, malicious spirit expressed itself in a style of penetrating simplicity, and his works had great influence upon European life and thought

Zadig, the chief character in the story from which the following passages are taken, is a rich young man dwelling in the city of Babylon. He marries a beautiful maiden named Azora, who makes great profession of her faithfulness, but when, to test her, Zadig feigns to be dead, she is soon ready not only to wed someone else, but even to cut off the nose of her supposed deceased husband in order to cure a sickness of her new lover—who, in fact, was a disguised friend of Zadig

The translation is by Mrs G. Sampson

SOME ADVENTURES OF ZADIG

I

The Dog and the Horse

Zadig found that, as it is written in the Zend-Avesta, the first month of marriage is a month of honey, but the second is a month of wormwood. He was soon obliged to get rid of Azora, who had become too difficult to live with, and he sought happiness in the study of nature. "Nobody," said he, "is happier than a philosopher who reads the great book that God has spread before us. The truths that he discovers are his own; he feeds and elevates his soul, he lives in peace, he fears no man, and his gentle wife does not come to cut off his nose."

Full of these ideas he retired to a country house on the banks of the Euphrates. He did not spend his time there in reckoning how many inches of water ran in one second under the arches of a bridge, or if a cubic foot more rain fell in the mouse-month, than in the sheep-month. He did not try to make silk out of spiders' webs, nor porcelain out of broken bottles, but he studied specially the characteristics of animals and plants, and soon acquired a discernment that showed him a thousand differences where ordinary men would perceive none.

One day, while walking near a little wood, he saw running towards him one of the queen's men-servants, followed by several officers who seemed to be in the greatest anxiety, and who ran wildly hither and thither like men seeking a precious possession which they have lost. "Young man," said the chief servant "have you seen the queen's dog?" Zadig replied modestly, "It is a very small female spaniel, she limps with the left fore-foot, and has very long ears." "Then you have seen her?" said the chief servant breathlessly. "No," replied Zadig, "I have never seen her and I did not even know that the queen had a dog."

Exactly at the same time by one of fortune's usual freaks, the finest horse in the king's stable had escaped from the hands of a groom on the plains of Babylon. The grand huntsman and all the other officers ran after it with as much anxiety as the chief servant had run after the dog. The grand huntsman came to Zadig and asked if he had seen the king's horse. "It is the best galloper," said Zadig, "it is five feet high, it has small hoofs, it has a tail three and a half feet long, its bit is embossed with twenty-three carat gold, its shoes are of eleven pennyweight silver." "Which way did it go? Where is it?" demanded the grand huntsman, "I have not seen it at all," replied Zadig, "and have never even heard it mentioned."

The grand huntsman and the chief servant were certain that

VOLTAIRE
Moreau le jeune

Zadig had stolen the king's horse and the queen's dog; so they took him before the assembly of the Grand Desterham who condemned him to be knouted and sent to Siberia for life. The sentence had scarcely been passed when the horse and the dog were found. The judges were under the grievous necessity of amending their decision; but they sentenced Zadig to pay four hundred ounces of gold for having denied seeing what he had seen: Zadig was at first obliged to pay this fine, after which he was allowed to plead his cause in the council of the Grand Desterham; he spoke as follows:

"Stars of justice, unfathomable wells of wisdom, mirrors of truth, who have the weightiness of lead, the hardness of iron, the brilliance of the diamond, and great affinity with gold, since I am permitted to speak before this august assembly I swear to you by Ormuzd that I have never seen the queen's most respectable dog nor the sacred horse of the king of kings. This is what happened. I was walking towards the little wood where I afterwards met the venerable chief servant and the illustrious grand huntsman. I saw on the sand the traces of an animal and I easily discerned that they were the foot-prints of a small dog. Certain marks which had disturbed the surface of the sand at the sides of the front feet told me that she had very long ears, and as I noticed that the sand was less indented by one foot than by the other three I inferred that the dog of our august queen was a little lame, if I may dare to say so.

"With regard to the horse of the king of kings, you must know that, while walking in the paths of this wood, I saw the marks of a horse's shoes; they were all at equal distances. 'That,' said I, 'is a horse who has a perfect gallop.' In a narrow path only seven feet across, the dust of the trees was brushed off a little to right and left, three and a half feet from the middle of the path. 'This horse,' said I, 'has a tail three and a half feet long which by its waving from side to side has swept off the dust.' Under the trees which formed a bower five feet high I saw leaves newly broken from the branches; I knew that the horse had touched them and that therefore he was five feet high. As to his bit, it must be of twenty-three carat gold for he knocked the bosses of it against a touchstone which I have tested. By the marks which his shoes left on some pebbles of another kind, I decided that he was shod with silver of eleven pennyweights."

All the judges admired Zadig's profound and subtle discernment; the fame of it reached the king and queen. Nothing but Zadig was talked of in the ante-chambers, the throne-room, and the private apartments; and although several of the Magi thought he ought to be burnt as a sorcerer, the king ordered him to be given back the fine of four hundred ounces of gold which he had had to pay. The recorder, the ushers, and the attorneys came to his house in grand array to bring back his four hundred ounces, they kept only three hundred and ninety-eight for the law expenses, and their servants demanded fees.

Zadig saw how dangerous it is sometimes to be too clever, and resolved on the next occasion to keep silent about what he had seen. This opportunity soon occurred. A state prisoner escaped: he passed under the windows of Zadig's house. Zadig was questioned: he gave no answer, but it was proved that he had looked out of the window. For this crime he was condemned to pay five hundred ounces of gold, and he thanked the judges for their clemency, according to Babylonian custom. "Good heavens!" said he to himself, "how distressing it is to walk in a wood where the queen's dog and the king's horse have passed; how dangerous it is even to stand at a window· and how difficult it is ever to be happy in this life!"

II

The Envious Man

To console himself for his ill-fortune Zadig turned to philosophy and friendship. In one of the suburbs of Babylon he had a house, adorned with taste, where he gathered all the arts and pastimes worthy of a cultivated man. In the morning his library was open to all the learned men; in the evening his table was free to good company. But he soon discovered how dangerous learned men can be. A great discussion arose about a law of Zoroaster which forbade the eating of the griffin. "How can the griffin be forbidden if no such animal exists?" said some. "It must exist," said the others, "since Zoroaster does not wish it to be eaten." Zadig tried to reconcile them by saying, "If there are griffins do not let us eat them; if there are none still less will we eat them; and in that way we shall all obey Zoroaster."

A scholar who had written thirteen volumes on the peculiar

properties of the griffin and who was, too, a great magician hastened to go and accuse Zadig before an archimage named Yebor, the most stupid and fanatical of the Chaldeans. This man would have impaled Zadig for the greater glory of the sun, and would then have recited the breviary of Zoroaster with a more gratified air; but friend Cador (one friend is worth a hundred priests) sought out old Yebor and said to him:

"Long live the sun and the griffins! Beware of punishing Zadig; he is a saint; he has griffins in his back-yard and does not eat them; his accuser is a heretic who dares to maintain that rabbits have cloven feet and are not unclean." "Well," said Yebor, wagging his bald head, "Zadig must be impaled for having thought badly of griffins and the other for having spoken badly of rabbits." Cador, however, settled the matter. Nobody was impaled, although several doctors grumbled and prophesied the downfall of Babylon "Where is happiness?" cried Zadig, "everyone persecutes me in this world, even creatures that don't exist." He cursed the learned men and determined to live in future only in good company.

He gathered at his house the most agreeable men and the most charming women in Babylon; he gave dainty suppers, often preceded by concerts, and enlivened by interesting conversations, from which he was careful to banish the anxiety to be witty, which is the surest way of being dull and of spoiling the most brilliant society. His choice neither of friends nor of dishes was made out of vanity; for in everything he preferred the reality to the appearance, and by this he won a real esteem to which he laid no claim.

Opposite his house lived Ahrimazd, a man whose wicked soul was depicted on his coarse face. He was eaten up with envy and puffed up with pride, and to crown all was a thoroughly tiresome person. Never having been able to succeed in the world he took his revenge by slandering it. Rich as he was, he could hardly get even flatterers to visit him. To hear carriages going to Zadig's house in the evening annoyed him, and to hear Zadig praised irritated him still more. Sometimes he went to Zadig's house and sat at his table uninvited, spoiling all the gaiety of the company, as harpies, it is said, taint the food they touch. One day it happened that Ahrimazd wished to entertain a lady who, instead, went to sup with Zadig. Another day while talking together in the palace, they met a minister who invited

Zadig to supper, but did not ask Ahrimazd. The most bitter hatreds often have a basis just as trivial. This man, called "the envious man" in Babylon, wished to ruin Zadig because he was called "the happy man." Opportunities of doing harm occur a hundred times a day while the chance of doing good comes only once in a year, as Zoroaster says.

The envious man went to Zadig's house and found him walking in the garden with two friends, and a lady to whom he was paying compliments without any serious intention. The conversation turned on a war which the king had just happily ended against the Prince of Hyrcania his vassal. Zadig, who had shown his courage in this short campaign, praised the king much, but the lady more. He took his tablets and wrote four lines of verse that he composed at the moment and gave them to the lady to read. His friends begged to be allowed to see them, but modesty, or rather a natural pride, made him refuse. He knew that impromptu verses are good only to those in whose honour they are made. He broke in two the tablet on which he had written, and threw the pieces into a thicket of roses where one might seek for them in vain. A light shower drove the guests indoors. The envious man, who had stayed in the garden, searched until he found one piece of the tablet. It had been broken in such a way that each half-line of verse made sense, and even poetry in a shorter metre; but by a still stranger chance this little verse was found to contain horrible accusations against the king; it read:

> Through the foulest of crimes
> Firmly placed on the throne,
> In these soft peaceful times
> He the foe is alone

The envious man was happy for the first time in his life; he had in his hands the means of ruining a kind and noble gentleman. Full of this cruel joy he took care that this lampoon written in Zadig's hand should reach the king. Zadig, his two friends and the lady were all imprisoned. He was tried at once without even a hearing. When he went to receive his sentence, the envious man met him on his way and said aloud that his verses were worthless. Zadig did not pride himself on being a good poet, but he was in despair at being condemned as guilty of high-treason, and at seeing a fair lady and two of his friends kept in prison for a crime that he had not committed. He was not allowed to speak because his tablets spoke for him. Such was the law of Babylon. He was obliged to go to his execution through an inquisitive mob, not one of whom dared to pity him, but who only rushed to stare at his face to see if he would die bravely. Only his parents were distressed, because they inherited nothing, three quarters of his goods were confiscated by the king and the other quarter went to the envious man.

While he was preparing himself for death, the king's parrot flew from its balcony and alighted in Zadig's garden upon a rose bush. A peach from a neighbouring tree had been blown there by the wind; it had fallen on a piece of a writing tablet to which it had stuck. The bird picked up the peach and the tablet with it and carried it to the king's lap. The monarch's curiosity was aroused by the sight of some words which made no sense, and which seemed to be the ends of rhymed lines. He loved poetry, and princes who love poetry are never dull his parrot's adventure set him thinking. The queen, who remembered what Zadig had written on the broken tablet, sent for it. The two pieces were put together and fitted perfectly. The lines then appeared as Zadig had composed them:

> Through the foulest of crimes I have seen the world smart,
> Firmly placed on the throne, our king is our shield.
> In these soft peaceful times none but Love wields the dart,
> He the foe is alone : to him only we yield.

The king immediately ordered that Zadig should be brought before him, and that his two friends and the fair lady should be set free. Zadig prostrated himself before the king and queen, and humbly asked their pardon for having written such poor verses. He spoke with so much wit, wisdom, and eloquence that the king and queen wished to see more of him. He came again and won still greater favour. He was given all the goods of the envious man who had unjustly accused him, but Zadig gave them back and the envious man was touched, but only by the joy of not losing his possessions. The king's good opinion of Zadig grew from day to day. He included him in all his pleasures and consulted him in all his business. The queen henceforth regarded him with an affection which bid fair to become dangerous for her, for the king her august consort, for Zadig, and for the kingdom itself. Zadig began to think that it is not difficult to be happy

[Zadig becomes prime minister, but he arouses the jealousy of the king and has to flee for his life. He wanders into distant countries and has many adventures. He returns to Babylon and takes part in a tournament, the victor at which is to marry the Queen (the king having perished in battle) if he can prove his wisdom by answering certain riddles. Zadig, clad in white armour, overcomes the great champion Otama, but while he is resting after the battle, a green-armoured rival named Itobad steals his white armour and claims to have been the victor. In despair he leaves the city and wanders away to the river Euphrates.]

III

The Hermit

As he was walking he met a hermit whose white and venerable beard hung down to his waist. In his hand he held a book which he was reading attentively. Zadig stopped and made him a low bow. The hermit saluted him in so noble and kind a manner that Zadig had the curiosity to engage him in conversation. He asked what book he was reading. "It is the book of fate," said the hermit; "would you like to read therein?" He handed the book to Zadig who, well-versed as he was in several languages, could not decipher a single letter of it. This increased his curiosity. "You seem cast down," said the good father. "Alas! I have cause to be," replied Zadig. "If you will allow me to accompany you perhaps I can be of some use," rejoined the old man, "I have sometimes brought consolation to an unhappy soul." Zadig felt respect for the manner, the beard, and the book of the hermit and found that he conversed like a superior being. The hermit spoke of fate, of justice, of morals, of sovereign good, of human weakness, of virtues and vices, with an eloquence so moving, that Zadig felt himself drawn towards him by an irresistible spell. He begged the hermit not to leave him until they returned to Babylon. "I myself ask you this favour," said the old man. "Swear by Ormuzd that you will not part from me for several days, whatever I do." Zadig promised and they set out together.

The two travellers arrived that evening at a splendid castle. The hermit besought hospitality for himself and the young man who accompanied him. The door-keeper, who might have been taken for a lord, admitted them with condescending good-nature They were presented to the head-servant who showed them his master's magnificent apartments. They were seated at the lower end of the table without the lord of the castle's honouring them with a glance: but they were served like the rest with taste and profusion. They were given a golden bowl, set with emeralds and rubies, to wash in; they were put to sleep in a fine room, and the next morning a servant brought each of them a piece of gold; after which they were dismissed upon their way.

"The master of the house," said Zadig, as they walked along, "seems a generous man though rather proud; he dispenses hospitality nobly." As he spoke he noticed that a large pocket that the hermit wore seemed prominent and distended; in it he saw the jewelled golden bowl, which the hermit had stolen He was astounded, but dared not take any notice of it at first.

Towards midday the hermit presented himself at the door of a very small house in which lived a rich miser; he asked hospitality for a few hours An old badly-dressed servant received him roughly, and took him and Zadig to a stable, where they were given some rotten olives, mouldy bread and sour beer. The hermit ate and drank as contentedly as on the previous day; then turning to the old servant, who was watching them both to see that they stole nothing, and kept urging them to go, he gave him the two gold pieces that he had received in the morning and thanked him for all his attentions. "I pray you," added the hermit, "let me speak to your master." The astonished servant took the travellers into him. "Illustrious lord," said the hermit, "I can but offer you our very humble thanks for the noble manner in which you have received us; deign to accept this golden bowl as a slight token of my gratitude." The miser nearly collapsed. The hermit gave him no time to recover from his seizure, but set off swiftly with his young companion. "Father," said Zadig, "what is all this that I see? You seem to be unlike other men in all things; you steal a jewelled golden bowl from a lord who receives you magnificently and you give it to a miser who treats you with indignity." "My son," replied the old man, "this fine lord, who receives strangers only out of vanity that they may admire his wealth, will become wiser. The miser will learn to be hospitable. Do not

9—2

be surprised at anything, and follow me." Zadig scarcely knew if he was dealing with the maddest or the wisest of men; but the hermit spoke with so much authority that Zadig, bound besides by his vow, was forced to follow him

They arrived that evening at a pleasantly built but simple house, where nothing proclaimed either prodigality or avarice. The master was a philosopher retired from the world, who peacefully cultivated wisdom and virtue and was never bored. It had pleased him to build this retreat, where he received strangers with a generosity that was quite unostentatious He went himself to meet the two travellers, whom he conducted to a pleasant room to rest, some time afterwards he came to invite them to a neat and well-served meal, during which he spoke discreetly of the latest revolutions in Babylon. He seemed sincerely attached to the queen and wished that Zadig had been in the lists to compete for the crown; "but men," added he, "do not deserve to have a king like Zadig" The latter blushed and felt his wrongs more keenly than ever. They agreed, as they talked, that the things of this world do not always go according to the wishes of the wise. The hermit maintained that no one knew the ways of providence and that men are wrong to try to judge a whole of which they see only the smallest part. They spoke of the passions. "Ah! how fatal they are," said Zadig. "They are the winds that fill the sails of a ship," replied the hermit, "sometimes they wreck it, but without them it could not move Bile makes us hot-tempered and ill, but without bile man could not exist On this earth all is dangerous, but all is necessary."

They spoke of pleasure, and the hermit proved that it is a divine gift, "for," said he, "man cannot create for himself either sensations or ideas; he receives them all; pain and pleasure come to him from without, as his existence does."

Zadig wondered how a man who had done such extravagant things could reason so well At last after a discourse as instructive as it was agreeable the host led his two guests to their apartment again, blessing heaven that had sent him two men so virtuous and wise He offered them money in a manner so noble and yet so friendly that they could not be offended. The hermit declined it and said that he must take his leave as he purposed to set out for Babylon before daybreak. Their farewell was tender, Zadig especially was full of esteem and affection for so worthy a man. When the hermit and he were in their room they spoke long in praise of their host At dawn the old man woke his comrade. "We must depart," said he, "but while everybody is still asleep I am going to leave this man a token of my respect and regard." Saying these words he took a torch and set the house on fire. Zadig, uttering cries of dismay, tried to prevent him from committing such an atrocious act. The hermit carried him off by superior strength; the house was in flames, the hermit, already some distance off with his companion, tranquilly watched it burn. "Thank heaven!" said he, "there is my dear host's house destroyed from top to bottom! Happy man!" At these words Zadig was tempted to burst out laughing, to heap insults upon the reverend father, to thrash him, and to flee from him. But he did nothing, and still over-awed by the power of the hermit he followed him, in spite of himself, to their last resting place.

This was at the house of a good and kind widow who had a nephew aged fourteen, a charming boy, and her only hope. She did the honours of her house as well as she could. The next morning she told her nephew to accompany the travellers as far as a bridge which, having recently been broken, had become dangerous. The lad walked eagerly before them When they were on the bridge the hermit said to the youth, "Come, I must show my gratitude to your aunt." He then took him by the hair and threw him in the river. The boy fell, reappeared for an instant, and was engulfed by the torrent. "O monster! O most infamous of all mankind!" exclaimed Zadig. "You promised to be more patient," said the hermit interrupting him: "Know that under the ruins of that house which Providence set on fire the master has found an immense treasure, know that this youth whom Providence has killed would have murdered his aunt in a year, and you in two." "Who told you so, ruffian?" cried Zadig, "and even if you were able to read this event in your book of destiny are you permitted to drown a child who has done you no harm?"

While the Babylonian was speaking he noticed that the old man no longer had a beard, that his face took the features of youth; his hermit's robe disappeared, four beautiful wings covered a majestic form radiant with light. "O heavenly messenger! Angel Divine!" cried Zadig prostrating himself, "hast thou then descended from the empyrean to teach a weak mortal to submit to the decrees of providence?" "Man," said the angel Jesrad, "judges everything without knowing anything. Of all men thou wert he who most deserved to be enlightened." Zadig asked permission to speak. "I distrust myself," said he, "but dare I ask to have a doubt dispelled? Would it not have been better to correct this youth and make him virtuous than to drown him?" Jesrad replied, "If he had been virtuous and had lived, his fate was to be murdered with the wife he would have married and the son who would have been born to him." "What!" said Zadig, "is it then inevitable that there should be crimes and misfortunes, and that misfortunes should fall on the good?" "The wicked," answered Jesrad, "are always unhappy; they serve as a test of the few just persons scattered over the world, there is no evil from which good does not come." "But," said Zadig, "suppose there were only good and no evil." "Then," replied Jesrad, "this earth would be another earth; the chain of events would belong to another order of wisdom, and that order, which would be perfect, can exist only in the eternal dwelling of the Supreme Being, whom no evil can approach. He has created millions of worlds not one of which is like another; this infinite variety is an attribute of His divine power. There are not two leaves of a tree on earth, nor two spheres in the vast fields of heaven which are alike; and all that you see on the little atom where you were born must exist in its place, and at its fixed time, according to the immutable laws of Him who enfolds all. Men think that this child who has just perished fell into the water by chance; that it is by the same chance that the house was burnt; but there is no chance; everything is trial or punishment, reward or foresight....Feeble mortal, cease to rebel against that which you must adore." "But," said Zadig —— As he said the word the angel was already winging his flight towards the tenth sphere. Zadig on his knees adored Providence and submitted to it. The angel cried to him from on high, "Take your way towards Babylon."

IV

The Riddles

Zadig, beside himself, and like a man near whom a thunderbolt has fallen, walked on at random. He entered Babylon on the day when those who had fought in the lists were already assembled in the great hall of the palace to solve the riddles and answer the questions of the chief magician. All the knights had arrived except the one in green armour. As soon as Zadig appeared in the city crowds gathered round him; their eyes were never tired of gazing at him, their mouths of blessing him, or their hearts of wishing him the kingdom. The envious man saw him pass; he trembled and turned away: the people carried Zadig to the place of assembly The queen, who had been informed of his arrival, was a prey to mingled hope and fear. She was devoured by anxiety. She could not understand why Zadig was unarmed, nor why Itobad wore the white armour. A confused murmur arose at the sight of Zadig; they were surprised and delighted to see him again, but only knights who had fought were allowed to appear in the assembly.

"I fought like the rest," said he, "but another here wears my armour; and while waiting until I have the honour to prove it, I ask permission to present myself to solve the riddles." It was put to the vote; his reputation for integrity was still so deeply imprinted on their minds that no one hesitated to permit him.

The chief magician propounded this question first. "Of all things in the world, what is at once the longest and the shortest, the quickest and the slowest, the most minutely divided and the most extensive, the most neglected and the most regretted, without which nothing can be done, which swallows up all trivial things and preserves all great things?"

Itobad was to speak first; he replied that a man of his kind did not understand riddles, and that he was satisfied with having conquered by the blows of his lance. Some said that the enigma meant fortune, others said the earth, others, light: Zadig said it was time. "Nothing is so long," added he, "since it is the measure of eternity, nothing is so short since we never have enough for all our plans; nothing is so slow to those who wait, nothing so quick to those who revel, it stretches to infinite greatness, but its divisions are infinitely small; all men waste it and all regret its loss; nothing can be done without it; it obliterates all things unworthy of posterity and it immortalises all great things." The assembly agreed that Zadig was right.

They were next asked, "What is that which we receive without thanks, that we enjoy without knowing how we do so, that we give to others without knowing what it is, and that we lose without having understood it?"

Each said his word. Zadig alone guessed that it was life. He solved all the other riddles just as easily. Itobad said every time that nothing was simpler, and that he could have completed the test just as easily if he had taken the trouble. Questions were asked about justice, the highest good and the art of governing. Zadig's replies were judged the wisest. "It is a great pity," they said, "that one who has such sound judgment should be such a bad knight."

"Illustrious lords," said Zadig, "I had the honour of conquering in the lists. The white armour belongs to me. The lord Itobad took possession of it while I slept. He apparently thought it would suit him better than the green. I am ready to prove, here and now, with my robe and sword against all this beautiful white armour that he has taken from me, that it was I who had the honour of conquering the brave Otama."

Itobad accepted the challenge with the greatest confidence; he did not doubt that being fully armed he would easily put an end to an adversary in a night-cap and dressing-gown.

Zadig drawing his sword saluted the queen who, full of joy and fear, was watching him. Itobad drew his without saluting anyone. He advanced on Zadig like a man who has nothing to fear. He was about to split his head open when Zadig parried the blow by opposing the thick part of his blade to the thin part of his opponent's in such a way that Itobad's sword was broken. Then Zadig, seizing his enemy round the middle, hurled him to the ground and thrusting the point of his sword into a chink in the breast-plate, cried "Yield, or I kill you!"

Itobad, always astonished that any disgrace could befal such a man as he, surrendered to Zadig, who quietly removed his magnificent helmet, his superb breast-plate, his beautiful armlets, and his brilliant thigh-pieces, and, dressing himself in them once more, ran thus arrayed to throw himself at Astarte's feet. Cador easily proved that the armoui belonged to Zadig. He was acclaimed king by universal consent, and above all by that of Astarte who, after so many adversities, tasted the sweetness of seeing her lover worthy in the eyes of the world to be her consort. Itobad went to hear himself called lord in his own house. Zadig was king and was happy. He kept in his heart all that the angel Jesrad had told him. The envious man died of rage and shame. The kingdom enjoyed peace, prosperity and glory; it was the most splendid age of the world, when love and justice ruled All men blessed Zadig, and Zadig blessed heaven.

WALT WHITMAN

(The poem that follows is a lament for the death of President Lincoln)

O CAPTAIN! MY CAPTAIN!

O Captain! my Captain! our fearful trip is done,
The ship has weather'd every rack, the prize we sought is won,
The port is near, the bells I hear, the people all exulting,
While follow eyes the steady keel, the vessel grim and daring,
    But O heart! heart! heart!
      O the bleeding drops of red,
        Where on the deck my Captain lies,
        Fallen cold and dead.

O Captain! my Captain! rise up and hear the bells;
Rise up—for you the flag is flung—for you the bugle trills,
For you bouquets and ribbon'd wreaths—for you the shores a-crowding,
For you they call, the swaying mass, their eager faces turning;
    Here Captain! dear father!
      This arm beneath your head!
        It is some dream that on the deck,
        You've fallen cold and dead

My Captain does not answer, his lips are pale and still,
My father does not feel my arm, he has no pulse nor will,
The ship is anchor'd safe and sound, its voyage closed and done,
From fearful trip the victor ship comes in with object won;

Exult O shores, and ring O bells!
But I with mournful tread
Walk the deck my Captain lies,
Fallen cold and dead.

PATROLLING BARNEGAT

Wild, wild the storm, and the sea high running,
Steady the roar of the gale, with incessant undertone muttering,
Shouts of demoniac laughter fitfully piercing and pealing,
Waves, air, midnight, their savagest trinity lashing,
Out in the shadows there milk-white combs careering,
On beachy slush and sand spirts of snow fierce slanting,
Where through the murk the easterly death-wind breasting,
Through cutting swirl and spray watchful and firm advancing,
(That in the distance! is that a wreck? is the red signal flaring?)
Slush and sand of the beach tireless till daylight wending,
Steadily, slowly, through hoarse roar never remitting,
Along the midnight edge by those milk-white combs careering,
A group of dim, weird forms, struggling, the night confronting,
That savage trinity warily watching.

CHARLES DICKENS

CHARLES DICKENS (1812–70) was born at Landport (Portsmouth), the son
of a clerk at the Dockyard. The family moved about a great deal, and,
after two residences in Chatham, settled in London when Charles was nine.
The boy was early acquainted with trouble. His father's thriftless and
unbusinesslike character is reproduced in Micawber (*David Copperfield*), and
the boy's unhappy experiences, including employment at ten years of age
in a blacking factory, are used with beautiful effect in the same novel. The
father was arrested for debt and sent to the Marshalsea, a prison for debtors
described fully in *Little Dorrit*. Another debtor's prison, the Fleet, figures
largely in *Pickwick*. Like David Copperfield, Charles Dickens went to school
again after he had been to work. Later, he taught himself shorthand in order
to become a reporter. The rich nature of Dickens was able to turn all his
experiences to good account. What he had himself suffered he utilised with
great skill in his books. He began his literary career by writing short sketches
at the age of twenty-one. At twenty-four he began *Pickwick* and from that
time forward became a highly successful writer. He led an active life.
He travelled much, he gave public readings from his books, he played a

prominent part in the public life of his time and was able, by his influence, to put an end to many abuses. He died quite suddenly. His fame, great while he lived, has steadily increased.

The passage that follows is from *David Copperfield* Mr Peggotty, a Yarmouth fisherman, had turned an old boat on the beach into a comfortable little house where he lived with his relative Ham Peggotty, a noble hearted young fisherman, and "Little Em'ly" his niece. Ham and Emily were betrothed and were soon to be married. A handsome young gentleman, Steerforth, friend and schoolfellow of David Copperfield, became intimate with the family in the old houseboat, and basely destroyed the happiness of all by persuading Emily to desert her friends and run away with him. At the point where the extract begins, Emily had been found by Mr Peggotty after weary search, and was leaving with him for a new home and life in Australia

TEMPEST

I now approach an event in my life, so indelible, so awful, so bound by an infinite variety of ties to all that has preceded it, in these pages, that, from the beginning of my narrative, I have seen it growing larger and larger as I advanced, like a great tower in a plain, and throwing its forecast shadow even on the incidents of my childish days.

For years after it occurred I dreamed of it often. I have started up so vividly impressed by it, that its fury has yet seemed raging in my quiet room, in the still night. I dream of it sometimes, though at lengthened and uncertain intervals, to this hour. I have an association between it and a stormy wind, or the lightest mention of a sea-shore, as strong as any of which my mind is conscious. As plainly as I behold what happened, I will try to write it down. I do not recall it, but see it done; for it happens again before me.

The time drawing on rapidly for the sailing of the emigrant ship, my good old nurse (almost broken-hearted for me, when we first met) came up to London. I was constantly with her, and her brother, and the Micawbers (they being very much together); but Emily I never saw.

One evening, when the time was close at hand, I was alone with Peggotty and her brother. Our conversation turned on Ham. She described to us how tenderly he had taken leave of her, and how manfully and quietly he had borne himself—most of all, of late, when she believed he was most tried. It was a subject of which the affectionate creature never tired; and our interest in

hearing the many examples which she, who was so much with
him, had to relate, was equal to hers in relating them.

My aunt and I were at that time vacating the two cottages at
Highgate—I intending to go abroad, and she to return to her
house at Dover. We had a temporary lodging in Covent Garden.
As I walked home to it, after this evening's conversation, reflecting
on what had passed between Ham and myself when I was last at
Yarmouth, I wavered in the original purpose I had formed, of
leaving a letter for Emily when I should take leave of her uncle
on board the ship, and thought it would be better to write to
her now. She might desire, I thought, after receiving my communication, to send some parting word by me to her unhappy
lover. I ought to give her the opportunity.

I therefore sat down in my room, before going to bed, and
wrote to her. I told her that I had seen him, and that he had
requested me to tell her what I have already written in its place
in these sheets. I faithfully repeated it. I had no need to enlarge
upon it, if I had had the right. Its deep fidelity and goodness
were not to be adorned by me or any man. I left it out, to be sent
round in the morning, with a line to Mr Peggotty, requesting him
to give it to her; and went to bed at daybreak.

I was weaker than I knew then; and not falling asleep until
the sun was up, lay late, and unrefreshed, next day. I was roused
by the silent presence of my aunt at my bedside. I felt it in my
sleep, as I suppose we all do feel such things.

"Trot, my dear," she said, when I opened my eyes, "I couldn't
make up my mind to disturb you. Mr Peggotty is here; shall he
come up?"

I replied yes, and he soon appeared.

"Mas'r Davy," he said, when we had shaken hands, "I giv
Em'ly your letter, sir, and she writ this here; and begged of me
fur to ask you to read it, and if you see no hurt in't, to be so kind
as take charge on't"

"Have you read it?" said I.

He nodded sorrowfully. I opened it, and read as follows:—

" I have got your message. Oh, what can I write, to thank you
for your good and blessed kindness to me !

" I have put the words close to my heart. I shall keep them till I
die. They are sharp thorns, but they are such comfort. I have

prayed over them, oh, I have prayed so much! When I find what you are, and what uncle is, I think what God must be, and can cry to Him.

"Good-bye for ever. Now, my dear, my friend, good-bye for ever in this world. In another world, if I am forgiven, I may wake a child and come to you. All thanks and blessings. Farewell, evermore."

This, blotted with tears, was the letter.

"May I tell her as you doen't see no hurt in't, and as you'll be so kind as take charge on't, Mas'r Davy?" said Mr Peggotty, when I had read it.

"Unquestionably," said I; "but I am thinking——"

"Yes, Mas'r Davy?"

. "I am thinking," said I, "that I'll go down again to Yarmouth. There's time and to spare for me to go and come back before the ship sails. My mind is constantly running on him, in his solitude. To put this letter of her writing in his hand at this time, and to enable you to tell her, in the moment of parting, that he has got it, will be a kindness to both of them. I solemnly accepted his commission, dear good fellow, and cannot discharge it too completely. The journey is nothing to me. I am restless, and shall be better in motion. I'll go down to-night"

Though he anxiously endeavoured to dissuade me, I saw that he was of my mind; and this, if I had required to be confirmed in my intention, would have had the effect. He went round to the coach-office, at my request, and took the box-seat for me on the mail. In the evening I started, by that conveyance, down the road I had traversed under so many vicissitudes.

"Don't you think that," I asked the coachman, in the first stage out of London, "a very remarkable sky? I don't remember to have seen one like it."

"Nor I—not equal to it," he replied "That's wind, sir. There'll be mischief done at sea, I expect, before long."

It was a murky confusion—here and there blotted with a colour like the colour of the smoke from damp fuel—of flying clouds tossed up into most remarkable heaps, suggesting greater heights in the clouds than there were depths below them to the bottom of the deepest hollows in the earth, through which the wild moon seemed to plunge headlong, as if, in a dread disturbance of the laws of nature, she had lost her way and were frightened. There had been a wind all day; and it was rising then, with an extraordinary great sound. In another hour it had much increased, and the sky was more overcast, and it blew hard

But as the night advanced, the clouds closing in and densely overspreading the whole sky, then very dark, it came on to blow harder and harder. It still increased, until our horses could scarcely face the wind Many times, in the dark part of the night (it was then late in September, when the nights were not short), the leaders turned about, or came to a dead stop, and we were often in serious apprehension that the coach would be blown over. Sweeping gusts of rain came up before this storm, like showers of steel; and, at those times, when there was any shelter of trees or lee walls to be got, we were fain to stop, in a sheer impossibility of continuing the struggle.

When the day broke, it blew harder and harder. I had been in Yarmouth when the seamen said it blew great guns; but I had never known the like of this, or anything approaching to it. We came to Ipswich—very late, having had to fight every inch of ground since we were ten miles out of London—and found a cluster of people in the market-place, who had risen from their beds in the night, fearful of falling chimneys. Some of these, congregating about the inn-yard while we changed horses, told us of great sheets of lead having been ripped off a high church tower, and flung into a by-street, which they then blocked up Others had to tell of country people, coming in from neighbouring villages, who had seen great trees lying torn out of the earth, and whole ricks scattered about the roads and fields Still, there was no abatement in the storm, but it blew harder.

As we struggled on, nearer and nearer to the sea, from which this mighty wind was blowing dead on shore, its force became more and more terrific. Long before we saw the sea, its spray was on our lips, and showered salt rain upon us. The water was out, over miles and miles of the flat country adjacent to Yarmouth; and every sheet and puddle lashed its banks, and had its stress of little breakers setting heavily towards us When we came within sight of the sea, the waves on the horizon, caught at intervals above the rolling abyss, were like glimpses of another shore with towers and buildings. When at last we got into the town, the

people came out to their doors, all aslant, and with streaming hair, making a wonder of the mail that had come through such a night

I put up at the old inn, and went down to look at the sea; staggering along the street, which was strewn with sand and seaweed, and with flying blotches of sea-foam; afraid of falling slates and tiles; and holding by people I met, at angry corners. Coming near the beach, I saw, not only the boatmen, but half the people of the town, lurking behind buildings; some now and then braving the fury of the storm to look away to sea, and blown sheer out of their course in trying to get zigzag back.

Joining these groups, I found bewailing women whose husbands were away in herring or oyster boats, which there was too much reason to think might have foundered before they could run in anywhere for safety. Grizzled old sailors were among the people, shaking their heads, as they looked from water to sky, and muttering to one another; shipowners, excited and uneasy, children, huddling together, and peering into older faces; even stout mariners, disturbed and anxious, levelling their glasses at the sea from behind places of shelter, as if they were surveying an enemy.

The tremendous sea itself, when I could find sufficient pause to look at it, in the agitation of the blinding wind, the flying stones and sand, and the awful noise, confounded me. As the high watery walls came rolling in, and, at their highest, tumbled into surf, they looked as if the least would engulf the town. As the receding wave swept back with a hoarse roar, it seemed to scoop out deep caves in the beach, as if its purpose were to undermine the earth When some white-headed billows thundered on, and dashed themselves to pieces before they reached the land, every fragment of the late whole seemed possessed by the full might of its wrath, rushing to be gathered to the composition of another monster. Undulating hills were changed to valleys, undulating valleys (with a solitary storm-bird sometimes skimming through them) were lifted up to hills; masses of water shivered and shook the beach with a booming sound; every shape tumultuously rolled on, as soon as made, to change its shape and place, and beat another shape and place away; the ideal shore on the horizon, with its towers and buildings, rose and fell; the clouds flew fast and thick; I seemed to see a rending and upheaving of all nature.

Not finding Ham among the people whom this memorable wind—for it is still remembered down there, as the greatest ever known to blow upon that coast—had brought together, I made my way to his house. It was shut; and as no one answered to my knocking, I went, by back ways and by-lanes, to the yard where he worked. I learned there that he had gone to Lowestoft, to meet some sudden exigency of ship-repairing in which his skill was required, but that he would be back to-morrow morning, in good time.

I went back to the inn; and when I had washed and dressed, and tried to sleep, but in vain, it was five o'clock in the afternoon. I had not sat five minutes by the coffee-room fire, when the waiter coming to stir it, as an excuse for talking, told me that two colliers had gone down, with all hands, a few miles away; and that some other ships had been seen labouring hard in the Roads, and trying, in great distress, to keep off shore. Mercy on them, and on all poor sailors, said he, if we had another night like the last!

I was very much depressed in spirits, very solitary, and felt an uneasiness in Ham's not being there, disproportionate to the occasion. I was seriously affected, without knowing how much, by late events; and my long exposure to the fierce wind had confused me. There was that jumble in my thoughts and recollections, that I had lost the clear arrangement of time and distance. Thus, if I had gone out into the town, I should not have been surprised, I think, to encounter some one who I knew must be then in London. So to speak, there was in these respects a curious inattention in my mind. Yet it was busy, too, with all the remembrances the place naturally awakened, and they were particularly distinct and vivid.

In this state, the waiter's dismal intelligence about the ships immediately connected itself, without any effort of my volition, with my uneasiness about Ham. I was persuaded that I had an apprehension of his returning from Lowestoft by sea, and being lost. This grew so strong with me, that I resolved to go back to the yard before I took my dinner, and ask the boatbuilder if he thought his attempting to return by sea at all likely? If he gave me the least reason to think so, I would go over to Lowestoft and prevent it by bringing him with me.

I hastily ordered my dinner, and went back to the yard. I was none too soon, for the boatbuilder, with a lantern in his hand, was locking the yard-gate. He quite laughed when I asked him the question, and said there was no fear; no man in his senses, or out of them, would put off in such a gale of wind, least of all Ham Peggotty, who had been born to seafaring.

So sensible of this, beforehand, that I had really felt ashamed of doing what I was nevertheless impelled to do, I went back to the inn. If such a wind could rise, I think it was rising. The howl and roar, the rattling of the doors and windows, the rumbling in the chimneys, the apparent rocking of the very house that sheltered me, and the prodigious tumult of the sea, were more fearful than in the morning. But there was now a great darkness besides, and that invested the storm with new terrors, real and fanciful.

I could not eat, I could not sit still, I could not continue stead-fast to anything. Something within me, faintly answering to the storm without, tossed up the depths of my memory, and made a tumult in them. Yet, in all the hurry of my thoughts, wild running with the thundering sea—the storm, and my uneasiness regarding Ham, were always in the foreground.

My dinner went away almost untasted, and I tried to refresh myself with a glass or two of wine. In vain. I fell into a dull slumber before the fire, without losing my consciousness, either of the uproar out of doors or of the place in which I was. Both became overshadowed by a new and indefinable horror; and when I awoke—or rather when I shook off the lethargy that bound me in my chair—my whole frame thrilled with objectless and un-intelligible fear.

I walked to and fro; tried to read an old gazetteer; listened to the awful noises; looked at faces, scenes, and figures in the fire. At length, the steady ticking of the undisturbed clock on the wall tormented me to that degree that I resolved to go to bed.

It was reassuring, on such a night, to be told that some of the inn-servants had agreed together to sit up until morning. I went to bed, exceedingly weary and heavy; but, on my lying down, all such sensations vanished, as if by magic, and I was broad awake, with every sense refined.

For hours I lay there, listening to the wind and water—imagining, now, that I heard shrieks out at sea; now, that I distinctly heard the firing of signal guns; and now, the fall of houses in the town. I got up several times and looked out; but could see nothing, except the reflection in the window-panes of the faint candle I had left burning, and of my own haggard face looking in at me from the black void.

At length my restlessness attained to such a pitch that I hurried on my clothes, and went downstairs. In the large kitchen, where I dimly saw bacon and ropes of onions hanging from the beams, the watchers were clustered together, in various attitudes, about a table, purposely moved away from the great chimney, and brought near the door. A pretty girl, who had her ears stopped with her apron, and her eyes upon the door, screamed when I appeared, supposing me to be a spirit; but the others had more presence of mind, and were glad of an addition to their company. One man, referring to the topic they had been discussing, asked me whether I thought the souls of the collier-crews who had gone down were out in the storm?

I remained there, I dare say, two hours. Once, I opened the yard gate, and looked into the empty street. The sand, the seaweed, and the flakes of foam were driving by, and I was obliged to call for assistance before I could shut the gate again, and make it fast against the wind.

There was a dark gloom in my solitary chamber when I at length returned to it; but I was tired now, and, getting into bed again, fell—off a tower and down a precipice—into the depths of sleep. I have an impression that for a long time, though I dreamed of being elsewhere and in a variety of scenes, it was always blowing in my dream. At length I lost that feeble hold upon reality, and was engaged with two dear friends, but who they were I don't know, at the siege of some town in a roar of cannonading.

The thunder of the cannon was so loud and incessant, that I could not hear something I much desired to hear, until I made a great exertion, and awoke. It was broad day—eight or nine o'clock; the storm raging, in lieu of the batteries; and some one knocking and calling at my door.

"What is the matter?" I cried.

"A wreck! Close by!"

I sprung out of bed, and asked, what wreck?

"A schooner, from Spain or Portugal, laden with fruit and wine. Make haste, sir, if you want to see her! It's thought, down on the beach, she'll go to pieces every moment."

The excited voice went clamouring along the staircase, and I wrapped myself in my clothes as quickly as I could, and ran into the street.

Numbers of people were there before me, all running in one direction—to the beach. I ran the same way, outstripping a good many, and soon came facing the wild sea.

The wind might by this time have lulled a little, though not more sensibly than if the cannonading I had dreamed of had been diminished by the silencing of half a dozen guns out of hundreds. But the sea, having upon it the additional agitation of the whole night, was infinitely more terrific than when I had seen it last. Every appearance it had then presented bore the expression of being *swelled*; and the height to which the breakers rose, and, looking over one another, bore one another down, and rolled in, in interminable hosts, was most appalling.

In the difficulty of hearing anything but wind and waves, and in the crowd, and the unspeakable confusion, and my first breathless efforts to stand against the weather, I was so confused that I looked out to sea for the wreck, and saw nothing but the foaming heads of the great waves. A half-dressed boatman, standing next me, pointed with his bare arm (a tattooed arrow on it, pointing in the same direction) to the left. Then, O great Heaven, I saw it, close in upon us!

One mast was broken short off, six or eight feet from the deck, and lay over the side, entangled in a maze of sail and rigging; and all that ruin, as the ship rolled and beat—which she did without a moment's pause, and with a violence quite inconceivable—beat the side as if it would stave it in. Some efforts were even then being made to cut this portion of the wreck away; for, as the ship, which was broadside on, turned towards us in her rolling, I plainly descried her people at work with axes, especially one active figure with long curling hair, conspicuous among the rest. But a great cry, which was audible even above the wind and water, rose from the shore at this moment: the sea, sweeping over the rolling wreck, made a clean breach, and carried men, spars, casks, planks, bulwarks, heaps of such toys, into the boiling surge.

The second mast was yet standing, with the rags of a rent sail and a wild confusion of broken cordage flapping to and fro. The ship had struck once, the same boatman hoarsely said in my ear, and then lifted in and struck again. I understood him to add that she was parting amidships, and I could readily suppose so, for the rolling and beating were too tremendous for any human work to suffer long. As he spoke, there was another great cry of pity from the beach: four men arose with the wreck out of the deep, clinging to the rigging of the remaining mast—uppermost, the active figure with the curling hair.

There was a bell on board, and as the ship rolled and dashed, like a desperate creature driven mad, now showing us the whole sweep of her deck, as she turned on her beam-ends towards the shore, now nothing but her keel, as she sprang wildly over and turned towards the sea, the bell rang; and its sound, the knell of those unhappy men, was borne towards us on the wind. Again we lost her, and again she rose. Two men were gone. The agony on shore increased. Men groaned, and clasped their hands; women shrieked, and turned away their faces. Some ran wildly up and down along the beach, crying for help where no help could be. I found myself one of these, frantically imploring a knot of sailors whom I knew not to let those two lost creatures perish before our eyes.

They were making out to me, in an agitated way—I don't know how, for the little I could hear I was scarcely composed enough to understand—that the lifeboat had been bravely manned an hour ago, and could do nothing; and that as no man would be so desperate as to attempt to wade off with a rope, and establish a communication with the shore, there was nothing left to try; when I noticed that some new sensation moved the people on the beach, and saw them part, and Ham come breaking through them to the front.

I ran to him, as well as I know, to repeat my appeal for help. But, distracted though I was by a sight so new to me and terrible, the determination in his face, and his look out to sea—exactly the same look as I remembered in connection with the morning after Emily's flight—awoke me to a knowledge of his danger. I held him back with both arms, and implored the men with whom I had been speaking not to listen to him, not to do murder, not to let him stir from off that sand!

Another cry arose on shore; and looking to the wreck, we saw the cruel sail, with blow on blow, beat off the lower of the two men, and fly up in triumph round the active figure left alone upon the mast.

Against such a sight, and against such determination as that of the calmly-desperate man who was already accustomed to lead half the people present, I might as hopefully have entreated the wind. "Mas'r Davy," he said, cheerily grasping me by both hands, "if my time is come, 'tis come. If 't an't, I'll bide it. Lord above bless you, and bless all! Mates, make me ready; I'm a-going off!"

I was swept away, but not unkindly, to some distance, where the people around me made me stay—urging, as I confusedly perceived, that he was bent on going, with help or without, and that I should endanger the precautions for his safety by troubling those with whom they rested. I don't know what I answered, or what they rejoined; but I saw hurry on the beach, and men running with ropes from a capstan that was there, and penetrating into a circle of figures that hid him from me. Then I saw him standing alone in a seaman's frock and trousers, a rope in his hand, or slung to his wrist, another round his body; and several of the best men holding, at a little distance, to the latter, which he laid out himself, slack upon the shore, at his feet.

The wreck, even to my unpractised eye, was breaking up. I saw that she was parting in the middle, and that the life of the solitary man upon the mast hung by a thread. Still, he clung to it. He had a singular red cap on—not like a sailor's cap, but of a finer colour; and as the few yielding planks between him and destruction rolled and bulged, and his anticipative death-knell rung, he was seen by all of us to wave it. I saw him do it now, and thought I was going distracted when his action brought an old remembrance to my mind of a once dear friend

Ham watched the sea, standing alone, with the silence of suspended breath behind him, and the storm before, until there was a great retiring wave, when, with a backward glance at those who held the rope which was made fast round his body, he dashed in after it, and in a moment was buffeting with the water—rising with the hills, falling with the valleys, lost beneath the foam, then drawn again to land. They hauled in hastily.

He was hurt. I saw blood on his face, from where I stood; but he took no thought of that. He seemed hurriedly to give them some directions for leaving him more free—or so I judged from the motion of his arm—and was gone as before.

And now he made for the wreck, rising with the hills, falling with the valleys, lost beneath the rugged foam, borne in towards the shore, borne on towards the ship, striving hard and valiantly. The distance was nothing, but the power of the sea and wind made the strife deadly. At length he neared the wreck. He was so near that with one more of his vigorous strokes he would be clinging to it—when a high, green, vast hillside of water moving on shoreward from beyond the ship, he seemed to leap up into it with a mighty bound, and the ship was gone!

Some eddying fragments I saw in the sea, as if a mere cask had been broken, in running to the spot where they were hauling in. Consternation was in every face. They drew him to my very feet —insensible—dead. He was carried to the nearest house, and, no one preventing me now, I remained near him, busy, while every means of restoration were tried; but he had been beaten to death by the great wave, and his generous heart was stilled for ever.

As I sat beside the bed, when hope was abandoned and all was done, a fisherman, who had known me when Emily and I were children, and ever since, whispered my name at the door.

"Sir," said he, with tears starting to his weather-beaten face, which, with his trembling lips, was ashy pale, "will you come over yonder?"

The old remembrance that had been recalled to me was in his look. I asked him, terror-stricken, leaning on the arm he held out to support me,—

"Has a body come ashore?"

He said, "Yes."

"Do I know it?" I asked then.

He answered nothing.

But he led me to the shore. And on that part of it where she and I had looked for shells, two children—on that part of it where some lighter fragments of the old boat, blown down last night, had been scattered by the wind—among the ruins of the home he had wronged—I saw him lying with his head upon his arm, as I had often seen him lie at school.

WORDSWORTH

WILLIAM WORDSWORTH (1770–1850) was born at Cockermouth and educated at Hawkeshead School and at Cambridge. He describes his boyhood days and his life at Cambridge in some fine passages of his autobiographical poem, *The Prelude*, of which *The Simplon Pass* and *There was a Boy* form part. *Nutting* was at first meant to be included. A volume entitled *Lyrical Ballads* (1798, enlarged to two volumes in 1800) aroused much ridicule and opposition owing to the simple language of the poems and the lowly character of the subjects—the kind of poetry then in fashion being very artificial and ornamented. Wordsworth's best short poems and sonnets, full of noble thought and great beauty, are among the finest in our tongue. His longest poem is *The Excursion.*

NUTTING

It seems a day
(I speak of one from many singled out)
One of those heavenly days that cannot die;
When, in the eagerness of boyish hope,
I left our cottage-threshold, sallying forth
With a huge wallet o'er my shoulders slung,
A nutting-crook in hand; and turned my steps
Tow'rd some far-distant wood, a Figure quaint,
Tricked out in proud disguise of cast-off weeds
Which for that service had been husbanded,
By exhortation of my frugal Dame—
Motley accoutrement, of power to smile
At thorns, and brakes, and brambles,—and in truth
More ragged than need was! O'er pathless rocks,
Through beds of matted fern, and tangled thickets,
Forcing my way, I came to one dear nook
Unvisited, where not a broken bough
Drooped with its withered leaves, ungracious sign
Of devastation; but the hazels rose
Tall and erect, with tempting clusters hung,
A virgin scene!—A little while I stood,
Breathing with such suppression of the heart
As joy delights in; and with wise restraint
Voluptuous, fearless of a rival, eyed

The banquet;—or beneath the trees I sate
Among the flowers, and with the flowers I played;
A temper known to those who, after long
And weary expectation, have been blest
With sudden happiness beyond all hope.
Perhaps it was a bower beneath whose leaves
The violets of five seasons re-appear
And fade, unseen by any human eye;
Where fairy water-breaks do murmur on
For ever; and I saw the sparkling foam,
And—with my cheek on one of those green stones
That, fleeced with moss, under the shady trees,
Lay round me, scattered like a flock of sheep—
I heard the murmur and the murmuring sound,
In that sweet mood when pleasure loves to pay
Tribute to ease; and, of its joy secure,
The heart luxuriates with indifferent things.
Wasting its kindliness on stocks and stones,
And on the vacant air. Then up I rose,
And dragged to earth both branch and bough, with crash
And merciless ravage: and the shady nook
Of hazels, and the green and mossy bower,
Deformed and sullied, patiently gave up
Their quiet being: and unless I now
Confound my present feelings with the past,
Ere from the mutilated bower I turned
Exulting, rich beyond the wealth of kings,
I felt a sense of pain when I beheld
The silent trees, and saw the intruding sky.—
Then, dearest Maiden, move along these shades
In gentleness of heart; with gentle hand
Touch—for there is a spirit in the woods.

THERE WAS A BOY

There was a Boy; ye knew him well, ye cliffs
And islands of Winander!—many a time,
At evening, when the earliest stars began
To move along the edges of the hills,

Rising or setting, would he stand alone,
Beneath the trees, or by the glimmering lake;
And there, with fingers interwoven, both hands
Pressed closely palm to palm and to his mouth
Uplifted, he, as through an instrument,
Blew mimic hootings to the silent owls,
That they might answer him —And they would shout
Across the watery vale, and shout again
Responsive to his call,—with quivering peals,
And long halloos, and screams, and echoes loud
Redoubled and redoubled; concourse wild
Of jocund din! And, when there came a pause
Of silence such as baffled his best skill:
Then sometimes, in that silence, while he hung
Listening, a gentle shock of mild surprise
Has carried far into his heart the voice
Of mountain-torrents; or the visible scene
Would enter unawares into his mind
With all its solemn imagery, its rocks,
Its woods, and that uncertain heaven received
Into the bosom of the steady lake....

THE SIMPLON PASS

Brook and road
Were fellow-travellers in this gloomy Pass,
And with them did we journey several hours
At a slow step. The immeasurable height
Of woods decaying, never to be decayed,
The stationary blasts of waterfalls,
And in the narrow rent, at every turn,
Winds thwarting winds bewildered and forlorn,
The torrents shooting from the clear blue sky,
The rocks that muttered close upon our ears,
Black drizzling crags that spake by the wayside
As if a voice were in them, the sick sight
And giddy prospect of the raving stream,
The unfettered clouds and region of the heavens,

Tumult and peace, the darkness and the light—
Were all like workings of one mind, the features
Of the same face, blossoms upon one tree,
Characters of the great Apocalypse,
The types and symbols of Eternity,
Of first, and last, and midst, and without end.

BENJAMIN DISRAELI

BENJAMIN DISRAELI (1804–81) was born in London. The boy came of Jewish race but was baptised in the Christian faith. He began writing novels at an early age, and gained much notice for his rather affected manner of writing and his very elaborate costumes. He was greatly influenced by a year of travel in Southern Europe and the East. As he grew older his style of writing improved, and his best work is brilliant and witty. He was already famous as a "dandy" and a novelist when he entered parliament in 1837. His Jewish blood, his affected manners and his foreign appearance were all obstacles to success in politics: but beneath his affectations and his languid manner he concealed high spirit, courage and a powerful will, which he steadily exerted till he forced his way into the front rank of statesmen. He became Chancellor of the Exchequer and was twice Prime Minister. He received the title "Earl of Beaconsfield" in 1876. His best novels are *Coningsby, Sybil, Henrietta Temple, Lothair* and *Endymion*. The passage that follows is taken from *Coningsby*.

CONINGSBY AND SIDONIA

There are few things more full of delight and splendour, than to travel during the heat of a refulgent summer in the green district of some ancient forest.

In one of our midland counties, there is a region of this character, to which during a season of peculiar lustre we would introduce the reader.

It was a fragment of one of those vast sylvan tracts wherein Norman kings once hunted, and Saxon outlaws plundered; and although the plough had for centuries successfully invaded brake and bower, the relics retained all their original character of wildness and seclusion. Sometimes the green earth was thickly studded with groves of huge and vigorous oaks, intersected with those smooth and sunny glades that seem as if they must be cut for dames and knights to saunter on. Then again the undulating ground spread on all sides, far as the eye could range, covered with copse and fern of immense growth. Anon, you found yourself in a turfy wilderness girt in apparently by dark woods. And when you had wound your way a little through this gloomy belt, the landscape, still strictly sylvan, would beautifully expand with every combination and variety of woodland; while in its centre, the wild fowl covered the waters of a lake, and the deer basked on the knolls that abounded on its banks.

It was in the month of August, some six or seven years ago, that a traveller on foot, touched as he emerged from the dark wood by the beauty of this scene, threw himself under the shade of a spreading tree, and stretched his limbs on the turf for enjoyment rather than repose. The sky was deep coloured and without a cloud, save here and there a minute, sultry, burnished vapour, almost as glossy as the heavens. Everything was as still as it was bright. All seemed brooding and basking. The bee upon its wing was the only stirring sight, and its song the only sound.

The traveller fell into a reverie. He was young, and therefore his musings were of the future. He had felt the pride of learning, so ennobling to youth; he was not a stranger to the stirring impulses of a high ambition, though the world to him was as yet only a world of books, and all that he knew of the schemes of statesmen and the passions of the people were to be found in their annals. Often had his fitful fancy dwelt with fascination on visions of personal distinction, of future celebrity, perhaps even of enduring fame. But his dreams were of another colour now. The surrounding scene, so fair, so still, and sweet; so abstracted from all the tumult of the world, its strife, its passions, and its cares, had fallen on his heart with its soft and subduing spirit: had fallen on a heart still pure and innocent; the heart of one, who, notwithstanding all his high resolves and daring thoughts, was blessed with that tenderness of soul which is sometimes linked with an ardent imagination and a strong will. The traveller was an orphan, more than that—a solitary orphan. The sweet sedulousness of a mother's love, a sister's mystical affection, had not cultivated his early susceptibility. No soft pathos of expression had appealed to his childish ear. He was alone, among strangers, calmly and coldly kind. It must indeed have been a truly gentle disposition that could have withstood such hard neglect. All that he knew of the power of the softer passions might be found in the fanciful and romantic annals of school-boy friend-ship.

And those friends too, so fond, so sympathising, so devoted, where were they now? Already they were dispersed. The first great separation of life had been experienced. The former school-boy had planted his foot on the threshold of manhood. True, many of them might meet again. Many of them the University must again unite. But never with the same feelings. The space of time, passed in the world before they again met, would be an age of sensation, passion, experience to all of them. They would meet again with altered mien; with different manners, different voices. Their eyes would not shine with the same light; they would not speak the same words. The favourite phrases of their intimacy, the mystic sounds that spoke only to their initiated ear, they would be ashamed to use them. Yes! they might meet again; but the gushing and secret tenderness was gone for ever.

Nor could our pensive youth conceal it from himself that it was affection, and mainly affection, that had bound him to these dear companions. They could not be to him what he had been to them. His had been the inspiring mind that had guided their opinions, formed their tastes, directed the bent and tenor of their lives and thoughts. Often indeed had he needed, sometimes indeed he had sighed for the companionship of an equal, or superior mind; one who by the comprehension of his thought, and the richness of his knowledge, and the advantage of his experience, might strengthen and illuminate and guide his obscure or hesitating or unpractised intelligence. He had scarcely been fortunate in this respect, and he deeply regretted it; for he was one of those who was not content with excelling in his own circle, if he thought there was one superior to it. Absolute, not relative distinction, was his noble aim.

Alone, in a lonely scene, he doubly felt the solitude of his life and mind. His heart and his intellect seemed both to need a companion. Books, and action, and deep thought, might in time supply the want of that intellectual guide; but for the heart where was he to find solace?

Ah! if she would but come forth from that shining lake like a beautiful Ondine! Ah! if she would but step out from the green shade of that secret grove like a Dryad of sylvan Greece! O!

mystery of mysteries! when the youth dreams his first dream over some imaginary heroine!

Suddenly the brooding wild-fowl rose from the bosom of the lake, soared in the air, and uttering mournful shrieks, whirled in agitated tumult. The deer started from their knolls, no longer sunny, stared around, and rushed into the woods. Coningsby raised his eyes from the turf on which they had been long fixed in abstraction, and he observed that the azure sky had vanished, a thin white film had suddenly spread itself over the heavens, and the wind moaned with a sad and fitful gust.

He had some reason to believe that on the other side of the opposite wood, the forest was intersected by a public road, and that there were some habitations Immediately rising, he descended at a rapid pace into the valley, passed the lake, and then struck into the ascending wood of the bank opposite to that on which he had mused away some precious time

The wind howled, the branches of the forest stirred, and sent forth sounds like an incantation. Soon might be distinguished the various voices of the mighty trees, as they expressed their terror or their agony. The oak roared, the beech shrieked, the elm sent forth its deep and long-drawn groan; while ever and anon, amid a momentary pause, the passion of the ash was heard in moans of thrilling anguish.

Coningsby hurried on, the forest became less close. All that he aspired to was to gain more open country. Now he was in a rough flat land covered only here and there with some dwarf underwood; the horizon bounded at no great distance by a barren hill of moderate elevation. He gained its height with ease. He looked over a vast open country, like a wild common; in the extreme distance hills covered with woods; the plain intersected by two good roads; the sky entirely clouded, but in the distance black as ebony.

A place of refuge too was at hand: screened from his first glance by some elm trees, the ascending smoke now betrayed a roof which Coningsby reached before the tempest broke. The forest inn was also a farm-house. There was a comfortable-enough-looking kitchen; but the ingle nook was full of smokers, and Coningsby was glad to avail himself of the only private room for the simple meal which they offered him. Only eggs and bacon; but very welcome to a pedestrian, and a hungry one.

As he stood at the window of his little apartment, watching the large drops that were the heralds of a coming hurricane, and waiting for his repast, a flash of lightning illumined the whole country, and a horseman at full speed, followed by his groom, galloped up to the door

The remarkable beauty of the animal so attracted Coningsby's attention, that it prevented him catching even a glimpse of the rider, who rapidly dismounted and entered the inn. The host shortly after came in and asked Coningsby whether he had any objection to a gentleman, who was driven there by the storm, sharing his room until it subsided. The consequence of the immediate assent of Coningsby was, that the landlord retired and soon returned ushering in an individual, who though perhaps ten years older than Coningsby, was still, according to Hippocrates, in the period of lusty youth. He was above the middle height, and of a distinguished air and figure; pale, with an impressive brow, and dark eyes of great intelligence.

"I am glad that we have both escaped the storm," said the stranger; "and I am greatly indebted to you for your courtesy." He slightly and graciously bowed as he spoke in a voice of remarkable clearness; and his manner, though easy, was touched with a degree of dignity that was engaging.

"The inn is a common home," replied Coningsby, returning his salute.

"And free from cares," added the stranger. Then looking through the window, he said: "A strange storm this. I was sauntering in the sunshine, when suddenly I found I had to gallop for my life. 'Tis more like a white squall in the Mediterranean than anything else."

"I never was in the Mediterranean," said Coningsby. "There is nothing that I should like so much as to travel."

"You are travelling," rejoined his companion. "Every movement is travel, if understood."

"Ah! but the Mediterranean!" exclaimed Coningsby. "What would I not give to see Athens!"

"I have seen it," said the stranger, slightly shrugging his shoulders; "and more wonderful things. Phantoms and spectres! The Age of Ruins is past. Have you seen Manchester?"

"I have seen nothing," said Coningsby; "this is my first

wandering. I am about to visit a friend who lives in this county, and I have sent on my baggage as I could. For myself, I determined to trust to a less common-place conveyance."

"And seek adventures," said the stranger, smiling. "Well, according to Cervantes, they should begin in an inn."

"I fear that the age of adventures is past, as well as that of ruins," replied Coningsby.

"Adventures are to the adventurous," said the stranger.

At this moment, a pretty serving-maid entered the room. She laid the dapper cloth and arranged the table with a self-possession quite admirable. She seemed unconscious that any being was in the chamber except herself, or that there were any other duties to perform in life beyond filling a salt-cellar or folding a napkin.

"She does not even look at us," said Coningsby when she had quitted the room; "and I dare say is only a prude."

"She is calm," said the stranger, "because she is mistress of her subject; 'tis the secret of self-possession. She is here, as a Duchess at Court."

They brought in Coningsby's meal, and he invited the stranger to join him. The invitation was accepted with cheerfulness.

"'Tis but simple fare," said Coningsby, as the maiden uncovered the still hissing bacon and the eggs that looked like tufts of primroses.

"Nay, a national dish," said the stranger, glancing quickly at the table, "whose fame is a proverb. And what more should we expect under a simple roof! How much better than an omelette or a greasy olla, that they would give us in a posada! 'Tis a wonderful country this England! What a napkin! How spotless! And so sweet, I declare 'tis a perfume. There is not a princess throughout the South of Europe served with the cleanliness that meets us in this cottage."

"An inheritance from our Saxon fathers?" said Coningsby. "I apprehend the northern nations have a greater sense of cleanliness—of propriety—of what we call comfort?"

"By no means," said the stranger, "the East is the land of the Bath. Moses and Mahomet made cleanliness religion."

"You will let me help you," said Coningsby, offering him a plate which he had filled.

"I thank you," said the stranger, "but it is one of my bread days. With your permission this shall be my dish," and he cut from the large loaf a supply of crusts.

"'Tis but unsavoury fare after a gallop," said Coningsby.

"Ah! you are proud of your bacon and your eggs," said the stranger, smiling, "but I love corn and wine. They are our chief and our oldest luxuries. Time has brought us substitutes, but how inferior! Man has deified corn and wine! but not even the Chinese or the Irish have raised temples to tea and potatoes."

"But Ceres without Bacchus," said Coningsby, "how does that do? Think you, under this roof we could invoke the god?"

"Let us swear by his body that we will try," said the stranger.

Alas! the landlord was not a priest of Bacchus But then these inquiries led to the finest perry in the world. The young men agreed they had seldom tasted anything more delicious; they sent for another bottle Coningsby, who was much interested by his new companion, enjoyed himself amazingly.

A cheese, such as Derby can alone produce, could not induce the stranger to be even partially inconstant to his crusts. But his talk was as vivacious, as if the talker had been stimulated by the juices of the finest banquet. Coningsby had never met or read of any one like this chance companion. His sentences were so short, his language so racy, his voice rang so clear, his elocution was so complete. On all subjects his mind seemed to be instructed, and his opinions formed. He flung out a result in a few words; he solved with a phrase some deep problem that men muse over for years. He said many things that were strange, yet they immediately appeared to be true Then, without the slightest air of pretension or parade, he seemed to know everybody as well as everything Monarchs, statesmen, authors, adventurers of all descriptions and of all climes—if their names occurred in the conversation, he described them in an epigrammatic sentence, or revealed their precise position, character, calibre, by a curt dramatic trait. All this, too, without any excitement of manner; on the contrary with repose amounting almost to nonchalance. If his address had a fault in it, it was rather a deficiency of earnestness. A slight spirit of mockery played over his speech even when you deemed him most serious; you were startled by his sudden transitions from profound thought to poignant sarcasm. A very singular freedom from passion and prejudice on every topic on which they treated might be some compensation for this want of earnestness, perhaps was its consequence. Certainly it was difficult to ascertain his precise opinions on many subjects, though his manner was frank even to abandonment. And yet throughout his whole conversation, not a stroke of egotism, not a word, not a circumstance, escaped him by which you could judge of his position or purposes in life. As little did he seem to care to discover those of his companion He did not by any means monopolise the conversation Far from it; he continually asked questions, and while he received answers, or had engaged his fellow traveller in any exposition of his opinions or feelings, he listened with a serious and fixed attention, looking Coningsby in the face with a steadfast glance.

"I perceive," said Coningsby, pursuing a train of thought which the other had indicated, "that you have great confidence in the influence of individual character. I also have some confused persuasions of that kind. But it is not the Spirit of the Age "

"The age does not believe in great men, because it does not possess any," replied the stranger. "The Spirit of the Age is the very thing that a great man changes."

"But does not he rather avail himself of it?" inquired Coningsby.

"Parvenus do," rejoined his companion; "but not prophets, great legislators, great conquerors. They destroy and they create."

"But are these times for great legislators and great conquerors?" urged Coningsby.

"When were they more wanted?" asked the stranger. "From the throne to the hovel all call for a guide. You give monarchs constitutions to teach them sovereignty, and nations Sunday-schools to inspire them with faith."

"But what is an individual," exclaimed Coningsby, "against a vast public opinion?"

"Divine," said the stranger "God made man in his own image, but the Public is made by Newspapers, Members of Parliament, Excise Officers, Poor Law Guardians. Would Philip have succeeded, if Epaminondas had not been slain? And if Philip had not succeeded? Would Prussia have existed had Frederick not been born? And if Frederick had not been born? What would have been the fate of the Stuarts if Prince Henry had not died, and Charles I, as was intended, had been Archbishop of Canterbury?"

"But when men are young, they want experience," said Coningsby; "and when they have gained experience, they want energy."

"Great men never want experience," said the stranger.

"But everybody says that experience——"

"Is the best thing in the world—a treasure for you, for me, for millions. But for a creative mind, less than nothing. Almost everything that is great has been done by youth."

"It is at least a creed flattering to our years," said Coningsby with a smile.

"Nay," said the stranger; "for life in general there is but one decree. Youth is a blunder; Manhood a struggle; old Age a regret. Do not suppose," he added, smiling, "that I hold that youth is genius; all that I say is, that genius, when young, is divine. Why, the greatest captains of ancient and modern times both conquered Italy at five and twenty! Youth, extreme youth, overthrew the Persian Empire. Don John of Austria won Lepanto at twenty-five—the greatest battle of modern time; had it not been for the jealousy of Philip, the next year he would have been Emperor of Mauritania. Gaston de Foix was only twenty-two when he stood a victor on the plain of Ravenna. Every one remembers Condé and Rocroy at the same age. Gustavus Adolphus died at thirty-eight. Look at his captains: that wonderful Duke of Weimar, only thirty-six when he died. Banier himself, after all his miracles, died at forty-five. Cortes was little more than thirty when he gazed upon the golden cupolas of Mexico. When Maurice of Saxony died at thirty-two, all Europe acknowledged the loss of the greatest captain and the profoundest statesman of the age. Then there is Nelson, Clive—but these are warriors, and perhaps you may think there are greater things than war. I do not; I worship the Lord of Hosts. But take the most illustrious achievements of civil prudence. Innocent III, the greatest of the Popes, was the despot of Christendom at thirty-seven. John de Medici was a Cardinal at fifteen, and Guicciardini tells us baffled with his statecraft Ferdinand of Aragon himself. He was Pope as Leo X at thirty-seven. Luther robbed even him of his richest province at thirty-five. Take Ignatius Loyola and John Wesley, they worked with young brains Ignatius was only thirty when he made his pilgrimage and wrote the 'Spiritual Exercises.' Pascal wrote a great work at sixteen, the greatest of Frenchmen, and died at thirty-seven!

"Ah! that fatal thirty-seven, which reminds me of Byron, greater even as a man than a writer. Was it experience that guided the pencil of Raphael when he painted the palaces of Rome! He died too at thirty-seven. Richelieu was Secretary of State at thirty-one. Well then, there are Bolingbroke and Pitt, both Ministers before other men leave off cricket. Grotius was in great practice at seventeen, and Attorney-General at twenty-four. and Acquaviva—Acquaviva was General of the Jesuits, ruled every cabinet in Europe, and colonised America before he was thirty-seven. What a career!" exclaimed the stranger, rising from his chair and walking up and down the room, "the secret sway of Europe! That was indeed a position! But it is needless to multiply instances The history of Heroes is the history of Youth."

"Ah!" said Coningsby, "I should like to be a great man!"

The stranger threw at him a scrutinising glance. His countenance was serious. He said in a voice of almost solemn melody:

"Nurture your mind with great thoughts. To believe in the heroic makes heroes."

"You seem to me a hero," said Coningsby in a tone of real feeling, which, half-ashamed of his emotion, he tried to turn into playfulness

"I am, and must ever be," said the stranger, "but a dreamer of dreams." Then going towards the window and changing into a familiar tone, as if to divert the conversation, he added: "What a delicious afternoon! I look forward to my ride with delight. You rest here?"

"No; I go on to Nottingham, where I shall sleep."

"And I in the opposite direction." And he rang the bell and ordered his horses.

"I long to see your mare again," said Coningsby "She seemed to me so beautiful."

"She is not only of pure race," said the stranger, "but of the highest and rarest breed in Arabia Her name is the 'Daughter of the Star.' She is a foal of that famous mare which belonged to the Prince of the Wahabees, and to possess which, I believe, was one of the principal causes of war between that tribe and the Egyptians. The Pacha of Egypt gave her to me, and I would not change her for her statue in pure gold, even carved by Lysippus. Come round to the stable and see her."

They went out together. It was a soft sunny afternoon; the air fresh from the rain, but mild and exhilarating.

The groom brought forth the mare. The "Daughter of the Star" stood before Coningsby with her sinewy shape of matchless symmetry; her burnished skin, black mane, legs like those of an antelope, her little ears, dark speaking eye, and tail worthy of a pacha. And who was her master, and whither was she about to take him?

Coningsby was so naturally well-bred, that we may be sure it was not curiosity; no, it was a finer feeling that made him hesitate and think a little, and then say:

"I am sorry to part."

"I also," said the stranger. "But life is constant separation."

"I hope we may meet again," said Coningsby.

"If our acquaintance be worth preserving," said the stranger, "you may be sure it will not be lost."

"But mine is not worth preserving," said Coningsby earnestly. "It is yours that is the treasure. You teach me things of which I have long mused."

The stranger took the bridle of the "Daughter of the Star," and turning round with a faint smile, extended his hand to his companion.

"Your mind at least is nurtured with great thoughts," said Coningsby, "your actions should be heroic."

"Action is not for me," said the stranger, "I am of that faith that the Apostles professed before they followed their Master."

He vaulted into his saddle, the "Daughter of the Star" bounded away as if she scented the air of the desert from which she and her rider had alike sprung, and Coningsby remained in profound meditation.

WORDSWORTH

Composed upon Westminster Bridge, Sept 2, 1802

Earth has not anything to show more fair:
Dull would he be of soul who could pass by
A sight so touching in its majesty:
This City now doth, like a garment, wear
The beauty of the morning; silent, bare,
Ships, towers, domes, theatres, and temples lie
Open unto the fields, and to the sky;
All bright and glittering in the smokeless air.
Never did sun more beautifully steep
In his first splendour, valley, rock, or hill;
Ne'er saw I, never felt, a calm so deep!
The river glideth at his own sweet will:
Dear God! the very houses seem asleep;
And all that mighty heart is lying still!

MILTON

JOHN MILTON (1608–74) was born in London and educated at St Paul's
School and Cambridge His careful studies made him one of the most learned
men of his time *L'Allegro, Il Penseroso, Comus* and *Lycidas* are among his
beautiful earlier poems He spent many months travelling in Italy, and
when he returned to England he wrote pamphlets on the side of the parliament In middle life he became totally blind, and to this trouble was added
the danger that threatened him when the puritan cause was overthrown
and Charles II became king It was during his blindness and distress that
Paradise Lost, the greatest of his poems, was written Milton died in London,
and was buried at St Giles's, Cripplegate.

ON HIS BLINDNESS

When I consider how my light is spent,
Ere half my days in this dark world and wide,
And that one talent which is death to hide
Lodged with me useless, though my soul more bent

To serve therewith my Maker, and present
My true account, lest He returning chide;
'Doth God exact day-labour, light denied?'
I fondly ask.   But Patience, to prevent

That murmur, soon replies, 'God doth not need
Either man's work or His own gifts. Who best
Bear His mild yoke, they serve Him best.   His state

Is kingly: thousands at His bidding speed
And post o'er land and ocean without rest;
They also serve who only stand and wait.'

THE BLINDNESS OF SAMSON

(From *Samson Agonistes*)

>   But, chief of all,
O loss of sight, of thee I most complain!
Blind among enemies! Oh worse than chains,
Dungeon, or beggary, or decrepit age!
Light, the prime work of God, to me is extinct,
And all her various objects of delight
Annull'd, which might in part my grief have eased,
Inferior to the vilest now become
Of man or worm; the vilest here excel me.
They creep, they see; I, dark in light, exposed
To daily fraud, contempt, abuse, and wrong,
Within doors, or without, still as a fool,
In power of others, never in my own;
Scarce half I seem to live, dead more than half.
O dark, dark, dark, amid the blaze of noon,
Irrecoverably dark, total eclipse
Without all hope of day!
O first-created beam, and thou great Word,
"Let there be light," and light was over all,
Why am I thus bereaved thy prime decree?
The Sun to me is dark
And silent as the Moon,
When she deserts the night,
Hid in her vacant interlunar cave.

ON HIS BLINDNESS

(From *Paradise Lost*)

Hail, holy Light, offspring of Heaven first born!...
Thee I revisit now with bolder wing...
And feel thy vital sovran lamp; but thou
Revisit'st not these eyes, that roll in vain
To find thy piercing ray, and find no dawn,
So thick a drop serene hath quencht their orbs,
Or dim suffusion veil'd. Yet not the more
Cease I to wander where the Muses haunt
Clear spring, or shady grove, or sunny hill,
Smit with the love of sacred song; but chief
Thee, Sion, and the flowery brooks beneath,
That wash thy hallow'd feet, and warbling flow,
Nightly I visit...
Then feed on thoughts that voluntary move
Harmonious numbers; as the wakeful bird
Sings darkling, and, in shadiest covert hid
Tunes her nocturnal note. Thus with the year
Seasons return; but not to me returns
Day, or the sweet approach of even or morn,
Or sight of vernal bloom, or summer's rose,
Or flocks, or herds, or human face divine;
But cloud instead and ever-during dark
Surrounds me, from the cheerful ways of men
Cut off, and, for the book of knowledge fair,
Presented with a universal blank
Of Nature's works, to me expunged and rased,
And wisdom at one entrance quite shut out.
So much the rather thou, celestial Light,
Shine inward, and the mind through all her powers
Irradiate: there plant eyes, all mist from thence
Purge and disperse, that I may see and tell
Of things invisible to mortal sight.

ARNOLD BENNETT

ARNOLD BENNETT is the author of *The Old Wives' Tale*, *Clayhanger*, *Hilda Lessways*, *What the Public Wants*, *The Great Adventure* and many other novels, plays and essays. The following sketch of child labour in the days before humane laws prevented such slavery is taken from *Clayhanger*.

THE BOY MAN

I

The earliest memory of Darius Clayhanger had to do with the capital letters Q W and S. Even as the first steam-printer in Bursley, even as the father of a son who had received a thoroughly sound middle-class education, he never noticed a capital Q.W. or S without recalling the widow Susan's school, where he had wonderingly learnt the significance of those complicated characters. The school consisted of the entire ground floor of her cottage, namely, one room, of which the far corner was occupied by a tiny winding staircase that led to the ancient widow's bedchamber. The furniture comprised a few low forms for scholars, a table, and a chair; and there were some brilliant coloured prints on the whitewashed walls At this school Darius acquired a knowledge of the alphabet, and from the alphabet passed to Reading-Made-Easy, and then to the Bible He made such progress that the widow soon singled him out for honour He was allowed the high and envied privilege of raking the ashes from under the fire-place and carrying them to the ash-pit, which ash-pit was vast and lofty, being the joint production of many cottages To reach the summit of the ash-pit, and thence to fling backwards down its steep sides all assailants who challenged your supremacy, was a precious joy The battles of the ash-pit, however, were not battles of giants, as no children had leisure for ash-carrying after the age of seven A still greater honour accorded to Darius was permission to sit, during lessons, on the topmost visible step of the winding stair The widow Susan, having taught Darius to read brilliantly, taught him to knit, and he would knit stockings for his father, mother, and sister.

At the age of seven, his education being complete, he was summoned into the world It is true that he could neither write nor deal with the multiplication table, but there were always night-schools which studious adults of seven and upwards might attend if business permitted. Further, there was the Sunday school, which Darius had joyously frequented since the age of three, and which he had no intention of leaving. As he grew older the Sunday school became more and more enchanting to him Sunday morning was the morning which he lived for during six days; it was the morning when his hair was brushed and combed, and perfumed with a delightful oil, whose particular fragrance he remembered throughout his life. At Sunday school he was petted and caressed. His success at Sunday school was shining. He passed over the heads of bigger boys, and at the age of six he was in a Bible class.

Upon hearing that Darius was going out into the world, the superintendent of the Sunday school, a grave whiskered young man of perhaps thirty, led him one morning out of the body of the Primitive Methodist Chapel which served as schoolroom before and after chapel service, up into the deserted gallery of the chapel, and there seated him on a stair, and knelt on the stair below him, and caressed his head, and called him a good boy, and presented him with an old battered Bible. This volume was the most valuable thing that Darius had ever possessed He ran all the way home with it, half suffocated by his triumph Sunday-school prizes had not then been invented. The young superintendent of the Sunday school was Mr Shushions.

II

The man Darius was first taken to work by his mother. It was the winter of 1835, January. They passed through the market-place of the town of Turnhill, where they lived Turnhill lies a couple of miles north of Bursley. One side of the market-place was barricaded with stacks of coal, and the other with loaves of a species of rye and straw bread This coal and these loaves were being served out by meticulous and haughty officials, all invisibly braided with red-tape, to a crowd of shivering, moaning, and weeping wretches, men, women and children—the basis of the population of Turnhill. Although they were all endeavouring to make a noise, they made scarcely any noise, from mere lack of strength. Nothing could be heard, under the implacable bright sky, but faint ghosts of sound, as though people were sighing and crying from within the vacuum of a huge glass bell.

The next morning, at half-past five, Darius began his career in earnest He was "mould-runner" to a "muffin-maker," a muffin being not a comestible but a small plate, fashioned by its maker on a mould. The business of Darius was to run as hard as he could with the mould, and a newly created plate adhering thereto, into the drying-stove. This "stove" was a room lined with shelves, and having a red-hot stove and stove-pipe in the middle. As no man of seven could reach the upper shelves, a pair of steps was provided for Darius, and up these he had to scamper. Each mould with its plate had to be leaned carefully against the wall, and if the soft clay of a new-born plate was damaged, Darius was knocked down. The atmosphere outside the stove was chill, but owing to the heat of the stove, Darius was obliged to work half naked. His sweat ran down his cheeks, and down his chest, and down his back, making white channels, and lastly it soaked his hair.

When there were no moulds to be sprinted into the drying-stove, and no moulds to be carried less rapidly out, Darius was engaged in clay-wedging That is to say, he took a piece of raw clay weighing more than himself, cut it in two with a wire, raised one half above his head and crashed it down with all his force upon the other half, and he repeated the process until the clay was thoroughly soft and even in texture At a later period it was discovered that hydraulic machinery could perform this operation more easily and more effectually than the brawny arms of a man of seven At eight o'clock in the evening Darius was told that he had done enough for that day, and that he must arrive at five sharp the next morning to light the fire, before his master the muffin-maker began to work When he inquired how he was to light the fire his master kicked him jovially on the thigh and suggested that he should ask another mould-runner His master was not a bad man at heart, it was said, but on Tuesdays, after Sunday and Saint Monday, masters were apt to be capricious.

Darius reached home at a quarter to nine, having eaten nothing but bread all day. Somehow he had lapsed into the child again. His mother took him on her knee, and wrapped her sacking apron round his ragged clothes, and cried over him and cried into his supper of porridge, and undressed him and put him to bed. But he could not sleep easily because he was afraid of being late the next morning.

III

And the next morning, wandering about the yards of the manufactory in a storm of icy sleet a little before five o'clock, he learnt from a more experienced companion that nobody would provide him with kindling for his fire, that on the contrary everybody who happened to be on the place at that hour would unite to prevent him from getting kindling, and that he must steal it or expect to be thrashed before six o'clock. Near them a vast kiln of ware in process of firing showed a white flaming glow at each of its mouths in the black winter darkness. Darius's mentor crept up to the archway of the great hovel which protected the kiln, and pointed like a conspirator to the figure of the guardian fireman dozing near his monster. The boy had the handle-less remains of an old spade, and with it he crept into the hovel, dangerously abstracted fire from one of the scorching mouths, and fled therewith, and the fireman never stirred. Then Darius, to whom the mentor kindly lent his spade, attempted to do the same, but being inexpert woke the fireman, who held him spell-bound by his roaring voice and then flung him like a sack of potatoes bodily into the slush of the yard, and the spade after him. Happily the mentor, whose stove was now alight, lent fire to Darius, so that Darius's stove too was cheerfully burning when his master came. And Darius was too excited to feel fatigue.

By six o'clock on Saturday night Darius had earned a shilling for his week's work. But he could only possess himself of the shilling by going to a magnificent public-house with his master the muffin-maker. This was the first time that he had ever been inside a public-house. The place was crowded with men, women, and children eating the most lovely hot rolls and drinking beer, in an atmosphere exquisitely warm. And behind a high counter a stout jolly man was counting piles and piles and piles of silver. Darius's master, in company with other boys' masters, gave this stout man four sovereigns to change, and it was an hour before he changed them. Meanwhile Darius was instructed that he must eat a roll

like the rest, together with cheese. Never had he tasted anything
so luscious. He had a match with his mentor, as to which of them
could spin out his roll the longer, honestly chewing all the time;
and he won. Some one gave him half a glass of beer. At half-past
seven he received his shilling, which consisted of a sixpenny-piece
and four pennies; and, leaving the gay public-house, pushed his
way through a crowd of tearful women with babies in their arms
at the doors, and went home. And such was the attraction of the
Sunday school that he was there the next morning, with scented
hair, two minutes before the opening

iv

In about a year Darius's increasing knowledge of the world
enabled him to rise in it. He became a handle-maker in another
manufactory, and also he went about with the pride of one who
could form the letters of the alphabet with a pen. In his new work
he had to put a bit of clay between two moulds and then force the
top mould on to the bottom one by means of his stomach, which it
was necessary to press downwards and at the same time to wriggle
with a peculiar movement. The workman to whom he was
assigned, his new "master," attached these handles, with strange
rapid skill, to beer-mugs. For Darius the labour was much lighter
than that of mould-running and clay-wedging, and the pay was
somewhat higher. But there were minor disadvantages. He
descended by twenty steps to his toil, and worked in a long cellar
which never received any air except by way of the steps and a
passage, and never any daylight at all. Its sole illumination was
a stove used for drying. The "throwers'" and the "turners'"
rooms were also subterranean dungeons. When in full activity all
these stinking cellars were full of men, boys, and young women,
working close together in a hot twilight. Certain boys were
trained contrabandists of beer, and beer came as steadily into the
dungeons as though it had been laid on by a main pipe. It was not
honourable, even on the part of a young woman, to refuse beer,
particularly when the beer happened to arrive in the late afternoon.
On such occasions young men and women would often entirely
omit to go home of a night, and seasoned men of the world aged
eight, on descending into the dungeons early the next morning,

would have a full view of pandemonium, and they would witness during the day salutary scenes of remorse, and proofs of the existence of a profound belief in the homeopathic properties of beer.

But perhaps the worst drawback of Darius's new position was the long and irregular hours, due partly to the influences of Saint Monday and of the scenes above indicated but not described, and partly to the fact that the employés were on piece-work and entirely unhampered by grandmotherly legislation. The result was that six days' work was generally done in four. And as the younger the workman the earlier he had to start in the morning, Darius saw scarcely enough of his bed. It was not of course to be expected that a self-supporting man of the world should rigorously confine himself to an eight-hour day or even a twelve-hour day, but Darius's day would sometimes stretch to eighteen and nineteen hours: which on hygienic grounds could not be unreservedly defended.

V

One Tuesday evening his master, after three days of debauch, ordered him to be at work at three o'clock the next morning. He quickly and even eagerly agreed, for he was already intimate with his master's rope-lash. He reached home at ten o'clock on an autumn night, and went to bed and to sleep. He woke up with a start, in the dark. There was no watch or clock in the house, from which nearly all the furniture had gradually vanished, but he knew it must be already after three o'clock; and he sprang up and rushed out. Of course he had not undressed; his life was too strenuous for mere formalities. The stars shone above him as he ran along, wondering whether after all, though late, he could by unprecedented effort make the ordained number of handles before his master tumbled into the cellar at five o'clock.

When he had run a mile he met some sewage men on their rounds, who in reply to his question told him that the hour was half after midnight. He dared not risk a return to home and bed, for within two and a half hours he must be at work. He wandered aimlessly over the surface of the earth until he came to a tile-works, more or less unenclosed, whose primitive ovens showed a glare. He ventured within, and in spite of himself sat down on the ground near one of those heavenly ovens. And then he wanted to get up again, for he could feel the strong breath of his enemy, sleep. But he could not get up. In a state of terror he yielded himself to his enemy. Shameful cowardice on the part of a man now aged nine! God, however, is merciful, and sent to him an angel in the guise of a night-watchman, who kicked him into wakefulness and off the place. He ran on limping, beneath the stellar systems, and reached his work at half-past four o'clock.

Although he had never felt so exhausted in his long life, he set to work with fury. Useless! When his master arrived he had scarcely got through the preliminaries. He dully faced his master in the narrow stifling cellar, lit by candles impaled on nails and already peopled by the dim figures of boys, girls, and a few men. His master was of taciturn habit and merely told him to kneel down. He knelt. Two bigger boys turned hastily from their work to snatch a glimpse of the affair. The master moved to the back of the cellar and took from a box a piece of rope an inch thick and clogged with clay. At the same moment a companion offered him, in silence, a tin with a slim neck, out of which he drank deep, it contained a pint of porter owing on loan from the previous day. When the master came in due course with the rope to do justice upon the sluggard he found the lad fallen forward and breathing heavily and regularly. Darius had gone to sleep. He was awakened with some violence, but the public opinion of the dungeon saved him from a torn shirt and a bloody back.

TWO OLD BALLADS

It is not known who wrote these two old and rather ghostly ballads

THE WIFE OF USHER'S WELL

There lived a wife at Usher's Well,
    And a wealthy wife was she;
She had three stout and stalwart sons,
    And sent them o'er the sea.

They hadna been a week from her,
    A week but barely ane,
When word cam' to the carline wife
    That her three sons were gane.

They hadna been a week from her,
   A week but barely three,
When word cam' to the carline wife
   That her sons she'd never see.

"I wish the wind may never cease,
   Nor freshes in the flood,
Till my three sons come hame to me,
   In earthly flesh and blood.'"

It fell about the Martinmas,
   When nights are lang and mirk,
The carline wife's three sons cam' hame,
   And their hats were o' the birk[1].

It neither grew in syke[2] nor ditch,
   Nor yet in ony sheugh[3];
But at the gates o' Paradise
   That birk grew fair eneugh.

"Blow up the fire, my maidens,
   Bring water from the well!
For a' my house shall feast this night,
   Since my three sons are well."

And she has made to them a bed,
   She's made it large and wide;
And she's ta'en her mantle her about,
   Sat down at the bedside.

Up then crew the red, red cock,
   And up and crew the grey;
The eldest to the youngest said,
   "'Tis time we were away."

The cock he hadna crawed but once,
   And clapp'd his wings at a',
When the youngest to the eldest said,
   "Brother, we must awa'.

[1] birch.   [2] marsh.   [3] trench.

"The cock doth craw, the day doth daw,
    The channerin' worm doth chide;
Gin we be miss'd out o' our place,
    A sair pain we maun bide."

"Fare ye weel, my mother dear,
    Fareweel to barn and byre!
And fare ye weel, the bonny lass
    That kindles my mother's fire!"

THE LYKE-WAKE DIRGE

This ae night, this ae night,
    Every night and all,
Fire and fleet and candle-light,
    And Christ receive thy saule!

When thou from hence away art past,
    Every night and all
To Whinny-muir thou comest at last;
    And Christ receive thy saule!

If ever thou gavest hosen or shoon,
    Every night and all
Sit thee down and put them on;
    And Christ receive thy saule!

But if hosen nor shoon thou never gave none
    Every night and all
The Whins shall prick thee to the bare bone;
    And Christ receive thy saule!

From Whinny-muir when thou mayst pass
    Every night and all
To Brig o' Dread thou comest at last;
    And Christ receive thy saule!

From Brig o' Dread when thou mayst pass
  Every night and all
To Purgatory fire thou comest at last;
  And Christ receive thy saule!

If ever thou gavest milk or drink,
  Every night and all
The fire shall never make thee shrink;
  And Christ receive thy saule!

But if milk nor drink thou never gave none,
  Every night and all
The fire shall burn thee to the bare bone;
  And Christ receive thy saule!

This ae night, this ae night,
  Every night and all,
Fire and fleet and candle-light,
  And Christ receive thy saule!

MARK TWAIN

SAMUEL LANGHORNE CLEMENS (1835–1910) was born at Florida, Missouri
During his early manhood he was a pilot on the Mississippi river, and when
he began to write he took his pen-name from a pilot's call, "Mark Twain!"
He became a journalist and gained much reputation for his humorous
conversation and lectures. His first important book, *The Innocents Abroad*,
records his adventures on a journey to Europe and the east. A later journey
provided material for the much finer book, *A Tramp Abroad* These two
volumes, together with two stories, *Tom Sawyer* and *Huckleberry Finn*, are
his most deservedly famous books His best work ranks very high as excellent
writing, genuine humour, sound wisdom and sterling honesty The passage
that follows is taken from *Tom Sawyer*. Tom is a lively and mischievous boy
living with his aunt in a small village on the banks of the great river. Jim
is their negro servant Tom has been fighting and getting his clothes torn,
and his aunt punishes him by setting him to whitewash a fence on his
Saturday holiday.

WHITEWASHING A FENCE

Saturday morning was come and all the summer world was
bright and fresh, and brimming with life. There was a song in
every heart; and if the heart was young the music issued at the
lips. There was cheer in every face, and a spring in every step.

The locust trees were in bloom, and the fragrance of the blossoms filled the air.

Cardiff Hill, beyond the village and above it, was green with vegetation, and it lay just far enough away to seem a Delectable Land, dreamy, reposeful, and inviting.

Tom appeared on the side-walk with a bucket of whitewash and a long-handled brush. He surveyed the fence, and the gladness went out of nature, and a deep melancholy settled down upon his spirit. Thirty yards of broad fence nine feet high! It seemed to him that life was hollow, and existence but a burden Sighing he dipped his brush and passed it along the topmost plank; repeated the operation; did it again; compared the insignificant whitewashed streak with the far-reaching continent of unwhitewashed fence, and sat down on a tree-box discouraged Jim came skipping out at the gate with a tin pail, and singing "Buffalo Gals." Bringing water from the town pump had always been hateful work in Tom's eyes before, but now it did not strike him so. He remembered that there was company at the pump. White, mulatto and negro boys and girls were always there waiting their turns, resting, trading playthings, quarrelling, fighting, skylarking. And he remembered that although the pump was only a hundred and fifty yards off Jim never got back with a bucket of water under an hour; and even then somebody generally had to go after him. Tom said:

"Say, Jim, I'll fetch the water if you'll whitewash some."

Jim shook his head, and said:

"Can't, Ma'rs Tom. Ole missis she tole me I got to go an' git dis water an' not stop foolin' 'roun wid anybody. She say she spec' Ma'rs Tom gwyne to ax me to whitewash, an' so she tole me go 'long an' 'tend to my own business—she 'lowed *she'd* 'tend to de whitewashin'."

"Oh, never you mind what she said, Jim. That's the way she always talks. Gimme the bucket—I won't be gone only a minute. *She* won't ever know."

"Oh, I dasn't, Ma'rs Tom. Ole missis she'd take an' tar de head off'n me. 'Deed she would."

"*She!* she never licks anybody—whacks 'em over the head with her thimble, and who cares for that, I'd like to know? She talks awful, but talk don't hurt—anyways, it don't if

she don't cry. Jim, I'll give you a marble. I'll give you a
white alley!"

Jim began to waver.

"White alley, Jim; and it's a bully taw."

"My; dat's a mighty gay marvel, *I* tell you But, Ma'rs Tom,
I's powerful 'fraid ole missis——"

But Jim was only human—this attraction was too much for
him. He put down his pail, took the white alley. In another
minute he was flying down the street with his pail and a tingling
rear, Tom was whitewashing with vigour, and aunt Polly was
retiring from the field with a slipper in her hand and triumph in
her eye.

But Tom's energy did not last. He began to think of the fun
he had planned for this day, and his sorrows multiplied. Soon the
free boys would come tripping along on all sorts of delicious
expeditions, and they would make a world of fun of him for having
to work—the very thought of it burnt him like fire. He got out
his worldly wealth and examined it—bits of toys, marbles and
trash; enough to buy an exchange of work maybe, but not enough
to buy so much as half-an-hour of pure freedom. So he returned
his straitened means to his pocket, and gave up the idea of trying
to buy the boys. At this dark and hopeless moment an inspiration
burst upon him. Nothing less than a great, magnificent inspiration.
He took up his brush and went tranquilly to work Ben Rogers
hove in sight presently; the very boy of all boys whose ridicule
he had been dreading Ben's gait was the hop, skip and jump—
proof enough that his heart was light and his anticipations high.
He was eating an apple, and giving a long, melodious whoop at
intervals, followed by a deep-toned ding dong dong, ding dong
dong, for he was personating a steamboat. As he drew near he
slackened speed, took the middle of the street, leaned far over to
starboard, and rounded-to ponderously, and with laborious pomp
and circumstance, for he was personating the "Big Missouri,"
and considered himself to be drawing nine feet of water. He was
boat, and captain, and engine-bells combined, so he had to imagine
himself standing on his own hurricane deck giving the orders and
executing them ...

Tom went on whitewashing—paid no attention to the steamer.
Ben stared a moment, and then said·

"Hi-yi! You're up a stump, ain't you!"

No answer. Tom surveyed his last touch with the eye of an artist; then he gave his brush another gentle sweep, and surveyed the result as before. Ben ranged up alongside of him. Tom's mouth watered for the apple, but he stuck to his work. Ben said:

"Hello, old chap; you got to work, hey?"

"Why, it's you, Ben! I warn't noticing."

"Say, I'm going in a-swimming, I am. Don't you wish you could? But of course you'd druther work wouldn't you? 'Course you would!"

Tom contemplated the boy a bit, and said:

"What do you call work?"

"Why, ain't that work?"

Tom resumed his whitewashing, and answered carelessly·

"Well, maybe it is, and maybe it ain't. All I know, is, it suits Tom Sawyer."

"Oh, come now, you don't mean to let on that you like it?"

The brush continued to move.

"Like it? Well, I don't see why I oughtn't to like it. Does a boy get a chance to whitewash a fence every day?"

That put the thing in a new light. Ben stopped nibbling his apple. Tom swept his brush daintily back and forth—stepped back to note the effect—added a touch here and there—criticised the effect again, Ben watching every move, and getting more and more interested, more and more absorbed. Presently he said:

"Say, Tom, let me whitewash a little."

Tom considered; was about to consent; but he altered his mind: "No, no, I reckon it wouldn't hardly do, Ben. You see, aunt Polly's awful particular about this fence—right here on the street, you know—but if it was the back fence I wouldn't mind, and she wouldn't. Yes, she's awful particular about this fence; it's got to be done very careful; I reckon there ain't one boy in a thousand, maybe two thousand, that can do it the way it's got to be done."

"No—is that so? Oh, come now, lemme just try, only just a little. I'd let you, if you was me, Tom."

"Ben, I'd like to, honest injun; but aunt Polly—well, Jim wanted to do it, but she wouldn't let him. Sid wanted to do it, but she wouldn't let Sid. Now, don't you see how I am fixed?

If you was to tackle this fence, and anything was to happen
to it——"

"Oh, shucks; I'll be just as careful. Now lemme try. Say—
I'll give you the core of my apple."

"Well, here. No, Ben; now don't; I'm afeard——"

"I'll give you all of it!"

Tom gave up the brush with reluctance in his face, but alacrity
in his heart. And while the late steamer "Big Missouri" worked
and sweated in the sun, the retired artist sat on a barrel in the
shade close by, dangled his legs, munched his apple, and planned
the slaughter of more innocents. There was no lack of material;
boys happened along every little while; they came to jeer, but
remained to whitewash. By the time Ben was fagged out, Tom
had traded the next chance to Billy Fisher for a kite in good
repair; and when he played out, Johnny Miller bought in for a
dead rat and a string to swing it with; and so on, and so on, hour
after hour. And when the middle of the afternoon came, from being
a poor poverty-stricken boy in the morning, Tom was literally
rolling in wealth. He had, besides the things I have mentioned,
twelve marbles, part of a jew's harp, a piece of blue bottle-glass
to look through, a spool-cannon, a key that wouldn't unlock
anything, a fragment of chalk, a glass stopper of a decanter, a tin
soldier, a couple of tadpoles, six fire-crackers, a kitten with only
one eye, a brass door-knob, a dog-collar—but no dog—the handle
of a knife, four pieces of orange-peel, and a dilapidated old window-
sash. He had had a nice, good, idle time all the while—plenty of
company—and the fence had three coats of whitewash on it! If
he hadn't run out of whitewash, he would have bankrupted every
boy in the village.

Tom said to himself that it was not such a hollow world after
all. He had discovered a great law of human action, without
knowing it, namely, that, in order to make a man or a boy covet
a thing, it is only necessary to make the thing difficult to attain.
If he had been a great and wise philosopher, like the writer of
this book, he would now have comprehended that work consists
of whatever a body is obliged to do, and that play consists of
whatever a body is not obliged to do. And this would help him
to understand why constructing artificial flowers, or performing
on a tread-mill, is work, whilst rolling nine-pins or climbing

Mont Blanc is only amusement. There are wealthy gentlemen in England who drive four-horse passenger-coaches twenty or thirty miles on a daily line, in the summer, because the privilege costs them considerable money; but if they were offered wages for the service that would turn it into work, and then they would resign.

EMERSON

RALPH WALDO EMERSON (1803–82), a great American writer, was born at Boston and educated at Harvard University He was at first a Unitarian minister, but he preferred to teach mankind through lectures, essays and poems rather than from the pulpit He visited England and became a friend and correspondent of Carlyle. His chief works are *Essays, English Traits* and *Representative Men*

THE RHODORA
On being asked, whence is the flower?

In May, when sea-winds pierced our solitudes,
I found the fresh Rhodora in the woods,
Spreading its leafless blooms in a damp nook,
To please the desert and the sluggish brook
The purple petals, fallen in the pool,
Made the black water with their beauty gay,
Here might the red-bird come his plumes to cool,
And court the flower that cheapens his array
Rhodora ! if the sages ask thee why
This charm is wasted on the earth and sky,
Tell them, dear, that if eyes were made for seeing,
Then Beauty is its own excuse for being:
Why thou wert there, O rival of the rose !
I never thought to ask, I never knew
But, in my simple ignorance, suppose
The self-same Power that brought me there brought you

SIR THOMAS MORE and WILLIAM ROPER

THOMAS MORE (1478 -1535) was born in London, the son of a judge and educated at a school in London and at Oxford He became a lawyer and rose to high office. He was chosen Speaker of the House of Commons and made Lord Chancellor in succession to Wolsey He privately disapproved of Henry VIII's declaring himself Head of the Church The king tried to force him to make a public declaration of approval More refused to take the oath put to him, and, after a year's harsh imprisonment, was executed. His best and best-known book is *Utopia*, written in Latin and not translated into English till many years after his death One of his children, Margaret, married William Roper, a young Kentish lawyer, who compiled a very charming account of More's simple and attractive life The passage that follows is taken from this book.

THE EXECUTION OF SIR THOMAS MORE

Now, after his arraignment, departed he from the bar to the Tower again, led by Sir William Kingston, a tall, strong, and comely knight, Constable of the Tower, and his very dear friend. Who when he had brought him from Westminster to the Old Swan towards the Tower, there with a heavy heart, the tears running down his cheeks, bade him farewell Sir Thomas More, seeing him so sorrowful, comforted him with as good words as he could, saying: "Good Master Kingston, trouble not yourself, but be of good cheer: for I will pray for you and my good lady your wife, that we may meet in heaven together, where we shall be merry for ever and ever." Soon after Sir William Kingston, talking with me of Sir Thomas More, said: "In good faith, Mr Roper, I was ashamed of myself that at my departing from your father I found my heart so feeble and his so strong, that he was fain to comfort me that should rather have comforted him." When Sir Thomas More came from Westminster to the Tower-ward again, his daughter, my wife, desirous to see her father, whom she thought she would never see in this world after, and also to have his final blessing, gave attendance about the Tower Wharf, where she knew he should pass by, before he could enter into the Tower There tarrying his coming, as soon as she saw him, after his blessing upon her knees reverently received, she hasting towards him, without consideration or care of herself, pressing in amongst the midst of the throng and company of the guard, that with halberds and bills went round about him, hastily ran to him, and there openly in sight of them all, embraced him, and took him about the neck and kissed him. Who well liking her most natural and dear daughterly affection towards him, gave her his fatherly blessing, and many godly words of comfort besides From whom after she was departed, she not satisfied with the former sight of her dear father, and like one that had forgotten herself, being all ravished with the entire love of her dear father, having respect neither to herself, nor to the press of people and multitude that were there about him, suddenly turned back again, ran to him as before, took him about the neck, and divers times kissed him most lovingly; and at last, with a full and heavy heart, was fain to depart from him: the beholding whereof was to many of them that were present thereat so lamentable, that it made them for very sorrow thereof to weep and mourn.

So remained Sir Thomas More in the Tower, more than a seven-night after his judgment. From whence, the day before he suffered, his sent his shirt of hair, not willing to have it seen, to my wife, his dearly beloved daughter, and a letter written with a coal[1] (contained in the foresaid book of his works), plainly expressing the fervent desire he had to suffer on the morrow, in these words following: "I cumber you, good Margret, much, but would be sorry if it should be any longer than to-morrow. For to-morrow is St Thomas even, and the Utas[2] of St Peter, and therefore to-morrow I long to go to God: it were a day very meet and convenient for me. Dear Megg, I never liked your manner better towards me than when you kissed me last. For I like when daughterly love and dear charity hath no leisure to look to worldly courtesy." And so upon the next morrow, being Tuesday, Saint Thomas his eve, and the Utas of Saint Peter, in the year of our Lord 1535, according as he in his letter the day before had wished, early in the morning came to him Sir Thomas Pope, his singular good friend, on message from the king and his council, that he should before nine of the clock of the same morning suffer death; and that, therefore, he should forthwith prepare himself thereto. "Master Pope," quoth Sir Thomas More, "for your good tidings I heartily thank you. I have been always much bounden to the king's highness for the benefits and honours that he had still from time to time most bountifully heaped upon me; and yet more bounden am I to his grace for putting me into this place, where I have had convenient time and space to have remembrance of my end. And so help me God, most of all, Master Pope, am I bounden to his highness that it pleaseth him so shortly to rid me out of the miseries of this wretched world, and therefore will I

---

[1] with a piece of charcoal—he had been deprived of writing material.
[2] Octave—the eighth day after a feast.

not fail earnestly to pray for his grace, both here, and also in the world to come." "The king's pleasure is farther," quoth Master Pope, "that at your execution you shall not use many words." "Master Pope," quoth he, "you do well to give me warning of his grace's pleasure, for otherwise, at that time, had I purposed somewhat to have spoken; but of no matter wherewith his grace, or any other, should have had cause to be offended. Nevertheless, whatsoever I intended, I am ready obediently to conform myself to his grace's commandment; and I beseech you, good Master Pope, to be a mean to his highness, that my daughter Margaret may be at my burial." "The king is content already," quoth Master Pope, "that your wife, children and other friends shall have liberty to be present thereat." "Oh, how much beholden then," said Sir Thomas More, "am I unto his grace, that unto my poor burial vouchsafeth to have so gracious consideration!" Wherewithal Master Pope, taking his leave of him, could not refrain from weeping. Which Sir Thomas More perceiving, comforted him in this wise: "Quiet yourself, good Master Pope, and be not discomforted, for I trust that we shall once in heaven see each other full merrily, where we shall be sure to live and love together, in joyful bliss eternally." Upon whose departure, Sir Thomas More, as one that had been invited to some solemn feast, changed himself into his best apparel. Which Master Lieutenant espying, advised him to put it off, saying, that he that should have it was but a javill[1]. "What, Master Lieutenant?" quoth he, "shall I account him a javill that will do me this day so singular a benefit? Nay, I assure you, were it cloth of gold, I should think it well bestowed on him, as Saint Cyprian did, who gave his executioner thirty pieces of gold." And albeit, at length, through Master Lieutenant's importunate persuasion, he altered his apparel, yet, after the example of the holy Martyr St Cyprian, did he, of that little money that was left him send an angel of gold to his executioner. And so was he by Master Lieutenant brought out of the Tower, and from thence led towards the place of execution. Where, going up the scaffold, which was so weak that it was ready to fall, he said merrily to the Lieutenant: "I pray you, Master Lieutenant, see me safe up, and for my coming down let me shift for myself" Then desired he all the

---

[1] a common fellow

people thereabout to pray for him, and to bear witness with him, that he should now there suffer death in and for the faith of the holy Catholic Church. Which done, he kneeled down, and, after his prayers said, turned to the executioner with a cheerful countenance, and said unto him: "Pluck up thy spirits, man, and be not afraid to do thine office. my neck is very short, take heed, therefore, thou strike not away, for saving of thine honesty." So passed Sir Thomas More out of this world to God, upon the very same day which he most desired. Soon after his death came intelligence thereof to the Emperor Charles. Whereupon he sent for Sir Thomas Eliott, our English ambassador, and said to him: "My Lord ambassador, we understand that the king your master hath put his faithful servant, and grave wise councillor, Sir Thomas More, to death." Whereupon Sir Thomas Eliott answered that "he understood nothing thereof." "Well," said the Emperor, "it is too true: and this will we say, that had we been master of such a servant, of whose doings ourselves have had these many years no small experience, we would rather have lost the best city of our dominions, than have lost such a worthy councillor."

TENNYSON

BREAK, BREAK, BREAK

Break, break, break,
  On thy cold grey stones, O Sea!
And I would that my tongue could utter
  The thoughts that arise in me

O well for the fisherman's boy,
  That he shouts with his sister at play!
O well for the sailor lad,
  That he sings in his boat on the bay!

And the stately ships go on
  To their haven under the hill;
But O for the touch of a vanish'd hand,
  And the sound of a voice that is still!

Break, break, break,
 At the foot of thy crags, O Sea!
But the tender grace of a day that is dead
 Will never come back to me.

KINGLAKE

Alexander William Kinglake (1809–91) was born near Taunton and educated at Eton and Cambridge. He travelled to the east in 1835 and wrote an account of his adventures in *Eōthen* (meaning "from the east"), one of the most delightful books of travel ever written. It is from this book that the following passage is taken. He also wrote a long history of the Crimean war

CAIRO TO SUEZ

The "dromedary" of Egypt and Syria is not the two-humped animal described by that name in books of natural history, but is, in fact, of the same family as the camel, to which it stands in about the same relation as a racer to a cart-horse. The fleetness and endurance of this creature are extraordinary. It is not usual to force him into a gallop, and I fancy from his make that it would be quite impossible for him to maintain that pace for any length of time; but the animal is on so large a scale, that the jog-trot at which he is generally ridden implies a progress of perhaps ten or twelve miles an hour, and this pace, it is said, he can keep up incessantly, without food, or water, or rest, for three whole days and nights

Of the two dromedaries which I had obtained for this journey, I mounted one myself, and put Dthemetri on the other. My plan was to ride on with Dthemetri to Suez as rapidly as the fleetness of the beasts would allow, and to let Mysseri (who was still weak from the effects of his late illness) come quietly on with the camels and baggage.

The trot of the dromedary is a pace terribly disagreeable to the rider, until he becomes a little accustomed to it; but after the first half-hour I so far schooled myself to this new exercise, that I felt capable of keeping it up (though not without aching limbs) for several hours together. Now, therefore, I was anxious to dart forward, and annihilate at once the whole space that divided me from the Red Sea. Dthemetri, however, could not get on at all. Every attempt which he made to trot seemed to threaten the utter dislocation of his whole frame, and indeed I doubt whether any one of Dthemetri's age (nearly forty, I think), and unaccustomed to such exercise, could have borne it at all easily; besides, the dromedary which fell to his lot was evidently a very bad one; he every now and then came to a dead stop, and coolly knelt down, as though suggesting that the rider had better get off at once and abandon the attempt as one that was utterly hopeless.

When for the third or fourth time I saw Dthemetri thus planted, I lost my patience, and went on without him. For about two hours, I think, I advanced without once looking behind me. I then paused, and cast my eyes back to the western horizon. There was no sign of Dthemetri, nor of any other living creature. This I expected, for I knew that I must have far out-distanced all my followers. I had ridden away from my party merely by way of gratifying my impatience, and with the intention of stopping as soon as I felt tired, until I was overtaken. I now observed, however (this I had not been able to do whilst advancing so rapidly), that the track which I had been following was seemingly the track of only one or two camels. I did not fear that I had diverged very largely from the true route, but still I could not feel any reasonable certainty that my party would follow any line of march within sight of me.

I had to consider, therefore, whether I should remain where I was, upon the chance of seeing my people come up, or whether I would push on alone, and find my way to Suez. I had now learned that I could not rely upon the continued guidance of any track, but I knew that (if maps were right) the point for which I was bound bore just due east of Cairo, and I thought that, although I might miss the line leading most directly to Suez, I could not well fail to find my way sooner or later to the Red Sea. The worst of it was that I had no provision of food or water with me, and already I was beginning to feel thirst. I deliberated for a minute, and then determined that I would abandon all hope of seeing my party again in the Desert, and would push forward as rapidly as possible towards Suez.

It was not, I confess, without a sensation of awe that I swept with my sight the vacant round of the horizon, and remembered that I was all alone, and unprovisioned in the midst of the arid waste; but this very awe gave tone and zest to the exultation with which I felt myself launched. Hitherto, in all my wandering, I had been under the care of other people—sailors, Tatars, guides, and dragomen had watched over my welfare, but now at last I was here in this African desert, and I *myself, and no other, had charge of my life*. I liked the office well. I had the greatest part of the day before me, a very fair dromedary, a fur pelisse, and a brace of pistols, but no bread and no water; for that I must ride —and ride I did.

For several hours I urged forward my beast at a rapid though steady pace, but now the pangs of thirst began to torment me. I did not relax my pace, however, and I had not suffered long when a moving object appeared in the distance before me. The intervening space was soon traversed, and I found myself approaching a Bedouin Arab mounted on a camel, attended by another Bedouin on foot. They stopped. I saw that, as usual, there hung from the pack-saddle of the camel a large skin water-flask, which seemed to be well filled. I steered my dromedary close up alongside of the mounted Bedouin, caused my beast to kneel down, then alighted, and keeping the end of the halter in my hand, went up to the mounted Bedouin without speaking, took hold of his water-flask, opened it, and drank long and deep from its leathern lips. Both of the Bedouins stood fast in amazement and mute horror; and really, if they had never happened to see an European before, the apparition was enough to startle them. To see for the first time a coat and a waistcoat, with the semblance of a white human head at the top, and for this ghastly figure to come swiftly out of the horizon upon a fleet dromedary, approach them silently and with a demoniacal smile, and drink a deep draught from their water-flask—this was enough to make the Bedouins stare a little; they, in fact, stared a great deal—not as Europeans stare, with a restless and puzzled expression of countenance, but with features all fixed and rigid, and with still, glassy eyes. Before they had time to get decomposed from their state of petrifaction I had remounted my dromedary, and was darting away towards the east.

Without pause or remission of pace I continued to press forward, but after a while I found to my confusion that the slight track which had hitherto guided me now failed altogether. I began to fear that I must have been all along following the course of some wandering Bedouins, and I felt that if this were the case, my fate was a little uncertain.

I had no compass with me, but I determined upon the eastern point of the horizon as accurately as I could by reference to the sun, and so laid down for myself a way over the pathless sands.

But now my poor dromedary, by whose life and strength I held my own, began to show signs of distress: a thick, clammy, and glutinous kind of foam gathered about her lips, and piteous sobs burst from her bosom in the tones of human misery. I doubted for a moment whether I would give her a little rest, a relaxation of pace, but I decided that I would not, and continued to push forward as steadily as before.

The character of the country became changed. I had ridden away from the level tracts, and before me now, and on either side, there were vast hills of sand and calcined rocks, that interrupted my progress and baffled my doubtful road, but I did my best. With rapid steps I swept round the base of the hills, threaded the winding hollows, and at last, as I rose in my swift course to the crest of a lofty ridge, Thalatta! Thalatta! by Jove! I saw the sea!

My tongue can tell where to find a clue to many an old pagan creed, because that (distinctly from all mere admiration of the beauty belonging to nature's works) I acknowledge a sense of mystical reverence when first I look, to see some illustrious feature of the globe—some coast-line of ocean, some mighty river or dreary mountain range, the ancient barrier of kingdoms. But the Red Sea! It might well claim my earnest gaze by force of the great Jewish migration which connects it with the history of our own religion From this very ridge, it is likely enough, the panting Israelites first saw that shining inlet of the sea. Ay! ay! but moreover, and best of all, that beckoning sea assured my eyes, and proved how well I had marked out the east for my path, and gave me good promise that sooner or later the time would come for me to rest and drink It was distant, the sea, but I felt my own strength, and I had *heard* of the strength of dromedaries. I pushed forward as eagerly as though I had spoiled the Egyptians and were flying from Pharaoh's police.

I had not yet been able to discover any symptoms of Suez, but after a while I descried in the distance a large, blank, isolated building. I made towards this, and in time got down to it. The building was a fort, and had been built there for the protection of a well which it contained within its precincts. A cluster of small huts adhered to the fort, and in a short time I was receiving the hospitality of the inhabitants, who were grouped upon the sands near their hamlet. To quench the fires of my throat with about a gallon of muddy water, and to swallow a little of the food placed before me, was the work of few minutes, and before the astonishment of my hosts had even begun to subside, I was pursuing my onward journey. Suez, I found, was still three hours distant, and the sun going down in the west warned me that I must find some other guide to keep me in the right direction. This guide I found in the most fickle and uncertain of the elements. For some hours the wind had been freshening, and it now blew a violent gale; it blew not fitfully and in squalls, but with such remarkable steadiness, that I felt convinced it would blow from the same quarter for several hours. When the sun set, therefore, I carefully looked for the point from which the wind was blowing, and found that it came from the very west, and was blowing exactly in the direction of my route. I had nothing to do therefore but to go straight to leeward; and this was not difficult, for the gale blew with such immense force, that if I diverged at all from its line I instantly felt the pressure of the blast on the side towards which I was deviating. Very soon after sunset there came on complete darkness, but the strong wind guided me well, and sped me, too, on my way.

I had pushed on for about, I think, a couple of hours after nightfall when I saw the glimmer of a light in the distance, and this I ventured to hope must be Suez. Upon approaching it, however, I found that it was only a solitary fort, and I passed on without stopping.

On I went, still riding down the wind, when an unlucky accident occurred, for which, if you like, you can have your laugh against me. I have told you already what sort of lodging it is that you have upon the back of a camel. You ride the dromedary in the same fashion; you are perched rather than seated on a bunch of carpets or quilts upon the summit of the hump. It happened that my dromedary veered rather suddenly from her onward course. Meeting the movement, I mechanically turned my left wrist as though I were holding a bridle rein, for the complete darkness prevented my eyes from reminding me that I had nothing but a halter in my hand. The expected resistance failed, for the halter was hanging upon that side of the dromedary's neck towards which I was slightly leaning. I toppled over, head foremost, and then went falling and falling through air, till my crown came whang against the ground. And the ground too was perfectly hard (compacted sand), but the thickly wadded headgear which I wore for protection against the sun saved my life. The notion of my being able to get up again after falling head-foremost from such an immense height seemed to me at first too paradoxical to be acted upon, but I soon found that I was not a bit hurt. My dromedary utterly vanished. I looked round me, and saw the glimmer of a light in the fort which I had lately passed, and I began to work my way back in that direction. The violence of the gale made it hard for me to force my way towards the west, but I succeeded at last in regaining the fort. To this, as to the other fort which I had passed, there was attached a cluster of huts, and I soon found myself surrounded by a group of villainous, gloomy-looking fellows. It was a horrid bore for me to have to swagger and look big at a time when I felt so particularly small on account of my tumble and my lost dromedary; but there was no help for it, I had no Dthemetri now to "strike terror" for me. I knew hardly one word of Arabic, but somehow or other I contrived to announce it as my absolute will and pleasure that these fellows should find me the means of gaining Suez. They acceded, and having a donkey, they saddled it for me, and appointed one of their number to attend me on foot.

I afterwards found that these fellows were not Arabs, but Algerine refugees, and that they bore the character of being sad scoundrels. They justified this imputation to some extent on the following day. They allowed Mysseri with my baggage and the camels to pass unmolested, but an Arab lad belonging to the party happened to lag a little way in the rear, and him (if they were not maligned) these rascals stripped and robbed. Low indeed is the state of bandit morality when men will allow the sleek traveller with well-laden camels to pass in quiet, reserving

their spirit of enterprise for the tattered turban of a miserable
boy .

I reached Suez at last. The British agent, though roused from
his midnight sleep, received me in his home with the utmost
kindness and hospitality. Oh! by Jove, how delightful it was to
lie on fair sheets, and to dally with sleep, and to wake, and to
sleep, and to wake once more, for the sake of sleeping again!

WILLIAM MORRIS

WILLIAM MORRIS (1834–96) was born at Walthamstow and educated at
Marlborough and Oxford He is famous as a writer of romances in prose and
verse, as a craftsman concerned in the design and production of beautiful
furniture, stained glass, books and fabrics, and as a hard worker in the cause
of social reform. Among his best known long poems are *The Life and Death
of Jason*, *The Earthly Paradise* (a collection of twenty-four old stories in
narrative verse), and *The Story of Sigurd the Volsung and the Fall of the
Niblungs* Among his prose works may be named *News from Nowhere*.
a story of England in the future, made happy and beautiful, *The Roots of
the Mountains* and *The Story of the Glittering Plain* Morris was fond of
Old Norse literature and many of his writings deal with northern subjects.
The passage that follows is taken from *The Life and Death of Jason* Jason
has voyaged perilously in his ship *Argo* to recover the Golden Fleece from
King Æetes of Colchis The crafty king seeks to slay the hero, and sets him
the task of taming the Brazen Bulls, but Medea, the king's daughter, has
fallen in love with him, and gives him a magic liquid to protect him from
the fire of the Brazen Bulls and a crystal ball to throw amongst the
Earthborn

JASON AND THE GOLDEN FLEECE

I

Now when she woke again the bright sun glared
In at the window, and the trumpets blared,
Shattering the sluggish air of that hot day,
For fain the king would be upon his way
Then straight she called her maidens, who forthright
Did due observance to her body white,
And clad her in the raiment of a queen,
And round her crown they set a wreath of green.
But she descending, came into the hall,
And found her father clad in royal pall,

Holding the ivory rod of sovereignty,
And Jason and his folk were standing by.
   Now was Æetes saying: "Minyæ,
And you, my people, who are here by me,
Take heed, that by his wilful act to-day
This man will perish, neither will I slay
One man among you. Nay, Prince, if you will,
A safe return I give unto you still."
   But Jason answered, smiling in his joy:—
"Once more, Æetes, nay. Against this toy
My life is pledged, let all go to the end "
Then, lifting up his eyes, he saw his friend,
Made fresh and lovelier by her quiet rest,
And set his hand upon his mailéd breast,
Where in its covering lay the crystal ball.
   But the king said: "Then let what will fall, fall!
Since time it is that we were on the way;
And thou, O daughter, shalt be there to-day,
And see thy father's glory once more shown
Before our folk and those the wind has blown
From many lands to see this play played out."
   Then raised the Colchians a mighty shout,
And doubtful grew the Minyæ of the end,
Unwitting who on that day was their friend
But down the hall the king passed, who did hold
Medea's hand, and on a car of gold
They mounted, drawn anigh the carven door,
And spearmen of the Colchians went before
And followed after, and the Minyæ
Set close together followed solemnly,
Headed by Jason, at the heels of these.
   So passed they through the streets and palaces
Thronged with much folk, and o'er the bridges passed,
And to the open country came at last,
Nor there went far, but turning to the right,
Into a close they came, where there were dight
Long galleries about the fateful stead,
Built all of marble fair and roofed with lead,
And carved about with stories of old time,

Framed all about with golden lines of rhyme.
Moreover, midmost was an image made
Of mighty Mars who maketh kings afraid,
That looked down on an altar builded fair,
Wherefrom already did a bright fire glare
And made the hot air glassy with its heat.
    So in the gallery did the king take seat
With fair Medea, and the Colchians stood
Hedging the twain in with a mighty wood
Of spears and axes, while the Minyæ
Stood off a space the fated things to see.
    Ugly and rugged was that spot of ground,
And with an iron wall was closed around,
And at the further end a monstrous cage
Of iron bars, shut in the stupid rage
Of those two beasts, and therefrom ever came
The flashing and the scent of sulphurous flame,
As with their brazen clangorous bellowing
They hailed the coming of the Colchian king;
Nor was there one of the seafaring men
But trembled, gazing on the deadly pen,
But Jason only, who before the rest
Shone like a star, having upon his breast
A golden corslet from the treasury
Of wise King Phineus by the doubtful sea,
By an Egyptian wrought who would not stay
At Salmydessa more than for a day,
But on that day the wondrous breast-plate wrought,
Which, with good will and strong help, Jason bought;
And from that treasury his golden shoe
Came, and his thighs the king's gift covered too;
But on his head his father's helm was set
Wreathed round with bay leaves, and his sword lay yet
Within the scabbard, while his ungloved hand
Bore nought within it but an olive wand.
    Now King Æetes well beholding him,
Fearless of mien and so unmatched of limb,
Trembled a little in his heart as now
He bade the horn-blowers the challenge blow,

But thought, "what strength can help him—or what art,
Or which of all the Gods be on his part?"
Impious, who knew not through what doubtful days,
E'en from his birth, and perilous rough ways
Juno had brought him safely, nor indeed
Of his own daughter's quivering lips took heed,
And restless hands wherein the God so wrought,
The wise man seeing her had known her thought.
    Now Jason, when he heard the challenge blow,
Across the evil fallow 'gan to go
With face beyond its wont in nowise pale,
Nor footstep faltering, if that might avail
The doomed man aught; so to the cage he came,
Whose bars now glowed red hot with spouted flame,
In many a place, nor doubted any one
Who there beheld him that his days were done,
Except his love alone, and even she,
Sickening with doubt and terror, scarce could see
The hero draw the brazen bolt aside
And throw the glowing wicket open wide.

    But he alone, apart from his desire,
Stood unarmed, facing those two founts of fire,
Yet feared not aught, for hope and fear were dead
Within his heart, and utter hardihead
Had Juno set there; but the awful beasts
Beholding now the best of all their feasts,
Roared in their joy and fury, till from sight
They and the prince were hidden by the white,
Thick rolling clouds of sulphurous pungent smoke,
Through which upon the blinded man they broke
    But when within a yard of him they came,
Baffled they stopped, still bellowing, and the flame
Still spouting out from nostril and from mouth,
As from some island mountain in the south
The trembling mariners behold it cast;
But still to right and left of him it passed,
Breaking upon him as cool water might,
Nor harming more, except that from his sight

All corners of the cage were hidden now,
Nor knew he where to seek the brazen plough;
As to and fro about the quivering cage
The monsters rushed in blind and helpless rage.
   But as he doubted, to his eyes alone
Within the place a golden light outshone,
Scattering the clouds of smoke, and he beheld
Once more the Goddess who his head upheld
In rough Anaurus on that other tide;
She, smiling on him, beckoned, and 'gan glide
With rosy feet across the fearful floor,
Breathing cool odours round her, till a door
She opened to him in the iron wall,
Through which he passed, and found a grisly stall
Of iron still, and at one end of it,
By glimmering lamps with greenish flame half lit,
Beheld the yoke and shining plough he sought;
Which, seizing straight, by mighty strength he brought
Unto the door, nor found the Goddess there,
Who in the likeness of a damsel fair,
Colchian Metharma, through the spearmen passed,
Bearing them wine, and causeless terror cast
Into their foolish hearts, nor spared to go
And 'mid the close seafaring ranks to sow
Good hope of joyful ending, and then stood
Behind the maid unseen, and brought the blood
Back to her cheeks and trembling lips and wan,
With thoughts of things unknown to maid or man.
   Meanwhile upon the foreheads of the twain
Had Jason cast the yoke with little pain,
And drove them now with shouts out through the door
Which in such guise ne'er had they passed before,
For never were they made the earth to till,
But rather, feeding fat, to work the will
Of some all-knowing man; but now they went
Like any peasant's beasts, tamed by the scent
Of those new herbs Medea's hand had plucked,
Whose roots from evil earth strange power had sucked.
   Now in the open field did Jason stand

And to the plough-stilts set his unused hand,
And down betwixt them lustily he bent;
Then the bulls drew, and the bright ploughshare sent
The loathly fallow up on the right side,
Whilst o'er their bellowing shrilly Jason cried:—
"Draw nigh, O King, and thy new ploughman see,
Then mayst thou make me shepherd, too, to thee;
Nor doubt thou, doing so, from out thy flock
To lose but one, who ne'er shall bring thee stock,
Or ram or ewe, nor doubt the grey wolf, King,
Wood-haunting bear, dragon, or such like thing.
Ah the straight furrow! how it mindeth me
Of the smooth parting of the land-locked sea
Over against Euboea, and this fire
Of the fair altar where my joyful sire
Will pour out wine to Neptune when I come
Not empty-handed back unto my home."

Such mocks he said; but when the sunlight broke
Upon his armour through the sulphurous smoke,
And showed the lengthening furrow cutting through
The ugly fallow as anigh they drew,
The joyful Minyæ gave a mighty shout;
But pale the king sat with brows knit for doubt,
Muttering: "Whose counsel hast thou taken, then,
To do this thing, which not the best of men
Could do unholpen of some sorcery?
Whoso it is, wise were he now to die
Ere yet I know him, since for many a day
Vainly for death I hope to hear him pray."
Meanwhile, askance Medea eyed the king,
Thinking nought safe until that everything
Was finished in the Colchian land, and she
No more beheld its shores across the sea;
But he, beholding her pale visage, thought
Grief like to his such paleness on her brought,
And turning to her, said: "How pale thou art!
Let not this first foil go unto thine heart
Too deeply, since thou knowest certainly,

One way or other this vain fool must die."
"Father," she said, "a doubt is on me still,
Some God this is come here our wealth to spill;
Nor is this first thing easier than the rest."
Then stammering, she said: "Were it not best
To give him that which he must have at last,
Before he slays us?" But Æetes cast
A sharp glance at her, and a pang shot through
His weary heart as half the truth he knew.
But for one moment, and he made reply
In passionate words: "Then, daughter, let me die!
And, ere I die, behold thee led along
A wretched slave to suffer grief and wrong
In far-off lands, and Æa at thy back
Nought but a huge flame hiding woe and wrack,
Before from out my willing open hand
This wonder, and the safeguard of my land
A God shall take; and such this man is not.
What! dost thou think because his eyes are hot
On tender maidens he must be a God?
Or that because firmly this field he trod
Well-fenced with magic? Were he like to me,
Grey-haired and lean, what Godhead wouldst thou see
In such an one? Hold, then, thy peace of this,
And thou shalt see thy God full widely miss
The mark he aims at, when from out the earth
Spring up those brothers of an evil birth."
    And therewithal he gazed at her, and thought
To see the rosy flush by such words brought
Across her face; as in the autumn eve,
Just as the sun's last half begins to leave
The shivering world, both east and west are red.—
But calm and pale she turned about her head,
And said. "My father, neither were these words
My words, nor would I struggle with my lords;
Thou art full wise, whatso thine heart would have
That do, and heed me not, who fain would save
This glory of thy kingdom and of thee.
But now look up, and soothly thou shalt see

Mars' acre tilled: the field is ready then,
Bid them bring forth the seed that beareth men."
  Again with her last words the shouts out-broke
From the seafarers, for, beside the yoke,
Before Mars' altar did Prince Jason stand,
Holding the wand of olive in his hand,
And on the new-turned furrow shone the sun
Behind him, and his half-day's work was done.
  And now another marvel: for, behold,
As at the furrow's end he slacked his hold
Upon the plough-stilts, all the bellowing
Wherewith the beasts had made the grim close ring,
Fell suddenly, and all the fire died
That they were wont erewhile to scatter wide
From mouth and nostril, and their loins and knees
Stiffened, and they grew nought but images
Lifelike but lifeless, wonderful but dead,
Such as he makes, who many a day hath fed
His furnace with the beechwood, when the clay
Has grown beneath his deft hands day by day
And all is ready for the casting, then
Such things as these he makes for royal men.
  But 'mid the shouts turned Jason to the king,
And said: "Fair sir, behold a wondrous thing,
And since these beasts have been content to stay
Before Mars' altar, from this very day
His should they be if they were mine to give."
  "O Jason," said the king, "well mayst thou live
For many a day, since thou this deed hast done,
But for the Gods, not unto any one
Will I give gifts; but let them take from me
What once they gave, if so the thing must be.
But do thou take this sack from out my hand
And cast its seed about the new-tilled land,
And watch the issue; and keep words till then,
I counsel thee, O luckiest of men."

  Then Jason took the sack, and with it went
About that field new turned, and broadcast sent

The white teeth scattering, but or ere he came
Back to the altar, and the flickering flame,
He heard from 'neath the earth a muttered sound
That grew and grew, till all that piece of ground
Swelled into little hillocks, like as where
A stricken field was foughten, but that there
Quiet the heroes' bones lie underneath
The quivering grasses and the dusky heath;
But now these heaps the labouring earth upthrew
About Mars' acre, ever greater grew,
And still increased the noise, till none could hear
His fellow speak, and paleness and great fear
Fell upon all; and Jason only stood
As stands the stout oak in the poplar wood
When winds are blowing.
                                Then he saw the mounds
Bursten asunder, and the muttered sounds
Changed into loud strange shouts and warlike clang,
As with freed feet at last the earth-born sprang
On to the tumbling earth, and the sunlight
Shone on bright arms clean ready for the fight.
   But terribly they showed, for through the place
Not one there was but had his staring face,
With great wide eyes, and lips in a set smile,
Turned full on Jason, who, for a short while,
Forgot indeed Medea's warning word,
And from its golden sheath half drew his sword,
But then, remembering all, cried valiantly:
"New born ye are—new slain too shall ye be,
Take this, and round about it read your doom,
And bid them make new dwellings in the tomb,
Wherefrom ye came, nor ever should have passed."
   Therewith the ball among the host he cast,
Standing to watch what next that folk would do.
But he the ball had smitten turned unto
The one who stood by him and like a cup
Shattered his head; then the next lifted up
His axe and slew the slayer, and straightway
Among the rest began a deadly fray.

No man gave back a foot, no breathing space
One took or gave within that dreadful place,
But where the vanquished stood there was he slain,
And straight the conquering arm was raised again
To meet its match and in its turn to fall.
No tide was there of fainting and recall,
No quivering pennon o'er their heads to flit,
Nor name or eager shout called over it,
No groan of pain, and no despairing cry
From him who knows his time has come to die,
But passionless each bore him in that fight,
Scarce otherwise than as a smith might smite
On sounding iron or bright glittering brass.
  So, little by little, did the clamour pass
As one by one each fell down in his place,
Until at last, midmost the bloody space,
One man was left, alive but wounded sore,
Who, staring round about and seeing no more
His brothers' spears against him, fixed his eyes
Upon the queller of those mysteries.
Then dreadfully they gleamed, and with no word,
He tottered towards him with uplifted sword.
But scarce he made three paces down the field,
Ere chill death reached his heart, and on his shield
Clattering he fell. So satiate of fight
Quickly the earth-born were, and their delight
With what it fed on perished, and one hour
Ripened the deadly fruit of that fell flower.
  Then Jason, mocking, cried unto the king:—
"O wonderful, indeed, must be the thing
Thou guardest with such wondrous guards as these;
Make no delay, therefore, but bring the keys
That I may see this dear delight of all."
  But on Æetes' face a change did fall,
As though a mask had been set over it,
And smiles of little meaning 'gan to flit
O'er his thin lips, as he spake out at last:—
"No haste, dear guest, for surely now is passed
All enmity from 'twixt us, since I know

How like a God thou art; and thou shalt go
To-morrow to thy ship, to make for Greece,
And with no trial more, bear back the fleece
Along our streets, and like no conquered thing,
But with much scattered flowers and tabouring,
Bearing with it great gifts and all my love;
And in return, I pray thee, pray to Jove,
That I may have a few more years of life,
And end at last in honour, free from strife.
And now to-night be merry, and let time
Be clean forgotten, and bring Saturn's clime
And golden days upon our flower-crowned brows,
For of the unseen future what man knows?"

   "O King," said Jason, "for these words I praise
Thy wisdom much, and wish thee happy days.
And I will give thee honour as I can,
Naming thee ever as a noble man
Through all the lands I come to: and will take
Thy gifts, indeed, and thou, for Jason's sake,
Shalt have gifts too, whatso thy soul may wish,
From out our keel that has escaped the fish "

   So spake those wary foes, fair friends in look,
And so in words great gifts they gave and took,
And had small profit, and small loss thereby.
Nor less Medea feigned, but angrily
Regarded Jason, and across her brow
Drew close her veil, nor doubted the king now
Her faith and loyalty.
              So from the place
Back toward the town they turned at a soft pace,
In guise of folk that hold high festival,
Since straightly had Æetes bid that all
Should do the strangers pleasure on that day
But warily went Jason on the way,
And through his folk spread words, to take good heed
Of what might come, and ready be at need,
Nor yet to take Æetes for their friend,
Since even then he plotted how to end
Their quest and lives: therefore he bade them spare

The wine that night, nor look on damsels fair;
But that, the feast done, all should stealthily
Get to the quay, and round about to sea
Turn Argo's head, and wait like hounds in slip,
Holding the oars, within the hollow ship.

　"Nor doubt," said he, "that good and glorious
The end shall be, since all the Gods for us
Are fighting certainly: but should death come
Upon me in this land, then turn back home,
Nor wait till they shall lay your bones with mine,
Since now I think to go unto the shrine,
The while ye wait, and take therefrom the fleece,
Not all unholpen, and depart in peace,
While yet the barbarous king beholds us dead
In dreams alone, or through his waking head
The vile plots chase each other for our death."

　These things he said, but scarce above his breath,
Unto wise Nestor, who beside him went,
Who unto Butes straight the message sent,
And he to Phlias, so the words at last
Throughout the wondering seafarers had passed,
And so were all made ready for the night.

　But on that eve, with manifold delight,
Æetes feasted them in his fair hall;
But they, well knowing what might chance to fall,
Sat saying little, nor drank deep of wine;
Until at last the old king gave the sign
To break the feast up, and within a while
All seemed asleep throughout the mighty pile.

　All seemed asleep, but now Medea went
With beating heart to work out her intent,
Scarce doubtful of the end, since only two
In all the world, she and Æetes, knew
Where the keys were, far from the light of day,
Beneath the palace. So, in garments grey,
Like the soft creeping twilight did she go,
Until she reached a passage far below
The river, past whose oozing walls of stone

She and the king alone had ever gone.
   Now she, who thus far had come through the dark,
Stopped, and in haste striking a little spark
From something in her hand, lit up a lamp,
Whose light fell on an iron door, with damp
All rusted red, which with a key of brass
She opened, and there-through made haste to pass,
Shuddering a little, as her feet 'gan tread
Upon a dank cold floor, though overhead
High-arched the place was, fairly built enow.
   But she across the slippery floor did go
Unto the other wall, wherein was built
A little aumbrye, with a door o'er-gilt,
That with the story of King Athamas,
And Phryxus, and the ram all carven was.
There did she draw forth from her balmy breast
A yellow flowering herb, that straight she pressed
Upon the lock, low muttering the while;
But soon across her face there passed a smile,
As backward in the lock the bolts did turn,
And the door opened; then a golden urn
She saw within the aumbrye, whereon she
Drew out the thing she sought for eagerly,
The seven keys with sere-cloth done about.
Then through the dreary door did she pass out,
And made it fast, and went her way once more
Through the black darkness on from floor to floor.
   And so, being come to Jason, him she found
All armed, and ready; therefore, with no sound,
She beckoned him to follow, and the twain
Passed through the brazen doors, locked all in vain,
Such virtue had the herb Medea bore,
And passing, did they leave ajar each door,
To give more ease unto the Minyæ.
   So out into the fresh night silently
The lovers passed, the loveliest of the land;
But as they went, neither did hand touch hand,
Or face seek face; for, gladsome as they were,
Trembling with joy to be at last so near

The wished-for day, some God yet seemed to be
'Twixt the hard past and their felicity.

11

But when they reached the precinct of the God,
And on the hallowed turf their feet now trod,
Medea turned to Jason, and she said:—
"O love, turn round, and note the goodlihead
My father's palace shows beneath the stars.
Bethink thee of the men grown old in wars,
Who do my bidding; what delights I have,
How many ladies lie in wait to save
My life from toil and carefulness, and think
How sweet a cup I have been used to drink,
And how I cast it to the ground for thee.
Upon the day thou weariest of me,
I wish that thou mayst somewhat think of this,
And 'twixt thy new-found kisses, and the bliss
Of something sweeter than thine old delight,
Remember thee a little of this night
Of marvels, and this starlit, silent place,
And these two lovers standing face to face."
   "O love," he said, "by what thing shall I swear,
That while I live thou shalt not be less dear
Than thou art now?"
                    "Nay, sweet," she said, "let be;
Wert thou more fickle than the restless sea,
Still should I love thee, knowing thee for such;
Whom I know not, indeed, but fear the touch
Of Fortune's hand when she beholds our bliss,
And knows that nought is good to me but this.

   "But now be ready, for I long full sore
To hear the merry dashing of the oar,
And feel the freshness of the following breeze
That sets me free, and sniff the rough salt seas.

Look! yonder thou mayst see armed shadows steal
Down to the quays, the guiders of thy keel;
Now follow me, though little shalt thou do
To gain this thing, if Hecate be true
Unto her servant. Nay, draw not thy sword,
And, for thy life, speak not a single word
Until I bid thee, else may all be lost,
And of this game our lives yet pay the cost."
   Then toward the brazen temple-door she went,
Wherefrom, half-open, a faint gleam was sent;
For little need of lock it had forsooth,
Because its sleepless guardian knew no ruth,
And had no lust for precious things or gold,
Whom, drawing near, Jason could now behold,
As back Medea thrust the heavy door,
For prone he lay upon the gleaming floor,
Not moving, though his restless, glittering eyes
Left them no hope of wile or of surprise.
Hideous he was, where all things else were fair;
Dull-skinned, foul-spotted, with lank rusty hair
About his neck; and hooked yellow claws
Just showed from 'neath his belly and huge jaws,
Closed in the hideous semblance of a smile.
Then Jason shuddered, wondering with what guile
That fair king's daughter such a beast could tame,
And of his sheathed sword had but little shame.
   But being within the doors, both mantle grey
And heavy gown Medea cast away, .
And in thin clinging silk alone was clad,
And round her neck a golden chain she had,
Whereto was hung a harp of silver white.
Then the great dragon, at that glittering sight,
Raised himself up upon his loathly feet,
As if to meet her, while her fingers sweet
Already moved amongst the golden strings,
Preluding nameless and delicious things;
But now she beckoned Jason to her side,
For slowly towards them 'gan the beast to glide,
And when close to his love the hero came,

She whispered breathlessly. "On me the blame
If here we perish; if I give the word,
Then know that all is lost, and draw thy sword,
And manlike die in battle with the beast;
So dying shalt thou fail to see at least
This body thou desiredst so to see,
In thy despite here mangled wretchedly.
Peace, for he cometh, O thou Goddess bright,
What help wilt thou be unto me this night?"
　　So murmured she, while ceaselessly she drew
Her fingers through the strings, and fuller grew
The tinkling music, but the beast drawn nigh
Went slower still, and turning presently
Began to move around them in a ring.
And as he went, there fell a strange rattling
Of his dry scales; but as he turned, she turned,
Nor failed to meet the eyes that on her burned
With steadfast eyes, and, lastly, clear and strong
Her voice broke forth in sweet melodious song:—

　　　　"O evil thing, what brought thee here
　　To be a wonder and a fear
　　Unto the river-haunting folk?
　　Was it the God of Day that broke
　　The shadow of thy windless trees,
　　Gleaming from golden palaces,
　　And shod with light, and armed with light,
　　Made thy slime stone, and day thy night,
　　And drove thee forth unwillingly
　　Within his golden house to lie?
　　　　"Or was it the slim messenger,
　　Who, treading softly, free from fear
　　Beguiled thee with his smiling face
　　From out thy dim abiding place,
　　To follow him and set thee down
　　Midst of this twice-washed royal town?
　　　　"Or, was it rather the dread Lord
　　Who slayeth without spear or sword,
　　And with the flower-culling maid

Of Enna, dwelleth in the shade,
Who, with stern voice compelling thee,
Hath set thee here, our bane to be?
    "Or was it Venus, seeking far
A sleepless guard 'gainst grief and war,
Who, journeying through thy dismal land,
Beside the heavy lake did stand,
And with no word, but very sight
Of tender limbs and bosom white,
Drew forth thy scaly feet and hard,
To follow over rock and shard?
    "Or rather, thy dull, waveless lake
Didst thou not leave for her dread sake,
Who, passing swift from glade to glade,
The forest-dwellers makes afraid
With shimmering of her silver bow
And dreadful arrows? Even so
I bid thee now to yield to me,
Her maid, who overmastered thee,
The Three-formed dreadful one who reigns
In heaven and the fiery plains,
But on the green earth best of all.
    "Lo, now thine upraised crest let fall,
Relax thy limbs, let both thine eyes
Be closed, and bestial fantasies
Fill thy dull head till dawn of day
And we are far upon our way."

As thus she sung the beast seemed not to hear
Her words at first, but ever drew anear,
Circling about them, and Medea's face
Grew pale unto the lips, though still the place
Rung with the piercing sweetness of her song;
But slower soon he dragged his length along,
And on his limbs he tottered, till at last
All feebly by the wondering prince he passed,
And whining to Medea's feet he crept,
With eyes half closed, as though well-nigh he slept,
And there before her laid his head adown;

Who, shuddering, on his wrinkled neck and brown
Set her white foot, and whispered: "Haste, O love!
Behold the keys; haste! while the Gods above
Are friendly to us; there behold the shrine
Where thou canst see the lamp of silver shine.
Nay, draw not death upon both thee and me
With fearless kisses; fear, until the sea
Shall fold green arms about us lovingly,
And kindly Venus to thy keel be nigh."
    Then lightly from her soft side Jason stept,
While still upon the beast her foot she kept,
Still murmuring gently many an unknown word,
As when through half-shut casements the brown bird
We hearken when the night is come in June,
And thick-leaved woods are 'twixt us and his tune.

    But Jason, going swiftly with good heart
Came to the wished-for shrine built all apart
Midmost the temple, that on pillars stood
Of jasper green, and marble red as blood,
All white itself and carven cunningly
With Neptune bringing from the wavy sea
The golden shining ram to Athamas;
And the first door thereof of silver was,
Wrought over with a golden glittering sun
That seemed well-nigh alike the heavenly one.
Such art therein the cunningest of men
Had used, which little Jason heeded then,
But thrusting in the lock the smallest key
Of those he bore, it opened easily;
And then five others, neither wrought of gold,
Or carved with tales, or lovely to behold,
He opened; but before the last one stayed
His hand, wherein the heavy key he weighed,
And pondering, in low muttered words he said:—
    "The prize is reached, which yet I somewhat dread
To draw unto me; since I know indeed,
That henceforth war and toil shall be my meed.—
Too late to fear, it was too late, the hour

I left the grey cliffs and the beechen bower,
So here I take hard life and deathless praise,
Who once desired nought but quiet days,
And painless life, not empty of delight;
I, who shall now be quickener of the fight,
Named by a great name—a far-babbled name,
The ceaseless seeker after praise and fame.
    "May all be well, and on the noisy ways
Still may I find some wealth of happy days."
    Therewith he threw the last door open wide,
Whose hammered iron did the marvel hide,
And shut his dazzled eyes, and stretched his hands
Out toward the sea-born wonder of all lands,
And plunged them deep within the locks of gold,
Grasping the fleece within his mighty hold.

    Which when Medea saw, her gown of grey
She caught up from the ground, and drew away
Her wearied foot from off the rugged beast,
And while from her soft strain she never ceased,
In the dull folds she hid her silk from sight,
And then, as bending 'neath the burden bright,
Jason drew nigh, joyful, yet still afraid.
She met him, and her wide grey mantle laid
Over the fleece, whispering "Make no delay;
He sleeps, who never slept by night or day
Till now; nor will his charmed sleep be long.
Light-foot am I, and sure thine arms are strong;
Haste, then! No word! nor turn about to gaze
At me, as he who in the shadowy ways
Turned round to see once more the twice-lost face."

    Then swiftly did they leave the dreadful place,
Turning no look behind, and reached the street,
That with familiar look and kind did greet
Those wanderers, mazed with marvels and with fear.
And so, unchallenged, did they draw anear
The long white quays, and at the street's end now
Beheld the ships' masts standing row by row

Stark black against the stars: then cautiously
Peered Jason forth, ere they took heart to try
The open starlit place; but nought he saw
Except the night-wind twitching the loose straw
From half-unloaded keels, and nought he heard
But the strange twittering of a caged green bird
With an Indian ship, and from the hill
A distant baying: yea, all was so still,
Somewhat they doubted, natheless forth they passed,
And Argo's painted sides they reached at last.
   On whom down-looking, scarce more noise they heard
Than from the other ships; some muttered word,
Some creaking of the timbers, as the tide
Ran gurgling seaward past her shielded side.
Then Jason knelt, and whispered: "Wise be ye,
O fair companions on the pathless sea,
But come, Erginus, Nestor, and ye twain
Of Lacedæmon, to behold my gain;
Take me amongst you, neither be afraid
To take withal this gold, and this fair maid.
Yare!—for the ebb runs strongly towards the sea,
The east wind drives the rack to Thessaly,
And lightly do such kings as this one sleep
If now and then small watch their servants keep."
   Then saw Medea men like shadows grey,
Rise from the darksome decks, who took straightway
With murmured joy, from Jason's outstretched hands,
The conquered fleece, the wonder of all lands,
While with strong arms he raised the royal maid,
And in their hold the precious burthen laid,
And scarce her dainty feet could touch the deck,
Ere down he leapt, and little now did reck
That loudly clanged his armour therewithal.
   But, turning townward, did Medea call:—
"O noble Jason, and ye heroes strong,
To sea, to sea! nor pray ye loiter long;
For surely shall ye see the beacons flare
Ere in mid stream ye are, and running fair
On toward the sea with tide, and oar, and sail

My father wakes, nor bides he to bewail
His loss and me; I see his turret gleam
As he goes towards the beacon, and down stream
Absyrtus lurks before the sandy bar
In mighty keel well manned and dight for war."
    But as she spoke, rattling the cable slipped
From out the hawse-hole, and the long oars dipped
As from the quays the heroes pushed away,
And in the loosened sail the wind 'gan play;
But e'en as they unto the stroke leaned back,
And Nauplius, catching at the main-sheet slack
Had drawn it taut, out flared the beacon wide,
Lighting the waves, and they heard folk who cried:
"Awake, awake, awake, O Colchian folk!"
And all about the blare of horns outbroke,
As watch-tower answered watch-tower down the stream,
Where far below they saw the bale-fires gleam;
And galloping of horses now they heard,
And clang of arms, and cries of men afeard,
For now the merchant mariners who lay
About the town, thought surely an ill day
Had dawned upon them while they slept at ease,
And, half awake, pushed madly from the quays
With crash of breaking oars and meeting ships,
And cries and curses from outlandish lips,
So fell the quiet night to turmoil sore,
While in the towers, over the uproar,
Melodiously the bells began to ring.

    But Argo, leaping forward to the swing
Of measured oars, and, leaning to the breeze,
Sped swiftly 'twixt the dark and whispering trees;
Nor longer now the heroes silence kept,
So joyously their hearts within them leapt,
But loud they shouted, seeing the Gold Fell
Laid heaped before them, and longed sore to tell
Their fair adventure to the maids of Greece;
And as the mingled noises did decrease
With added distance, and behind them night

Grew pale with coming of the eastern light,
Across the strings his fingers Orpheus drew,
And through the woods his wingéd music flew:—

 "O surely, now the fisherman
Draws homeward through the water wan
Across the bay we know so well,
And in the sheltered chalky dell
The shepherd stirs; and now afield
They drive the team with white wand peeled,
Muttering across the barley-bread
At daily toil and dreary-head.
 "And 'midst them all, perchance, my love
Is waking, and doth gently move
And stretch her soft arms out to me,
Forgetting thousand leagues of sea;
And now her body I behold,
Unhidden but by hair of gold,
And now the silver water kiss,
The crown of all delight and bliss.
And now I see her bind her hair
And do upon her raiment fair,
And now before the altar stand,
With incense in her outstretched hand,
To supplicate the Gods for me;
Ah, one day landing from the sea,
Amid the maidens shall I hear
Her voice in praise, and see her near,
Holding the gold-wrapt laurel crown,
'Midst of the shouting, wondering town!"

So sung he joyously, nor knew that they
Must wander yet for many an evil day
Or ever the dread Gods should let them come
Back to the white walls of their long-left home.
But on the shouting heroes gazed adown
The foundress of their triumph and renown,
And to her lover's side still drew anear,
With heart now swelled with joy, now sick with fear,
And cheeks now flushed with love, now pale and wan,

As now she thought upon that goodly man,
And now on the uncertain, dreadful Gods,
And now upon her father, and the odds
He well might raise against the reckless crew,
For all his mighty power full well she knew;
No wonder therefore if her heart grew cold,
And if her wretched self she did behold,
Led helpless through some old familiar place,
With none to turn on her a pitying face,
Unto the death in life, she still might win;
And yet, if she should 'scape the meed of sin
This once, the world was fair and bright enough,
And love there was to lead her o'er the rough
Of life, and love to crown her head with flowers,
And fill her days and nights with happy hours.

Now swift beneath the oar-strokes Argo flew,
While the sun rose behind them, and they drew
Unto the river's mouth, nor failed to see
Absyrtus' galley waiting watchfully
Betwixt them and the white-topped turbid bar.
Therefore they gat them ready now for war,
With joyful heart, for sharp they sniffed the sea,
And saw the great waves tumbling green and free
Outside the bar upon the way to Greece,
The rough green way to glory and sweet peace.
  Then to the prow gat Jason, and the maid
Must needs be with him, though right sore afraid,
As nearing now the Colchian ship, they hung
On balanced oars; but the wild Arcas strung
His deadly bow, and clomb into the top.
  Then Jason cried: "Absyrtus, will ye stop
Our peaceful keel, or let us take the sea'
Soothly, have we no will to fight with thee
If we may pass unfoughten, therefore say,
What is it thou wilt have this dawn of day?"
  Now on the other prow Absyrtus stood,
His visage red with eager wrathful blood,
And in his right hand shook a mighty spear,

And said. "O seafarers, ye pass not here,
For gifts or prayers, but if it must be so,
Over our sunken bulwarks shall ye go;
Nor ask me why, for thus my father wills,
Yet, as I now behold you, my heart thrills
With wrath indeed; and hearken for what cause,
That ye against all friendship and good laws
Bear off my sister with you; wherefore now
Mars give you courage and a brazen brow!
That ye may try this dangerous pass in vain,
For soothly, of your slaughter am I fain."
　　Then Jason wrathfully threw up his head,
But ere the shout came, fair Medea said,
In trembling whisper thrilling through his ear:—
　　"Haste, quick upon them! if before is fear,
Behind is death!" Then Jason turning, saw
A tall ship staggering with the gusty flaw,
Just entering the long reach where they were,
And heard her horns through the fresh morning air.
　　Then lifted he his hand, and with a cry
Back flew the balanced oars full orderly,
And toward the doomed ship mighty Argo passed;
Thereon Absyrtus shouted loud, and cast
His spear at Jason, that before his feet
Stuck in the deck; then out the arrows fleet
Burst from the Colchians; and scarce did they spare
Medea's trembling side and bosom fair;
But Jason, roaring as the lioness
When round her helpless whelps the hunters press,
Whirled round his head his mighty brass-bound spear,
That flying, smote the prince beneath the ear,
As Arcas' arrow sunk into his side.
Then falling, scarce he met the rushing tide,
Ere Argo's mighty prow had thrust apart
The huddled oars, and through the fair ship's heart
Had thrust her iron beak, and the green wave
Rushed in as rush the waters through a cave
That tunnels half a sea-girt lonely rock.
Then drawing swiftly backward from the shock,

And heeding not the cries of fear and woe,
They left the waters dealing with their foe;
And at the following ship threw back a shout,
And seaward o'er the bar drave Argo out.
　　Then joyful felt all men as now at last
From hill to green hill of the sea they passed;
But chiefly joyed Medea, as now grew
The Colchian hills behind them faint and blue,
And like a white speck showed the following ship.
There 'neath the canopy, lip pressed to lip,
They sat and told their love, till scarce he thought
What precious burden back to Greece he brought
Besides the maid, nor for his kingdom cared,
As on her beauty with wet eyes he stared,
And heard her sweet voice soft as in a dream,
When all seems gained, and trouble dead does seem.
　　So passed this day, and she no less forgot
That wreck upon the bar, the evil spot,
Red with a brother's blood, where long was stayed
The wrathful king as from the stream he weighed
The bleeding body of his well-loved son.
　　Lo in such wise their journey was begun,
And so began short love and long decay,
Sorrow that bides and joy that fleets away.

SIR WALTER SCOTT

WALTER SCOTT (1771–1832) was the son of an Edinburgh lawyer. He was
educated for the law at the Edinburgh High School and the Edinburgh
University. Very early he became a great reader of history, romance and
ballad poetry—forms of writing in which he himself was to become famous.
He began authorship by translating from the German and collecting Border
ballads, and for the rest of his days was a most busy writer Poems like
The Lay of the Last Minstrel, Marmion and *The Lady of the Lake* interested
many thousands of readers in Scottish history and scenery, till then scarcely
known in England; and when from poems he turned to prose and wrote
the famous set of Waverley novels, his popularity grew to extraordinary
proportions. Whatever he wrote was not only good; it was new of its kind
and gave readers of the time quite fresh sensations of delight Sir Walter
was a great lover of books, but there were few aspects of life in which he

was not interested. He was a great writer and he was also a great gentleman. His life by Lockhart is a fine biography. The passage that follows is taken from one of his best novels, *The Antiquary*. Mr Jonathan Oldbuck of Monkbarns is an eccentric old Scottish "laird" with a great passion for antiquities and old learning. Sir Arthur Wardour is an old friend and neighbour, very proud of his ancestors. At the Antiquary's house is Mr Lovel, a young stranger, who has fallen in love with Miss Isabella Wardour, Sir Arthur's daughter. Miss Oldbuck and Miss M'Intyre are two of the Antiquary's relatives—his "womenkind" as he calls them. Edie Ochiltree, a shrewd old soldier, is now "a blue-gown," a wanderer licensed to beg. Sir Arthur and Miss Wardour come from their house at Knockwinnock to dine with the Antiquary at Monkbarns. After dinner, a discussion between the two old cronies over a point of antiquarian lore becomes soon a heated argument, and then something like a serious quarrel.

A RESCUE FROM THE ROCKS

I

"If you mean the observation as a sneer at my ancestry," said the knight, with an assumption of dignified superiority and composure, "I have the pleasure to inform you, that the name of my ancestor, Gamelyn de Guardover, Miles, is written fairly with his own hand in the earliest copy of the Ragman-roll."

"Which only serves to show that he was one of the earliest who set the mean example of submitting to Edward I. What have you to say for the stainless loyalty of your family, Sir Arthur, after such a backsliding as that?"

"It's enough, sir," said Sir Arthur, starting up fiercely, and pushing back his chair, "I shall hereafter take care how I honour with my company one who shows himself so ungrateful for my condescension."

"In that you will do as you find most agreeable, Sir Arthur; I hope, that as I was not aware of the extent of the obligation which you have done me, by visiting my poor house, I may be excused for not having carried my gratitude to the extent of servility."

"Mighty well—mighty well, Mr Oldbuck—I wish you a good evening. Mr a—a—a—Shovel—I wish you a very good evening."

Out of the parlour door flounced the incensed Sir Arthur, as if the spirit of the whole Round Table inflamed his single bosom, and traversed with long strides the labyrinth of passages which conducted to the drawing-room.

"Did you ever hear such an old tub-headed ass?" said Oldbuck, briefly apostrophising Lovel, "but I must not let him go in this mad-like way neither."

So saying, he pushed off after the retreating Baronet, whom he traced by the clang of several doors which he opened in search of the apartment for tea, and slammed with force behind him at every disappointment. "You'll do yourself a mischief," roared the Antiquary; "*Qui ambulat in tenebris, nescit quo vadit*—you'll tumble down the back-stair"

Sir Arthur had now got involved in darkness, of which the sedative effect is well known to nurses and governesses who have to deal with pettish children. It retarded the pace of the irritated Baronet, if it did not abate his resentment, and Mr Oldbuck, better acquainted with the *locale*, got up with him as he had got his grasp upon the handle of the drawing-room door.

"Stay a minute, Sir Arthur," said Oldbuck, opposing his abrupt entrance; "don't be quite so hasty, my good old friend—I was a little too rude with you about Sir Gamelyn—why, he is an old acquaintance of mine, man, and a favourite—he kept company with Bruce and Wallace—and, I'll be sworn on a black-letter Bible, only subscribed the Ragman-roll with the legitimate and justifiable intention of circumventing the false Southern—'twas right Scottish craft, my good knight—hundreds did it—come, come, forget and forgive—confess we have given the young fellow here a right to think us two testy old fools."

"Speak for yourself, Mr Jonathan Oldbuck," said Sir Arthur, with much majesty.

"A-well, a-well—a wilful man must have his way."

With that the door opened, and into the drawing-room marched the tall, gaunt form of Sir Arthur, followed by Lovel and Mr Oldbuck, the countenances of all the three a little discomposed.

"I have been waiting for you, sir," said Miss Wardour, "to propose we should walk forward to meet the carriage, as the evening is so fine."

Sir Arthur readily assented to this proposal, which suited the angry mood in which he found himself; and having, agreeably to the established custom in cases of pet, refused the refreshment of tea and coffee, he tucked his daughter under his arm; and, after taking a ceremonious leave of the ladies, and a very dry one of Oldbuck—off he marched.

"I think Sir Arthur has got the black dog on his back again," said Miss Oldbuck.

"Black dog!—black devil!—he's more absurd than woman-kind What say you, Lovel? Why, the lad's gone too."

"He took his leave, uncle, while Miss Wardour was putting on her things; but I don't think you observed him."

"The devil's in the people! This is all one gets by fussing and bustling, and putting one's self out of one's way in order to give dinners, besides all the charges they are put to! O Seged, Emperor of Ethiopia!" said he, taking up a cup of tea in the one hand, and a volume of the Rambler in the other—for it was his regular custom to read while he was eating or drinking in presence of his sister, being a practice which served at once to evince his contempt for the society of womankind, and his resolution to lose no moment of instruction—"O Seged, Emperor of Ethiopia! well hast thou spoken—No man should presume to say, This shall be a day of happiness."

Oldbuck proceeded in his studies for the best part of an hour, uninterrupted by the ladies, who each, in profound silence, pursued some female employment. At length, a light and modest tap was heard at the parlour door. "Is that you, Caxon?—come in, come in, man "

The old man opened the door, and thrusting in his meagre face, thatched with thin grey locks, and one sleeve of his white coat, said, in a subdued and mysterious tone of voice, "I was wanting to speak to you, sir."

"Come in then, you old fool, and say what you have got to say."

"I'll maybe frighten the ladies," said the ex-friseur.

"Frighten!" answered the Antiquary, "What do you mean?—never mind the ladies. Have you seen another ghaist at the Humlock-know?"

"Na, sir, it's no a ghaist this turn," replied Caxon; "but I'm no easy in my mind."

"Did you ever hear of any body that was?" answered Oldbuck; "what reason has an old battered powder-puff like you to be easy in your mind, more than all the rest of the world besides?"

"It's no for mysell, sir; but it threatens an awfu' night; and Sir Arthur, and Miss Wardour, poor thing——"

"Why, man, they must have met the carriage at the head of the loaning, or thereabouts; they must be home long ago."

"Na, sir; they didna gang the road by the turnpike to meet the carriage, they gaed by the sands."

The words operated like electricity on Oldbuck. "The sands!" he exclaimed; "impossible!"

"Ou, sir, that's what I said to the gardener; but he says he saw them turn down by the Musselcraig—in troth, says I to him, an that be the case, Davie, I am misdoubting——"

"An almanack! an almanack!" said Oldbuck, starting up in great alarm—"not that bauble!" flinging away a little pocket almanack which his niece offered him—"Great God! my poor dear Miss Isabella! Fetch me instantly the Fairport Almanack" It was brought, consulted, and added greatly to his agitation. "I'll go myself—call the gardener and ploughman—bid them bring ropes and ladders—bid them raise more help as they come along—keep the top of the cliffs, and halloo down to them—I'll go myself."

"What is the matter?" inquired Miss Oldbuck and Miss M'Intyre.

"The tide!—the tide!" answered the alarmed Antiquary.

"Had not Jenny better—but no, I'll run myself," said the younger lady, partaking in all her uncle's terrors—"I'll run myself to Saunders Mucklebackit, and make him get out his boat."

"Thank you, my dear, that's the wisest word that has been spoken yet—run! run! To go by the sands!" seizing his hat and cane; "was there ever such madness heard of!"

II

Pleased awhile to view
The watery waste, the prospect wild and new;
The now receding waters gave them space,
On either side, the growing shores to trace;
And then, returning, they contract the scene,
Till small and smaller grows the walk between.

CRABBE.

The information of Davie Dibble, which had spread such general alarm at Monkbarns, proved to be strictly correct. Sir Arthur and his daughter had set out, according to their first

proposal, to return to Knockwinnock by the turnpike road; but
when they reached the head of the loaning, as it was called, or
great lane, which on one side made a sort of avenue to the house of
Monkbarns, they discerned, a little way before them, Lovel, who
seemed to linger on the way as if to give him an opportunity to
join them Miss Wardour immediately proposed to her father
that they should take another direction; and, as the weather was
fine, walk home by the sands, which, stretching below a picturesque
ridge of rocks, afforded at almost all times a pleasanter passage
between Knockwinnock and Monkbarns than the high-road.

Sir Arthur acquiesced willingly. "It would be unpleasant," he
said, "to be joined by that young fellow, whom Mr Oldbuck had
taken the freedom to introduce them to." And his old-fashioned
politeness had none of the ease of the present day, which permits
you, if you have a mind, to *cut* the person you have associated with
for a week, the instant you feel or suppose yourself in a situation
which makes it disagreeable to own him. Sir Arthur only stipu-
lated, that a little ragged boy, for the guerdon of one penny
sterling, should run to meet his coachman, and turn his equipage
back to Knockwinnock.

When this was arranged, and the emissary despatched, the
knight and his daughter left the high-road, and following a
wandering path among sandy hillocks, partly grown over with
furze and the long grass called bent, soon attained the side of the
ocean. The tide was by no means so far out as they had computed,
but this gave them no alarm; there were seldom ten days in the
year when it approached so near the cliffs as not to leave a dry
passage. But, nevertheless, at periods of spring-tide, or even
when the ordinary flood was accelerated by high winds, this road
was altogether covered by the sea; and tradition had recorded
several fatal accidents which had happened on such occasions.
Still, such dangers were considered as remote and improbable;
and rather served, with other legends, to amuse the hamlet fireside,
than to prevent any one from going between Knockwinnock and
Monkbarns by the sands.

As Sir Arthur and Miss Wardour paced along, enjoying the
pleasant footing afforded by the cool moist hard sand, Miss
Wardour could not help observing that the last tide had risen
considerably above the usual water-mark Sir Arthur made the

same observation, but without its occurring to either of them to be alarmed at the circumstance The sun was now resting his huge disk upon the edge of the level ocean, and gilded the accumulation of towering clouds through which he had travelled the livelong day, and which now assembled on all sides, like misfortunes and disasters around a sinking empire, and falling monarch. Still, however, his dying splendour gave a sombre magnificence to the massive congregation of vapours, forming out of their unsubstantial gloom, the show of pyramids and towers, some touched with gold, some with purple, some with a hue of deep and dark red. The distant sea, stretched beneath this varied and gorgeous canopy, lay almost portentously still, reflecting back the dazzling and level beams of the descending luminary, and the splendid colouring of the clouds amidst which he was setting Nearer to the beach, the tide rippled onward in waves of sparkling silver, that imperceptibly, yet rapidly, gained upon the sand.

With a mind employed in admiration of the romantic scene, or perhaps on some more agitating topic, Miss Wardour advanced in silence by her father's side, whose recently offended dignity did not stoop to open any conversation. Following the windings of the beach, they passed one projecting point or headland of rock after another, and now found themselves under a huge and continued extent of the precipices by which that iron-bound coast is in most places defended. Long projecting reefs of rock, extending under water, and only evincing their existence by here and there a peak entirely bare, or by the breakers which foamed over those that were partially covered, rendered Knockwinnock bay dreaded by pilots and ship-masters. The crags which rose between the beach and the mainland, to the height of two or three hundred feet, afforded in their crevices shelter for unnumbered sea-fowl, in situations seemingly secured by their dizzy height from the rapacity of man Many of these wild tribes, with the instinct which sends them to seek the land before a storm arises, were now winging towards their nests with the shrill and dissonant clang which announces disquietude and fear The disk of the sun became almost totally obscured ere he had altogether sunk below the horizon, and an early and lurid shade of darkness blotted the serene twilight of a summer evening. The wind began next to arise; but its wild and moaning sound was heard for some time, and its effect became visible on the bosom of the sea before the gale was felt on shore. The mass of waters, now dark and threatening, began to lift itself in larger ridges, and sink in deeper furrows, forming waves that rose high in foam upon the breakers, or burst upon the beach with a sound resembling distant thunder.

Appalled by this sudden change of weather, Miss Wardour drew close to her father, and held his arm fast. "I wish," at length she said, but almost in a whisper, as if ashamed to express her increasing apprehensions—"I wish we had kept the road we intended, or waited at Monkbarns for the carriage."

Sir Arthur looked round, but did not see, or would not acknowledge, any signs of an immediate storm. They would reach Knockwinnock, he said, long before the tempest began. But the speed with which he walked, and with which Isabella could hardly keep pace, indicated a feeling that some exertion was necessary to accomplish his consolatory prediction.

They were now near the centre of a deep but narrow bay, or recess, formed by two projecting capes of high and inaccessible rock, which shot out into the sea like the horns of a crescent; and neither durst communicate the apprehension which each began to entertain, that, from the unusually rapid advance of the tide, they might be deprived of the power of proceeding by doubling the promontory which lay before them, or of retreating by the road which brought them thither.

As they pressed forward, longing doubtless to exchange the easy curving line, which the sinuosities of the bay compelled them to adopt, for a straighter and more expeditious path, though less conformable to the line of beauty, Sir Arthur observed a human figure on the beach advancing to meet them. "Thank God," he exclaimed, "we shall get round Halket-head! that person must have passed it"; thus giving vent to the feeling of hope, though he had suppressed that of apprehension.

"Thank God indeed!" echoed his daughter, half audibly, half internally, as expressing the gratitude which she strongly felt.

The figure which advanced to meet them made many signs, which the haze of the atmosphere, now disturbed by wind and a drizzling rain, prevented them from seeing or comprehending distinctly. Some time before they met, Sir Arthur could recognise the old blue-gowned beggar, Edie Ochiltree. It is said that even the brute creation lay aside their animosities and antipathies when pressed by an instant and common danger. The beach under Halket-head, rapidly diminishing in extent by the encroachments of the spring-tide and a north-west wind, was in like manner a neutral field, where even a justice of peace and a strolling mendicant might meet upon terms of mutual forbearance.

"Turn back! turn back!" exclaimed the vagrant; "why did ye not turn when I waved to you?"

"We thought," replied Sir Arthur, in great agitation, "we thought we could get round Halket-head."

"Halket-head! The tide will be running on Halket-head by this time like the Fall of Fyers! It was a' I could do to get round it twenty minutes since—it was coming in three feet abreast. We will maybe get back by Ballyburgh Ness Point yet. The Lord help us, it's our only chance. We can but try."

"My God, my child!" "My father! my dear father!" exclaimed the parent and daughter, as, fear lending them strength and speed, they turned to retrace their steps, and endeavoured to double the point, the projection of which formed the southern extremity of the bay.

"I heard ye were here, frae the bit callant[1] ye sent to meet your carriage," said the beggar, as he trudged stoutly on a step or two behind Miss Wardour, "and I couldna bide to think o' the dainty young leddy's peril, that has aye been kind to ilka forlorn heart that cam near her. Sae I lookit at the lift and the rin o' the tide, till I settled it that if I could get down time enough to gie you warning, we wad do weel yet. But I doubt, I doubt, I have been beguiled! for what mortal ee ever saw sic a race as the tide is rinning e'en now? See, yonder's the Ratton's Skerry[2]—he aye held his neb[3] abune[4] the water in my day—but he's aneath it now."

Sir Arthur cast a look in the direction in which the old man pointed. A huge rock, which in general, even in spring-tides, displayed a hulk like the keel of a large vessel, was now quite under water, and its place only indicated by the boiling and breaking of the eddying waves which encountered its submarine resistance

"Mak haste, mak haste, my bonny leddy," continued the old man, "mak haste, and we may do yet! Tak haud o' my arm—an

---

[1] little fellow.   [2] rock.   [3] nose.   [4] above.

auld and frail arm it's now, but it's been in as sair stress as this is yet. Tak haud o' my arm, my winsome leddy! D'ye see yon wee black speck amang the wallowing waves yonder? This morning it was as high as the mast o' a brig—it's sma' eneugh now—but, while I see as muckle black about it as the crown o' my hat, I winna believe but we'll get round the Ballyburgh Ness, for a' that's come and gane yet."

Isabella, in silence, accepted from the old man the assistance which Sir Arthur was less able to afford her. The waves had now encroached so much upon the beach, that the firm and smooth footing which they had hitherto had on the sand must be exchanged for a rougher path close to the foot of the precipice, and in some places even raised upon its lower ledges. It would have been utterly impossible for Sir Arthur Wardour or his daughter to have found their way along these shelves without the guidance and encouragement of the beggar, who had been there before in high tides, though never, he acknowledged, "in sae awsome a night as this."

It was indeed a dreadful evening. The howling of the storm mingled with the shrieks of the sea-fowl, and sounded like the dirge of the three devoted beings, who, pent between two of the most magnificent, yet most dreadful objects of nature—a raging tide and an insurmountable precipice—toiled along their painful and dangerous path, often lashed by the spray of some giant billow, which threw itself higher on the beach than those that had preceded it. Each minute did their enemy gain ground perceptibly upon them! Still, however, loth to relinquish the last hopes of life, they bent their eyes on the black rock pointed out by Ochiltree. It was yet distinctly visible among the breakers, and continued to be so, until they came to a turn in their precarious path, where an intervening projection of rock hid it from their sight. Deprived of the view of the beacon on which they had relied, they now experienced the double agony of terror and suspense. They struggled forward, however; but, when they arrived at the point from which they ought to have seen the crag, it was no longer visible The signal of safety was lost among a thousand white breakers, which, dashing upon the point of the promontory, rose in prodigious sheets of snowy foam, as high as the masts of a first-rate man-of-war, against the dark brow of the precipice.

The countenance of the old man fell. Isabella gave a faint shriek, and, "God have mercy upon us!" which her guide solemnly uttered, was piteously echoed by Sir Arthur—"My child! my child!—to die such a death!"

"My father! my dear father!" his daughter exclaimed, clinging to him—"and you too, who have lost your own life in endeavouring to save ours?"

"That's not worth the counting," said the old man. "I hae lived to be weary o' life; and here or yonder—at the back o' a dyke, in a wreath o' snaw, or in the wame o' a wave, what signifies how the auld gaberlunzie¹ dies?"

"Good man," said Sir Arthur, "can you think of nothing?—of no help? I'll make you rich—I'll give you a farm—I'll——"

"Our riches will be soon equal," said the beggar, looking out upon the strife of the waters—"they are sae already; for I hae nae land, and you would give your fair bounds and barony for a square yard of rock that would be dry for twal hours."

While they exchanged these words, they paused upon the highest ledge of rock to which they could attain; for it seemed that any further attempt to move forward could only serve to anticipate their fate. Here, then, they were to await the sure though slow progress of the raging element, something in the situation of the martyrs of the early church, who, exposed by heathen tyrants to be slain by wild beasts, were compelled for a time to witness the impatience and rage by which the animals were agitated, while awaiting the signal for undoing their grates, and letting them loose upon the victims.

Yet even this fearful pause gave Isabella time to collect the powers of a mind naturally strong and courageous, and which rallied itself at this terrible juncture. "Must we yield life," she said, "without a struggle? Is there no path, however dreadful, by which we could climb the crag, or at least attain some height above the tide, where we could remain till morning, or till help comes? They must be aware of our situation, and will raise the country to relieve us."

Sir Arthur, who heard, but scarcely comprehended, his daughter's question, turned, nevertheless, instinctively and eagerly to the old man, as if their lives were in his gift. Ochiltree paused "I

¹ beggar.

was a bauld craigsman," he said, "ance in my life, and mony a kittywake's and lungie's[1] nest hae I harried up amang thae very black rocks, but it's lang, lang syne, and nae mortal could speel[2] them without a rope—and if I had ane, my ee-sight, and my foot-step, and my hand-grip hae a' failed mony a day sinsyne—and then how could I save *you*? But there was a path here ance, though maybe, if we could see it, ye would rather bide where we are. His name be praised!" he ejaculated suddenly, "there's ane coming down the crag e'en now!" Then, exalting his voice, he hilloa'd out to the daring adventurer such instructions as his former practice and the remembrance of local circumstances suddenly forced upon his mind:—"Ye're right—ye're right? that gate—that gate!—fasten the rope weel round Crummie's-horn, that's the muckle black stane—cast twa plies round it—that's it! —now, weize[3] yoursell a wee easel-ward[4]—a wee mair yet to that ither stane—we ca'd it the Cat's-lug—there used to be the root o' an aik-tree there—that will do!—canny now, lad—canny now— tak tent and tak time—Lord bless ye, tak time. Vera weel! Now ye maun get to Bessy's Apron, that's the muckle braid flat blue stane—and then, I think, wi' your help and the tow thegither, I'll win at ye, and then we'll be able to get up the young leddy and Sir Arthur."

The adventurer, following the directions of old Edie, flung him down the end of the rope, which he secured around Miss Wardour, wrapping her previously in his own blue gown, to preserve her as much as possible from injury. Then, availing himself of the rope, which was made fast at the other end, he began to ascend the face of the crag—a most precarious and dizzy undertaking, which, however, after one or two perilous escapes, placed him safe on the broad flat stone beside our friend Lovel. Their joint strength was able to raise Isabella to the place of safety which they had attained. Lovel then descended in order to assist Sir Arthur, around whom he adjusted the rope; and again mounting to their place of refuge, with the assistance of old Ochiltree, and such aid as Sir Arthur himself could afford, he raised himself beyond the reach of the billows.

The sense of reprieve from approaching and apparently inevitable death had its usual effect. The father and daughter threw

---

[1] guillemot.   [2] climb.   [3] turn.   [4] eastward.

themselves into each other's arms, kissed and wept for joy, although their escape was connected with the prospect of passing a tempestuous night upon a precipitous ledge of rock, which scarce afforded footing for the four shivering beings, who now, like the sea-fowl around them, clung there in hopes of some shelter from the devouring element which raged beneath. The spray of the billows, which attained in fearful succession the foot of the precipice, overflowing the beach on which they so lately stood, flew as high as their place of temporary refuge; and the stunning sound with which they dashed against the rocks beneath, seemed as if they still demanded the fugitives in accents of thunder as their destined prey. It was a summer night doubtless; yet the probability was slender, that a frame so delicate as that of Miss Wardour should survive till morning the drenching of the spray; and the dashing of the rain, which now burst in full violence, accompanied with deep and heavy gusts of wind, added to the constrained and perilous circumstances of their situation.

"The lassie!—the puir sweet lassie!"—said the old man; "mony such a night have I weathered at hame and abroad, but, God guide us, how can she ever win through it!"

His apprehension was communicated in smothered accents to Lovel; for, with the sort of freemasonry by which bold and ready spirits correspond in moments of danger, and become almost instinctively known to each other, they had established a mutual confidence. "I'll climb up the cliff again," said Lovel, "there's daylight enough left to see my footing; I'll climb up and call for more assistance."

"Do so, do so, for heaven's sake!" said Sir Arthur, eagerly.

"Are ye mad?" said the mendicant: "Francie o' Fowlsheugh, and he was the best craigsman that ever speel'd heugh[1] (mair by token, he brake his neck upon the Dunbuy of Slaines), wadna hae ventured upon the Halket-head craigs after sundown—it's God's grace, and a great wonder besides, that ye are not in the middle o' that roaring sea wi' what ye hae done already—I didna think there was the man left alive would hae come down the craigs as ye did. I question an I could hae done it mysell, at this hour and in this weather, in the youngest and yaldest[2] of my

---

[1] ever climbed crag.   [2] most active.

strength. But to venture up again—it's a mere and a clear tempting o' Providence."

"I have no fear," answered Lovel, "I marked all the stations perfectly as I came down, and there is still light enough left to see them quite well—I am sure I can do it with perfect safety. Stay here, my good friend, by Sir Arthur and the young lady."

"Deil be in my feet then," answered the bedesman, sturdily; "if ye gang, I'll gang too, for between the twa o' us, we'll hae mair than wark eneugh to get to the tap o' the heugh."

"No, no—stay you here and attend to Miss Wardour—you see Sir Arthur is quite exhausted."

"Stay yoursell then, and I'll gae," said the old man; "let death spare the green corn, and take the ripe."

"Stay both of you, I charge you," said Isabella, faintly; "I am well, and can spend the night very well here—I feel quite refreshed." So saying, her voice failed her—she sunk down, and would have fallen from the crag, had she not been supported by Lovel and Ochiltree, who placed her in a posture half sitting, half reclining, beside her father, who, exhausted by fatigue of body and mind so extreme and unusual, had already sat down on a stone in a sort of stupor.

"It is impossible to leave them," said Lovel—"what is to be done? Hark! hark!—did I not hear a halloo?"

"The skreigh of a Tammie Norie[1]," answered Ochiltree, "I ken the skirl weel."

"No, by Heaven!" replied Lovel, "it was a human voice."

A distant hail was repeated, the sound plainly distinguishable among the various elemental noises, and the clang of the sea-mews by which they were surrounded. The mendicant and Lovel exerted their voices in a loud halloo, the former waving Miss Wardour's handkerchief on the end of his staff to make them conspicuous from above. Though the shouts were repeated, it was some time before they were in exact response to their own, leaving the unfortunate sufferers uncertain whether, in the darkening twilight and increasing storm, they had made the persons who apparently were traversing the verge of the precipice to bring them assistance, sensible of the place in which they had found

[1] scream of a puffin.

refuge. At length their halloo was regularly and distinctly answered, and their courage confirmed, by the assurance that they were within hearing, if not within reach, of friendly assistance.

III

There is a cliff, whose high and bending head
Looks fearfully on the confined deep;
Bring me but to the very brim of it,
And I'll repair the misery thou dost bear.

King Lear.

The shout of human voices from above was soon augmented, and the gleam of torches mingled with those lights of evening which still remained amidst the darkness of the storm. Some attempt was made to hold communication between the assistants above and the sufferers beneath, who were still clinging to their precarious place of safety; but the howling of the tempest limited their intercourse to cries as inarticulate as those of the winged denizens of the crag, which shrieked in chorus, alarmed by the reiterated sound of human voices, where they had seldom been heard.

On the verge of the precipice an anxious group had now assembled. Oldbuck was the foremost and most earnest, pressing forward with unwonted desperation to the very brink of the crag, and extending his head (his hat and wig secured by a handkerchief under his chin) over the dizzy height, with an air of determination which made his more timorous assistants tremble.

"Haud a care, haud a care, Monkbarns!" cried Caxon, clinging to the skirts of his patron, and withholding him from danger as far as his strength permitted—"God's sake, haud a care!—Sir Arthur's drowned already, and an ye fa' over the cleugh[1] too, there will be but ae wig left in the parish, and that's the minister's."

"Mind the peak there," cried Mucklebackit, an old fisherman and smuggler—"mind the peak. Steenie, Steenie Wilks, bring up the tackle—I'se warrant we'll sune heave them on board, Monkbarns, wad ye but stand out o' the gate."

"I see them," said Oldbuck—"I see them low down on that flat stone. Hilli-hilloa! hilli-ho-a!"

[1] precipice.

"I see them mysell weel eneugh," said Mucklebackit; "they are sitting down yonder like hoodie-craws in a mist; but d'ye think ye'll help them wi' skirling that gate[1] like an auld skart[2] before a flaw[3] o' weather? Steenie, lad, bring up the mast. Odd, I'se hae them up as we used to bouse[4] up the kegs o' gin and brandy lang syne. Get up the pickaxe, make a step for the mast—make the chair fast with the rattlin—haul taut and belay!"

The fishers had brought with them the mast of a boat, and as half the country fellows about had now appeared, either out of zeal or curiosity, it was soon sunk in the ground, and sufficiently secured. A yard, across the upright mast, and a rope stretched along it, and reeved through a block at each end, formed an extempore crane, which afforded the means of lowering an arm-chair, well secured and fastened, down to the flat shelf on which the sufferers had roosted. Their joy at hearing the preparations going on for their deliverance was considerably qualified when they beheld the precarious vehicle by means of which they were to be conveyed to upper air. It swung about a yard free of the spot which they occupied, obeying each impulse of the tempest, the empty air all round it, and depending upon the security of a rope, which, in the increasing darkness, had dwindled to an almost imperceptible thread. Besides the hazard of committing a human being to the vacant atmosphere in such a slight means of conveyance, there was the fearful danger of the chair and its occupant being dashed, either by the wind or the vibrations of the cord, against the rugged face of the precipice. But to diminish the risk as much as possible, the experienced seamen had let down with the chair another line, which, being attached to it, and held by the persons beneath, might serve by way of *gy*[5], as Mucklebackit expressed it, to render its descent in some measure steady and regular. Still, to commit one's self in such a vehicle, through a howling tempest of wind and rain, with a beetling precipice above and a raging abyss below, required that courage which despair alone can inspire. Yet, wild as the sounds and sights of danger were, both above, beneath, and around, and doubtful and dangerous as the mode of escaping appeared to be, Lovel and the old mendicant agreed, after a moment's consultation, and

---

| [1] way. | [2] cormorant. | [3] blast. |
| [4] hoist. | [5] guy or guide rope. | |

after the former, by a sudden strong pull, had, at his own imminent risk, ascertained the security of the rope, that it would be best to secure Miss Wardour in the chair, and trust to the tenderness and care of those above for her being safely craned up to the top of the crag.

"Let my father go first," exclaimed Isabella; "for God's sake, my friends, place him first in safety!"

"It cannot be, Miss Wardour," said Lovel; "your life must be first secured—the rope which bears your weight may——"

"I will not listen to a reason so selfish!"

"But ye maun listen to it, my bonnie lassie," said Ochiltree, "for a' our lives depend on it—besides, when ye get on the tap o' the heugh yonder, ye can gie' them a round guess o' what's ganging on in this Patmos o' ours—and Sir Arthur's far by that, as I am thinking."

Struck with the truth of this reasoning, she exclaimed, "True, most true; I am ready and willing to undertake the first risk— What shall I say to our friends above?"

"Just to look that their tackle does not graze on the face o' the craig, and to let the chair down, and draw it up hooly[1] and fairly— we will halloo when we are ready."

With the sedulous attention of a parent to a child, Lovel bound Miss Wardour with his handkerchief, neckcloth, and the mendicant's leathern belt to the back and arms of the chair, ascertaining accurately the security of each knot, while Ochiltree kept Sir Arthur quiet. "What are ye doing wi' my bairn?—what are ye doing? She shall not be separated from me. Isabel, stay with me, I command you!"

"Lordsake, Sir Arthur, haud your tongue, and be thankful to God that there's wiser folk than you to manage this job," cried the beggar, worn out by the unreasonable exclamations of the poor Baronet.

"Farewell, my father!" murmured Isabella—"farewell, my— my friends"; and, shutting her eyes, as Edie's experience recommended, she gave the signal to Lovel, and he to those who were above. She rose, while the chair in which she sat was kept steady by the line which Lovel managed beneath. With a beating heart

---

[1] cautiously.

he watched the flutter of her white dress, until the vehicle was on a level with the brink of the precipice

"Canny now, lads, canny now!" exclaimed old Mucklebackit, who acted as commodore; "swerve the yard a bit. Now—there! there she sits safe on dry land!"

A loud shout announced the successful experiment to her fellow-sufferers beneath, who replied with a ready and cheerful halloo. Monkbarns, in his ecstasy of joy, stripped his great-coat to wrap up the young lady, and would have pulled off his coat and waistcoat for the same purpose, had he not been withheld by the cautious Caxon. "Haud a care o' us! your honour will be killed wi' the hoast[1]—ye'll no get out o' your night-cowl this fortnight— and that will suit us unco ill. Na, na—there's the chariot down by; let twa o' the folk carry the young leddy there."

"You're right," said the Antiquary, readjusting the sleeves and collar of his coat, "'you're right, Caxon; this is a naughty night to swim in. Miss Wardour, let me convey you to the chariot."

"Not for worlds, till I see my father safe."

In a few distinct words, evincing how much her resolution had surmounted even the mortal fear of so agitating a hazard, she explained the nature of the situation beneath, and the wishes of Lovel and Ochiltree.

"Right, right, that's right too—I should like to see the son of Sir Gamelyn de Guardover on dry land myself—I have a notion he would sign the abjuration oath, and the Ragman-roll to boot, and acknowledge Queen Mary to be nothing better than she should be, to get alongside my bottle of old port that he ran away from, and left scarce begun. But he's safe now, and here a' comes" (for the chair was again lowered, and Sir Arthur made fast in it, without much consciousness on his own part)—"here a' comes—bowse away, my boys!—canny wi' him—a pedigree of a hundred links is hanging on a tenpenny tow—the whole barony of Knockwinnock depends on three plies of hemp—*respice finem, respice funem*— look to your end—look to a rope's end. Welcome, welcome, my good old friend, to firm land, though I cannot say to warm land or to dry land—a cord for ever against fifty fathom of water, though not in the sense of the base proverb—a fico for the phrase —better *sus. per funem* than *sus. per coll.*"

1 cough.

While Oldbuck ran on in this way, Sir Arthur was safely wrapped in the close embraces of his daughter, who, assuming that authority which the circumstances demanded, ordered some of the assistants to convey him to the chariot, promising to follow in a few minutes. She lingered on the cliff, holding an old countryman's arm, to witness probably the safety of those whose dangers she had shared.

"What have we here?" said Oldbuck, as the vehicle once more ascended. "What patched and weather-beaten matter is this?" Then, as the torches illumined the rough face and grey hairs of old Ochiltree—"What! is it thou?—come, old Mocker, I must needs be friends with thee—but who the devil makes up your party besides?"

"Ane that's weel worth ony twa o' us, Monkbarns—it's the young stranger lad they ca' Lovel—and he's behaved this blessed night as if he had three lives to rely on, and was willing to waste them a' rather than endanger ither folk's. Ca' hooly, sirs, as ye wad win an auld's man's blessing!—mind there's naebody below now to haud the gy—hae a care o' the Cat's-lug corner—bide weel aff Crummie's-horn?"

"Have a care indeed," echoed Oldbuck. "What! is it my *rara avis*—my black swan—my phoenix of companions in a post-chaise? Take care of him, Mucklebackit."

"As muckle care as if he were a greybeard o' brandy; and I canna take mair if his hair were like John Harlowe's. Yo ho, my hearts! bowse away with him!"

Lovel did, in fact, run a much greater risk than any of his pre-cursors. His weight was not sufficient to render his ascent steady amid such a storm of wind, and he swung like an agitated pendulum at the mortal risk of being dashed against the rocks. But he was young, bold, and active, and, with the assistance of the beggar's stout spiked staff, which he had retained by advice of the pro-prietor, contrived to bear himself from the face of the precipice, and the yet more hazardous projecting cliffs which varied its sur-face. Tossed in empty space, like an idle and unsubstantial feather, with a motion that agitated the brain at once with fear and with dizziness, he retained his alertness of exertion and presence of mind; and it was not until he was safely grounded upon the summit of the cliff, that he felt temporary and giddy sickness. As

he recovered from a sort of half swoon, he cast his eyes eagerly
around. The object which they would most willingly have sought
was already in the act of vanishing. Her white garment was just
discernible as she followed on the path which her father had taken
She had lingered till she saw the last of their company rescued
from danger, and until she had been assured by the hoarse voice
of Mucklebackit, that "the callant had come off wi' unbrizzed
banes, and that he was but in a kind of dwam[1]." But Lovel was
not aware that she had expressed in his fate even this degree of
interest, which, though nothing more than was due to a stranger
who had assisted her in such an hour of peril, he would have
gladly purchased by braving even more imminent danger than
he had that evening been exposed to. The beggar she had already
commanded to come to Knockwinnock that night. He made an
excuse. "Then to-morrow let me see you."

The old man promised to obey. Oldbuck thrust something into
his hand—Ochiltree looked at it by the torchlight, and returned
it—"Na, na! I never tak gowd—besides, Monkbarns, ye wad
maybe be rueing it the morn." Then turning to the group of
fishermen and peasants—"Now, sirs, wha will gie me a supper and
some clean pease-strae?"

"I," "and I," "and I," answered many a ready voice.

"Aweel, since sae it is, and I can only sleep in ae barn at ance.
I'll gae down wi' Saunders Mucklebackit—he has aye a soup o'
something comfortable about his biggin[2]—and, bairns, I'll maybe
live to put ilka ane o' ye in mind some ither night that ye hae
promised me quarters and my awmous[3];" and away he went with
the fisherman.

Oldbuck laid the hand of strong possession on Lovel—"Deil a
stride ye's go to Fairport this night, young man—you must go
home with me to Monkbarns Why, man, you have been a hero—
a perfect Sir William Wallace, by all accounts. Come, my good
lad, take hold of my arm—I am not a prime support in such a
wind—but Caxon shall help us out. Here, you old idiot, come on
the other side of me And how the deil got you down to that
infernal Bessy's Apron, as they call it? Bess, said they—why,
curse her, she has spread out that vile pennon or banner of

[1] swoon   [2] house   [3] alms.

womankind, like all the rest of her sex, to allure her votaries to death and headlong ruin."

"I have been pretty well accustomed to climbing, and I have long observed fowlers practise that pass down the cliff."

"But how, in the name of all that is wonderful, came you to discover the danger of the pettish Baronet and his far more deserving daughter?"

"I saw them from the verge of the precipice."

"From the verge!—umph—and what possessed you, *dumosa pendere procul de rupe?*—though *dumosa* is not the appropriate epithet—what the deil, man, tempted ye to the verge of the craig?"

"Why, I like to see the gathering and growling of a coming storm—or, in your own classical language, Mr Oldbuck, *suave mari magno*—and so forth—but here we reach the turn to Fairport. I must wish you good-night."

"Not a step, not a pace, not an inch, not a shathmont[1], as I may say; the meaning of which word has puzzled many that think themselves antiquaries. I am clear we should read *salmon-length* for *shathmont's length.* You are aware that the space allotted for the passage of a salmon through a dam, dike, or weir, by statute, is the length within which a full-grown pig can turn himself round—now I have a scheme to prove, that, as terrestrial objects were thus appealed to for ascertaining submarine measurement, so it must be supposed that the productions of the water were established as gauges of the extent of land. Shathmont—salmont—you see the close alliance of the sounds; dropping out two *h*'s and a *t*, and assuming an *l*, makes the whole difference I wish to Heaven no antiquarian derivation had demanded heavier concessions."

"But, my dear sir, I really must go home—I am wet to the skin "

"Shalt have my night-gown, man, and slippers, and catch the antiquarian fever as men do the plague, by wearing infected garments—nay, I know what you would be at—you are afraid to put the old bachelor to charges But is there not the remains of that glorious chicken-pie—which, *meo arbitrio*, is better cold than hot—and that bottle of my oldest port, out of which the silly brain-sick Baronet (whom I cannot pardon, since he has escaped breaking his neck) had just taken one glass when his infirm noddle went a wool-gathering after Gamelyn de Guardover?"

[1] six inches

So saying, he dragged Lovel forward, till the Palmer's-port of Monkbarns received them Never, perhaps, had it admitted two pedestrians more needing rest; for Monkbarns's fatigue had been in a degree very contrary to his usual habits, and his more young and robust companion had that evening undergone agitation of mind which had harassed and wearied him even more than his extraordinary exertions of body.

T. E. BROWN

THOMAS EDWARD BROWN (1830–97) was a master at Clifton He wrote *Betsy Lee*, *Fo'c'sle Yarns* and many charming poems. His letters, too, are delightful.

MY GARDEN

A garden is a lovesome thing, God wot!
Rose plot,
Fringed pool,
Fern'd grot—
The veriest school
Of peace; and yet the fool
Contends that God is not—
Not God! in gardens! When the eve is cool?
    Nay, but I have a sign;
    'Tis very sure God walks in mine.

FRANCIS BACON

FRANCIS BACON, Viscount St Albans (1561–1626) was born in London and educated at Cambridge He was famous as a lawyer, and became Lord Chancellor, but he is still more famous as a philosopher and writer. Of his works, the best known are *The Advancement of Learning* and his *Essays* —the latter being wonderful examples of wisdom in the briefest form. The passage that follows is the beginning of the essay "Of Gardens."

OF GARDENS

God Almighty first planted a Garden And indeed it is the purest of human pleasures. It is the greatest refreshment to the spirits of man, without which, buildings and palaces are but gross handiworks; and a man shall ever see that, when ages grow to

civility and elegancy, men come to build stately sooner than to
gaiden finely, as if gardening were the greater perfection. I do
hold it, in the royal ordering of gardens, there ought to be gardens
for all months in the year, in which, severally, things of beauty
may be then in season.

ADDISON

(*The Spectator*, No. 477, 6 Sept. 1712.)

An me ludit amabilis
Insania? Audire, et videor pios
Errare per lucos, amœnæ
Quos et aquæ subeunt et auræ.
                                        Hor. *Od.* iii. iv. 5.

Does airy fancy cheat
My mind well pleas'd with the deceit?
I seem to hear, I seem to move,
And wander through the happy grove,
Where smooth springs flow, and murm'ring breeze
Wantons through the waving trees.   Creech

"Sir,

"Having lately read your essay on The Pleasures of the Imagination, I was so taken with your thoughts upon some of our
English gardens, that I cannot forbear troubling you with a letter
upon that subject. I am one, you must know, who am looked upon
as a humourist in gardening. I have several acres about my house,
which I call my gaiden, and which a skilful gardener would not
know what to call It is a confusion of kitchen and parterre,
orchard and flower-garden, which he so mixt and interwoven with
one another, that if a foreigner who had seen nothing of our
country should be conveyed into my garden at his first landing,
he would look upon it as a natural wilderness, and one of the
uncultivated parts of our country. My flowers grow up in several
parts of the garden in the greatest luxuriancy and profusion. I
am so far from being fond of any particular one, by reason of its
rarity, that if I meet with any one in a field which pleases me,
I give it a place in my garden. By this means, when a stranger
walks with me, he is surprised to see several large spots of ground
covered with ten thousand different colours, and has often singled

out flowers that he might have met with under a common hedge, in a field, or in a meadow, as some of the greatest beauties of the place. The only method I observe in this particular, is to range in the same quarter the products of the same season, that they may make their appearance together, and compose a picture of the greatest variety. There is the same irregularity in my planta- tions, which run into as great a wildness as their natures will permit. I take in none that do not naturally rejoice in the soil, and am pleased when I am walking in a labyrinth of my own raising, not to know whether the next tree I shall meet with is an apple or an oak, an elm or a pear-tree. My kitchen has likewise its particular quarters assigned it; for besides the wholesome luxury which that place abounds with, I have always thought a kitchen-garden a more pleasant sight than the finest orangery, or artificial green-house. I love to see every thing in its perfection, and am more pleased to survey my rows of coleworts and cabbages, with a thousand nameless pot-herbs, springing up in their full fragrancy and verdure, than to see the tender plants of foreign countries kept alive by artificial heats, or withering in an air and soil that are not adapted to them. I must not omit, that there is a fountain rising in the upper part of my garden, which forms a little wandering rill, and administers to the pleasure as well as the plenty of the place. I have so conducted it, that it visits most of my plantations, and have taken particular care to let it run in the same manner as it would do in an open field, so that it generally passes through banks of violets and primroses, plats of willow, or other plants, that seem to be of its own producing. There is another circumstance in which I am very particular, or, as my neighbours call me, very whimsical: as my garden invites into it all the birds of the country, by offering them the conveniency of springs and shades, solitude and shelter, I do not suffer any one to destroy their nests in the spring, or drive them from their usual haunts in fruit-time. I value my garden more for being full of blackbirds than cherries, and very frankly give them fruit for their songs. By this means, I have always the music of the season in its perfection, and am highly delighted to see the jay or the thrush hopping about my walks, and shooting before my eye across the several little glades and alleys that I pass through. I think there are as many kinds of gardening as of poetry: your makers of parterres and flower-gardens are epigrammatists and sonneteers in this art, contrivers of bowers and grottos, treillages and cascades, are romance writers. Wise and London are our heroic poets; and if, as a critic, I may single out any passage of their works to commend, I shall take notice of that part in the upper garden at Kensington, which was at first nothing but a gravel-pit. It must have been a fine genius for gardening that could have thought of forming such an unsightly hollow into so beautiful an area, and to have hit the eye with so uncommon and agreeable a scene as that which it is now wrought into. To give this particular spot of ground the greater effect, they have made a very pleasing contrast, for, as on one side of the walk you see this hollow basin, with its several little plantations lying so conveniently under the eye of the beholder; on the other side of it there appears a seeming mount, made up of trees rising one higher than another, in proportion as they approach the centre. A spectator, who has not heard this account of it, would think this circular mount was not only a real one, but that it had been actually scooped out of that hollow place which I have before mentioned. I never yet met with any one who has walked in this garden, who was not struck with that part of it which I have here mentioned. As for myself, you will find, by the account which I have already given you, that my compositions in gardening are altogether after the Pindaric manner, and run into the beautiful wildness of nature, without affecting the nicer elegancies of art. What I am now going to mention will, perhaps, deserve your attention more than any thing I have yet said. I find that in the discourse which I spoke of at the beginning of my letter, you are against filling an English garden with evergreens; and indeed I am so far of your opinion, that I can by no means think the verdure of an evergreen comparable to that which shoots out annually, and clothes our trees in the summer season. But I have often wondered that those who are like myself, and love to live in gardens, have never thought of contriving a winter garden, which should consist of such trees only as never cast their leaves. We have very often little snatches of sunshine and fair weather in the most uncomfortable parts of the year, and have frequently several days in November and January that are as agreeable as any in the finest months. At such times, therefore, I think there could not be a greater pleasure than to walk in such a winter garden as I have proposed. In the summer season the whole country blooms, and is a kind of garden, for which reason we are not so sensible of those beauties that at this time may be every where met with; but when Nature is in her desolation, and presents us with nothing but bleak and barren prospects, there is something unspeakably cheerful in a spot of ground which is covered with trees that smile amidst all the rigours of winter, and give us a view of the most gay season in the midst of that which is the most dead and melancholy I have so far indulged myself in this thought, that I have set apart a whole acre of ground for the executing of it. The walls are covered with ivy instead of vines. The laurel, the horn-beam, and the holly, with many other trees and plants of the same nature, grow so thick in it, that you cannot imagine a more lively scene. The glowing redness of the berries, with which they are hung at this time, vies with the verdure of their leaves, and is apt to inspire the heart of the beholder with that vernal delight which you have somewhere taken notice of in your former papers. It is very pleasant, at the same time, to see the several kinds of birds retiring into this little green spot, and enjoying themselves among the branches and foliage, when my great garden, which I have before mentioned to you, does not afford a single leaf for their shelter.

"You must know, Sir, that I look upon the pleasure which we take in a garden as one of the most innocent delights in human life. A garden was the habitation of our first parents before the fall It is naturally apt to fill the mind with calmness and tranquillity, and to lay all its turbulent passions at rest. It gives us a great insight into the contrivance and wisdom of Providence, and suggests innumerable subjects for meditation. I cannot but think the very complacency and satisfaction which a man takes in these works of Nature to be a laudable, if not a virtuous habit of mind. For all which reasons I hope you will pardon the length of my present letter.

"I am, Sir," &c.

ANDREW MARVELL

ANDREW MARVELL (1621–78) was, like his friend and fellow-puritan Milton, a Cambridge man. He took a prominent part in the politics of the Commonwealth, and was for a time joint secretary with Milton to the Council of State. He wrote much in prose and verse, but is remembered now by a few short poems, the best being the *Horatian Ode on Cromwell's Return from Ireland*.

THE GARDEN

How vainly men themselves amaze,
To win the palm, the oak, or bays;
And their incessant labours see
Crowned from some single herb, or tree,
Whose short and narrow-vergéd shade
Does prudently their toils upbraid;
While all the flowers and trees do close,
To weave the garlands of repose!

Fair Quiet, have I found thee here,
And Innocence, thy sister dear?
Mistaken long, I sought you then
In busy companies of men.
Your sacred plants, if here below,
Only among the plants will grow;
Society is all but rude
To this delicious solitude.

No white nor red was ever seen
So amorous as this lovely green.
Fond lovers, cruel as their flame,
Cut in these trees their mistress' name.
Little, alas! they know or heed,
How far these beauties her's exceed!
Fair trees! wheres'e'er your bark I wound,
No name shall but your own be found.

When we have run our passion's heat,
Love hither makes his best retreat.
The gods, that mortal beauty chase,
Still in a tree did end their race;

Apollo hunted Daphne so,
Only that she might laurel grow;
And Pan did after Syrinx speed,
Not as a nymph, but for a reed.

What wondrous life is this I lead!
Ripe apples drop about my head;
The luscious clusters of the vine
Upon my mouth do crush their wine;
The nectarine, and curious peach,
Into my hands themselves do reach;
Stumbling on melons, as I pass,
Insnared with flowers, I fall on grass

Meanwhile the mind, from pleasure less,
Withdraws into its happiness;
The mind, that ocean where each kind
Does straight its own resemblance find;
Yet it creates, transcending these,
Far other worlds, and other seas,
Annihilating all that's made
To a green thought in a green shade.

Here at the fountain's sliding foot,
Or at some fruit-tree's mossy root,
Casting the body's vest aside,
My soul into the boughs does glide:
There, like a bird, it sits and sings,
Then whets and combs its silver wings,
And, till prepared for longer flight,
Waves in its plumes the various light

Such was that happy garden-state,
While man there walked without a mate:
After a place so pure and sweet,
What other help could yet be meet!
But 'twas beyond a mortal's share
To wander solitary there
Two paradises 'twere in one,
To live in paradise alone.

How well the skilful gardener drew
Of flowers, and herbs, this dial new;
Where, from above, the milder sun
Does through a fragrant zodiac run,
And, as it works, the industrious bee
Computes its time as well as we!
How could such sweet and wholesome hours
Be reckoned but with herbs and flowers?

TENNYSON

(From *In Memoriam*)

Ring out, wild bells, to the wild sky,
  The flying cloud, the frosty light:
  The year is dying in the night;
Ring out, wild bells, and let him die.

Ring out the old, ring in the new,
  Ring, happy bells, across the snow:
  The year is going, let him go;
Ring out the false, ring in the true.

Ring out the grief that saps the mind,
  For those that here we see no more;
  Ring out the feud of rich and poor,
Ring in redress to all mankind.

Ring out a slowly dying cause,
  And ancient forms of party strife;
  Ring in the nobler modes of life,
With sweeter manners, purer laws.

Ring out the want, the care, the sin,
  The faithless coldness of the times;
  Ring out, ring out, my mournful rhymes,
But ring the fuller minstrel in.

Ring out false pride in place and blood,
　　The civic slander and the spite;
　　Ring in the love of truth and right,
Ring in the common love of good.

Ring out old shapes of foul disease;
　　Ring out the narrowing lust of gold;
　　Ring out the thousand wars of old,
Ring in the thousand years of peace.

Ring in the valiant man and free,
　　The larger heart, the kindlier hand;
　　Ring out the darkness of the land,
Ring in the Christ that is to be.

H. C. BEECHING

HENRY CHARLES BEECHING (b. 1859), Dean of Norwich.

GOING DOWN HILL ON A BICYCLE

A Boy's Song

With lifted feet, hands still,
I am poised, and down the hill
Dart, with heedful mind;
The air goes by in a wind.

Swifter and yet more swift,
Till the heart with a mighty lift
Makes the lungs laugh, the throat cry:—
"O bird, see; see, bird, I fly!

"Is this, is this your joy?
O bird, then I, though a boy,
For a golden moment share
Your feathery life in air!"

Say, heart, is there aught like this
In a world that is full of bliss?
'Tis more than skating, bound
Steel-shod to the level ground

Speed slackens now, I float
Awhile in my airy boat;
Till when the wheels scarce crawl,
My feet to the treadles fall.

Alas, that the longest hill
Must end in a vale; but still,
Who climbs with toil, whereso'er,
Shall find wings waiting there.

NEWBOLT

Sir Henry Newbolt (b 1862) was born in Staffordshire and educated at Clifton and Oxford. He has written stories and essays in addition to his fine stirring poems.

THE BEST SCHOOL OF ALL

It's good to see the School we knew,
    The land of youth and dream,
To greet again the rule we knew
    Before we took the stream:
Though long we've missed the sight of her,
    Our hearts may not forget;
We've lost the old delight of her,
    We keep her honour yet.

We'll honour yet the School we knew,
    The best School of all:
We'll honour yet the rule we knew,
    Till the last bell call.
For, working days or holidays,
And glad or melancholy days,
They were great days and jolly days
    At the best School of all.

The stars and sounding vanities
    That half the crowd bewitch,
What are they but inanities
    To him that treads the pitch?

And where's the wealth, I'm wondering,
    Could buy the cheers that roll
When the last charge goes thundering
    Beneath the twilight goal?

The men that tanned the hide of us,
    Our daily foes and friends,
They shall not lose their pride of us,
    Howe'er the journey ends.
Their voice, to us who sing of it,
    No more its message bears,
But the round world shall ring of it
    And all we are be theirs.

To speak of Fame a venture is,
    There's little here can bide,
But we may face the centuries,
    And dare the deepening tide·
For though the dust that's part of us
    To dust again be gone,
Yet here shall beat the heart of us—
    The School we handed on!

We'll honour yet the School we knew.
    The best School of all.
We'll honour yet the rule we knew,
    Till the last bell call
For, working days or holidays,
And glad or melancholy days,
They were great days and jolly days
    At the best School of all

CAMBRIDGE PRINTED BY J B. PEACE, M A , AT THE UNIVERSITY PRESS

CPSIA information can be obtained at www.ICGtesting.com
Printed in the USA
LVOW10*2230120314

377107LV00004B/69/P